J. CALVIN MORELAND

PROPHECY AND RELIGION

PUBLISHED BY
THE SYNDICS OF THE CAMBRIDGE UNIVERSITY PRESS

London Office: Bentley House, N.W. 1
American Branch: New York

Agents for Canada, India, and Pakistan: Macmillan

First Edition 1922
Reprinted 1926
1930
1936
1940
1948
1951

Printed in Great Britain at the University Press, Cambridge
(Brooke Crutchley, University Printer)

PROPHECY & RELIGION

STUDIES IN THE LIFE OF JEREMIAH

BY

JOHN SKINNER, D.D.

CAMBRIDGE
AT THE UNIVERSITY PRESS
1951

TO
THE STUDENTS
PAST AND PRESENT
OF WESTMINSTER COLLEGE
THIS VOLUME IS RESPECTFULLY DEDICATED
IN GRATEFUL MEMORY OF THIRTY YEARS
OF WORK AND FELLOWSHIP

PREFACE

WHEN the Council of the Cunningham Lecture-ship did me the honour of inviting me to be the Lecturer for 1920, leaving the choice of a subject to myself, I gratefully accepted the appointment, and offered a course on the life and writings of Jeremiah. Had I been younger, I should have preferred, instead of adding another to the many books on Jeremiah which have recently appeared in English, to try and break ground in some less frequented field of Old Testament theology. As it was, my choice was influenced by a long-standing interest in the study of Jeremiah's work and personality, as well as a hope that I might still be able to contribute something to an understanding of his message to his own age and to us.

The Lectures were delivered, under the same title as the present volume, in New College, Edinburgh, in the spring of 1920, and are now published in accordance with the terms of the Lectureship. I have to express my regret that publication has been unavoidably delayed beyond the allotted period; and also to explain that in preparing the work for the press I have not only expanded the lectures but arranged the matter under other headings and in a somewhat different order. In general, however, the substance of the six original lectures will be found in Chapters I and II; III and IV; VIII; VI and VII; XI; XV and XVIII. The remaining nine chapters are added in order to present a fuller picture of Jeremiah (though still an incomplete one) than was possible in the lectures.

To three friends in particular my warmest acknow-
ledgments are due for help in planning the Lectures
and publishing the book: to Dr George Steven, Edinburgh, for wise counsel and criticisms on many points;
to the Rev. H. C. Carter, Cambridge, who read the
manuscript and prepared the Index; and to Mr T. W.
Manson, M.A., of Westminster College, who assisted
me in revising the proofs and compiled the list of
Scripture passages.

J. S.

April 1922

CONTENTS

CHAPTER I

INTRODUCTORY—THE PLACE OF PROPHECY IN THE RELIGION OF ISRAEL

THE alliance of Prophecy and Religion in the history of Israel has been one of the most influential factors in what Lessing called the Education of the Human Race. It is a phenomenon to which the history of religion affords no real parallel. It is true that Hebrew Prophecy has its roots and antecedents in widely diffused primitive ideas and customs which are found everywhere among peoples in the early stages of civilisation. There is a stage of human development at which the instinctive craving for supernatural guidance produces a class of professional persons supposed to be in intimate communication with the unseen powers which control human destiny, and therefore able to foretell the future and give direction in difficult matters of policy and conduct. If we take the word Prophecy in this wide and vague sense it may be said that prophecy was a universal phenomenon of the ancient world. The remarkable thing is not that prophecy of a sort should have appeared in Israel, but that it should have persisted so long as a vehicle of the best political guidance and the highest ethical and religious teaching. In the more progressive communities of antiquity (like Greece and Rome) the repute of prophecy or divination tended to decline with the advance of popular enlightenment, and matters of importance came to be settled more and more on broad grounds of reason and expediency, until the Roman statesman marvelled that two augurs could meet

in the street without laughing in each other's faces. The
peculiarity in the case of Israel is that this elsewhere
discredited institution reached a height of spirituality
and moral influence which makes its records full of
instruction even to the mind of to-day. The contrast to
the ethnic religions is emphasised by Dr Warde Fowler
in his lectures on *The Religious Experience of the Roman
People*. He writes:

For instead of developing, as did the wise man or seer of
Israel, into the mouthpiece of God in His demand for the
righteousness of man, the Roman diviner merely assisted the
pontifex in his work of robbing religion of the idea of righteousness. Divination seems to be a universal instinct of human nature,
a perfectly natural instinct, arising out of man's daily needs,
hopes, fears; but though it may have had the chance, even at
Rome, it has never been able, except among the Jews, to emerge
from its cramping chrysalis of magic, and become a really
valuable stimulant of morality (*op. cit.* p. 292).

This result is undoubtedly due to the essentially
ethical character of the religion of Israel, which purified
and ennobled every institution of the national life which
came under its influence. Even in religions of a much
more primitive type, the element of divination does not
cover the whole area of religious practice and belief.
There is always an established order of ritual, a recognised code of social morals, a system of *taboos*, and so
forth, on the due observance of which the maintenance
of good relations between the tribe and the tribal deity
is understood to depend. This constitutes religion in its
public and traditional aspect. The soothsayer is only
called in to answer particular questions of importance
for the individual or the community, for which the
ordinary rules of religious observance provide no solution, and it becomes necessary to resort to occult methods
in order to ascertain the mind of the god. The same
distinction in a more refined form meets us in the higher

religion of the Old Testament. We find it in the utterances of the prophets themselves. While they claim to possess an exclusive insight into the secret purpose of Yahwe in His providential dealings with His people, they constantly appeal to a traditional *Tôrā*, or revelation, of Yahwe, common to all Israelites, in which the character of Yahwe and the conditions of intercourse with Him are authoritatively declared[1]. Hosea speaks of the priests as the official custodians of this tradition; and to the sinful neglect of this function on the part of the priesthood he attributes the universal defection from the national faith (Hos. iv. 6). Now the prophets regard themselves as the exponents of the essential principles of this authentic revelation of Yahwe; and their clear intuitive perception of these moral and spiritual truths goes far to account for the supreme position they hold among the religious teachers of the world. Being men imbued with the spirit of revealed religion, and seeing all things in the light of its principles, they were able to develop those principles in their application to new situations as they arose, and bring forth new truth from the depths of their inspired insight into the mind and character of God. But this does not explain the singular fact that in Israel alone a spiritual religion allied itself with the prophetic impulse, finding in it its most effective means of expression and bringing its latent possibilities to a perfection nowhere else realised.

There is a tendency among modern writers to explain away this phenomenon by asserting that the higher prophecy of the Old Testament has nothing whatever in common with the earlier manifestations of prophetic inspiration in Israel, still less of course with the cruder forms of divination which prevailed among other peoples. From this point of view the prophet is simply an inspired

[1] On the sense in which the prophets speak of the *Tôrā* of Yahwe, see pp. 331 f. below.

religious personality, who is a true organ of revelation just in so far as he ceases to be what the ancient world meant by a prophet[1]. That view seems to me one-sided and unhistorical. The prophet was not merely nor in the first instance a teacher of religion, but a seer, who perceives and announces beforehand what Yahwe is about to do. Prediction is no secondary or accidental feature of Old Testament prophecy even in its highest manifestations, but a central interest round which all

[1] Among recent statements of this theory mention may be made of the able and suggestive treatment of the subject by Prof. Buttenwieser in his book on *The Prophets of Israel* (1914), *vide* pp. 138 ff. His argument rests partly on the emphatic declaration of Amos, the father of literary prophecy, that he was no *Nābî'* nor son of a *Nābî'* (vii. 14): i.e. he was not a member of a prophetic guild. But over against this declaration we have to set the fact that the same Amos instances the raising up of *Nĕbî'îm* as a proof of Yahwe's peculiar love for Israel (ii. 11). From the fact that Amos repudiates all connexion with the degenerate professional prophets of his own day it by no means follows that he did not regard himself as standing in the succession of inspired men through whom Yahwe had formerly made His presence known in the life of Israel; nor is there any reason to assume that he looked on the manner of his inspiration as essentially different from theirs: the verb which he uses to denote his own prophetic activity (*hinnābē'*, vii. 15) is that which was commonly applied to the *Nĕbî'îm*. The real point at issue, however, is whether a great and even sudden advance in religious enlightenment involves an absolute breach of continuity with the kind of experience which was admittedly characteristic of the earlier *nabi'ism*. The case is closely analogous to the development of self-conscious reason in man from the rudimentary intelligence of the lower animals. The two are separated by an immeasurable chasm, so that the higher can never be *explained* in terms of the lower; and yet the persistence of animal appetites and instincts in the mental life of man proves conclusively that somehow it has sprung from that of the animals. Similarly in the spiritual prophecy of the Old Testament we find traces of ecstasy, visions and auditions, which are obviously survivals of states of consciousness belonging to prophecy of a lower grade. And the fact that the great prophets far surpassed their predecessors in their apprehension of religious truth is no reason for denying the reality of the ecstatic element in their experience, or for explaining it away as a mere rhetorical accommodation to traditional modes of expression.

other forms of prophetic activity ranged themselves. It is assumed in the Old Testament that spiritual prophecy supplies in Israel the place which divination occupies in other religions. 'For there is no enchantment in Jacob, nor divination in Israel; at the (right) time it is said to Jacob and to Israel what God is about to do' (Num. xxiii. 23)[1]. 'Those nations which thou shalt dispossess listen to soothsayers and to diviners; but thee Yahwe thy God suffereth not so to do. A prophet from the midst of thy brethren will Yahwe thy God raise up to thee; unto him shall ye hearken' (Deut. xviii. 14 f.). This of course does not mean that prophecy had no higher aim than to procure oracles unveiling the secrets of the future, but it does imply that in displacing the diviner and magician the true prophet took over their functions on a purer religious basis, satisfying the legitimate needs to which they bore witness and to which they falsely ministered. There is no discontinuity in the development of prophecy from the older *Nabi'ism* of the period from Samuel to Elisha, to the new type of prophecy inaugurated by Amos. *Nabi'ism* had its unprogressive and degenerate representatives between whom and the true prophets there was an irreconcileable antagonism; but as the medium of Yahwe's intercourse with His people it had embodied the same fundamental principle, and served the same end, as the work of Amos and his successors. It is this close and permanent association between religion and prophecy which is the distinctive feature of the Old Testament dispensation, and we can see how each worked for the advancement of the other: the ethical genius of the religion directing the vision of the prophet to the eternal principles of the divine government, while the insight of the prophet

[1] The verse is exegetically difficult, and is widely regarded as an interpolation; but the meaning can hardly be other than the rendering here given; see Gray, *International Critical Commentary, ad loc.*

drew forth from the national faith the essential truth about God which at last gave the world a perfect religion.

It would seem, therefore, that there must have been something in the religion of Israel on the one hand, and something in the prophetic consciousness on the other hand, which established an enduring contact between them, and made their co-operation so fruitful in spiritual results. There are at all events certain aspects of the relation which may here be noted as contributing to a clearer understanding of the prophetic movement in Israel, and in particular of Jeremiah's position in the history of that movement.

First of all, as regards the Old Testament religion, we observe that it is a relation between a personal Being on one side and a national entity on the other. Its fundamental principle is, 'Yahwe the God of Israel, and Israel the people of Yahwe.' That may seem a barren and empty formula from the point of view of modern individualism, but it is one of profound significance in the thought of the Old Testament. It marks, indeed, no outward distinction between the religion of Israel and those of the neighbouring Semitic peoples, which were all of the national type, and in each of which the deity was conceived as personal. There was however a vital difference in the fact that Yahwe was revealed to Israel as a moral personality, whose character is reflected in the demands of the conscience, and who is inexorable in His requirement of a righteousness corresponding to His own. The religion represented by the prophets is one in which the God of the conscience enters into personal relations not with the individual directly but with the community: in other words the primary subject or 'unit' of religion is the *nation* in whose history God revealed Himself. To say this is not to deny that the Old Testament contains anticipations of the perfect

relationship in which God speaks directly to the heart
of the individual believer; but it is none the less true
that to the saints of the old Covenant the foundation of
all religious confidence was Yahwe's faithful love for
the people of His choice. We shall have opportunity
later to examine this conception more closely in its
bearing on the work of the prophets[1]: in the meantime
it is sufficient to note that in this limitation of religion
to the national consciousness of Israel we can see a
reason for the existence of a special order of men through
whom God makes known His will to the nation at
large. We are thus led to inquire in what ways prophecy
provided a method of revelation adapted to the needs
of a religion national on one side and personal on
another;—national in the sense that its primary subject
was a whole people, but personal inasmuch as the relations between this people and its God were relations of
an ethical and therefore personal kind.

The prophetic consciousness, as exhibited in the
great prophets of Israel, is a variety of the general
religious consciousness, involving like it an immediate
fellowship of the prophet with God; but both in the
sphere of its exercise and in the form of its experience
it presents several phenomena which do not belong to
the permanent essence of religion. There are perhaps
three chief features which differentiate the religious
experience of the prophets from the normal communion
of a Christian with God.

(1) The prophets are conscious of being intermediaries
between Yahwe and the nation of Israel. It is always as
representatives of Yahwe the national God of Israel—
the God who had known that people alone of all the
families of the earth (Amos iii. 2)—that they speak the
'word of Yahwe'; and the message they deliver in His
name is addressed not to themselves personally, nor to

                    [1] See pp. 72 f., 216 f.

each Israelite individually, but to the nation in its corporate capacity, conceived as an organic unity, and often idealised as a moral person. 'Go, prophesy to my people Israel' is the commission with which the Lord summoned Amos from following the flock to announce His purpose (Amos vii. 15); and that is the mandate under which every prophet worked. In this way God spoke to His people of old, revealing His purpose and character, and conveying moral guidance, through the instrumentality of men called to His service and initiated into His secret. On first thoughts this might seem to be nothing different from what is observed in all religions, viz. the spiritual leadership that naturally accrues to men whose vision of divine truth is clearer than that of their fellows. But that does not fully explain the peculiar function of prophecy in the Old Testament. The prophets are not merely the teachers and guides of a nation; they are official exponents of a religion in which the whole nation appears as the religious unit, expressing its common religious attitude in the recognised functions of national life. And if we reflect for a moment on the method by which spiritual intercourse could be maintained between a moral personality, such as Yahwe was to the prophets, and a nation in its corporate life, it is evident that the only possible channel of such intercourse was a succession of men of God, conversant with the purpose and character of Yahwe, standing as mediators between Him and His people. We thus see that from the fundamental constitution of the Old Testament religion spiritual prophecy was an essential institution for the development of the highest religious life in Israel [1].

[1] See W. Robertson Smith, *The Old Testament in the Jewish Church* (1892), p. 291: 'That this spirit [of prophecy], in the Old Covenant, rests only upon chosen organs of revelation, and not upon all the faithful, corresponds to the limitations of the dispensation, in which the primary

(2) The prophets of Israel appear to have been endowed with remarkable insight into the providential significance of the political events of their time. Not general truths of reason, nor facts of the spiritual life, but the great movements of contemporary history, are the writing in which they chiefly read the will and purpose of the Almighty. Few things in prophecy are more striking than the confidence with which it identifies current events with the direct action of Yahwe, or the certainty with which it reads their lesson and predicts their issue. For us history, especially contemporary history, is an inscrutable enigma; nothing is more precarious than the attempt to interpret the divine meaning of the history which unfolds itself before our eyes.

'God,' says Victor Hugo, 'makes visible to men his will in events, an obscure text, written in a mysterious language. Men make their translations of it forthwith; hasty translations, incorrect, full of faults, omissions and misreadings. Very few minds comprehend the divine tongue. The most sagacious, the most calm, the most profound, decipher slowly; and, when they arrive with their text, the need has long gone by: there are already twenty translations in the public square.'

Nothing could be truer of the philosophical historian, nothing less true of the prophet. Instead of being the last to arrive with his translation, the prophet is first on the spot; he is even beforehand with the event, and discerns the mind of God not so much in what He has done as in that which He is about to do.

This is not the place to discuss the origin or nature of this endowment of the prophetic consciousness: how

subject of religion is not the individual but the nation, so that Israel's personal converse with Jehovah can be adequately maintained, like other national functions, through the medium of certain chosen and representative persons. The prophet is thus a mediator, who not only brings God's word to the people but conversely makes intercession for the people with God.'

far it was a presentiment borne in on the mind of the
prophet by subtle perception of the secret forces that
shape the destiny of the world, and how far an inference
from general laws of the divine action[1]. It is sufficient
for our present purpose to call attention to the fact, and
to note its fitness as a vehicle of revelation on the level
of a national religion. History being to the nation what
experience is to the individual, it is only through His
providential ordering of history that God could express
His dealings with a nation, and only through the prophetic interpretation of providence that His mind could
be truly known. That idea runs through the whole Old
Testament. The fundamental facts on which the religious
relation rests are the mighty deeds of Yahwe in redeem-
ing the people from Egypt, in securing it in the
possession of the land of Canaan, in defending it against
its foes, and crowning it with the temporal blessings in
which national well-being consists. In the pre-exilic
literary prophecy the dissolution of this gracious relationship, and the consequent destruction of the State,
are announced as a moral necessity brought about by
the persistent disobedience of Israel on the one hand
and the inflexible righteousness of Yahwe on the other.
But this startling message of doom is still an interpretation of the divine purpose as about to be manifested
in an imminent crisis of history.

(3) The experience of the prophets contains a sub-
conscious element, appearing chiefly in the form of the
Vision, which is not characteristic of normal religious
life. The prophetic vision is undoubtedly a creation of
the sub-conscious mind, working uncontrolled by
voluntary reflexion, and producing subjective images
which have something of the vividness and reality of
actual sense perception. No one denies that such visions

[1] See below, pp. 53, 75 f.; and compare Giesebrecht, *Die Berufsbegabung der alttestamentlichen Propheten* (1897), pp. 72–87.

were frequent on the lower levels of Hebrew prophecy.
'If there be a prophet among you, in visions do I make
Myself known to him, in dreams do I speak with him'
(Num. xii. 6). The only question is whether or to what
extent they entered into the experience of the great
literary prophets, whose perception of religious truth
seems more akin to what we call intuition than to the
obscure psychological phenomena of the dream and the
vision. On that point there is room for difference of
opinion, and great difference exists. The recent tendency
of criticism has been on the whole to hold that the
visions recorded by the prophets were actually experienced by them in a condition of comparative ecstasy, in
which self-consciousness was not lost, although its
control of the visionary process was suspended. But it
is held by some that this literal interpretation of the
descriptions given by the prophets is not justified: that
they are simply using the traditional form of prophetic
experience to express ideas which they had apprehended
otherwise, either by pure spiritual intuition or by the
exercise of their reasoning and reflective powers. Of
these opposing views the former alone seems to me to
be consistent with the directness and objectivity of the
prophets' narration. It must be borne in mind that
whatever *we* may think, the claim to have had a vision
was taken seriously in ancient times as a proof of
inspiration; so that for a prophet to profess to have had
a vision when he had not would have been to deceive
his public with regard to the validity of his commission
to declare the word of God. That in many cases we have
a conventional use of stereotyped prophetic phraseology
without any corresponding visionary experience is undoubtedly true; but the deliberate report of a vision,
especially a vision on which the prophet's whole title
to speak in the name of Yahwe depends, stands on a
different footing, and cannot be fairly explained as a

conscious literary effort to express spiritual truth by the aid of poetic imagination.

The objection usually urged against this explanation of the visions—that it reduces them to the same level as the delusions of 'poor phrenetics' and connects the deity with the irrational part of man's nature—appears to lose much of its force in the light of recent psychological research. The so-called irrational part of man's nature has assumed a new importance under the name of the 'sub-conscious'; and, uncertain as the ultimate nature of the sub-conscious self may be, there are facts enough to dispel the notion that everything of value in the spiritual life of man must come by way of conscious intellectual effort. It is a fact that under strong emotion religious ideas and convictions do sometimes give rise to visual or audible representations hardly distinguishable from sense impressions; and there is ample evidence in Christian biography that this is compatible with perfect sanity of mind and balance of judgment. Of this nature we take the visions of the prophets to be. They are purely subjective phenomena, taking place wholly within the prophet's mind, and are projected from the mind under the emotional stress which accompanies the perception of a new spiritual truth or a fresh impression of the reality of things divine. There seems no reason why intuition should not initiate a process of this kind, creating spontaneously the images in which the new truth perceived finds its first expression. It is obvious that there can be nothing absolutely new in the sensuous material of which the vision is composed. It is only a new synthesis of images supplied by previous waking experience, each having its own aesthetic and emotional value, which were stored in the memory of the prophet: nevertheless (as we see most clearly from Isaiah's inaugural vision in ch. vi) the effect of the combination may be such as to produce an impression

of overwhelming novelty on the mind. And this is all
that is necessarily implied in the operation of sub-
conscious thought as it appears in the great prophets
of Israel. Whether, as Professor James taught, the sub-
consciousness be open to the direct influx of the divine[1],
or whether (as other psychologists maintain) it is but
the lumber-room of the soul in which are stored impressions that have slipped unobserved through the
portals of the active mind, makes no essential difference
so far as the form of the prophet's experience is concerned. On either theory the revelation wells up from
the hidden depths of his being, and clothes itself in
symbols before his inner eye.

It cannot be maintained that this aspect of the
prophetic consciousness has any special adaptation to
the needs of a public religion of the national type, such
as the Old Testament religion was. There were many
other ways (especially the priestly oracle) in which the
will of Yahwe was made known to ancient Israel; and
again the ecstasy might be the vehicle of any conviction,
true or false, which took overmastering possession of
the prophet's mind. There is certainly no exclusive
connexion between national religion and ecstatic or
semi-ecstatic inspiration. At the same time we may
believe that in a more general way the vision and related
psychical phenomena were the necessary authentication
of the prophet's standing, both to himself and to the
people whom he addressed. It may have been, although
we have no right to affirm it positively, that in those
days no honest man would have ventured to speak in
the name of Yahwe without some express warrant in
his own experience that he had stood in the council of
the Lord. No doubt, the prophets' certainty of the truth
of their message rested ultimately on the self-evidencing

---

[1] *Varieties of Religious Experience*, pp. 242, 515–519.

power of spiritual truth on minds morally sincere; but, for the fundamental conviction that they belonged to the circle of Yahwe's intimates, and had a commission to declare His word, they may well have been dependent on some striking event in their personal history, such as the inaugural vision which several of them relate. As for their public audience, the time had not yet come when the messenger of God could rely on manifestation of the truth to commend him to every man's conscience in the sight of God (2 Cor. iv. 2). It is doubtful if the prophets expected this, although some expressions might seem to have that implication (Isa. xxix. 9–12, etc.). In general they speak as men accredited by definite experiences through which they have passed to exhort and threaten and command in the name of Yahwe the God of Israel.

These considerations do not completely explain the unique position of prophecy in the religion of Israel; but they are sufficient to show that there is a real correspondence between the fundamental character of the Old Dispensation and the salient features of the prophetic consciousness as manifested in the leading representatives of pre-exilic prophecy. The general conclusion to which we are led is that the higher prophecy of the Old Testament represents a transitional phase in the development of religion from a nationalistic basis, on which history is the chief medium of divine revelation, to an individual and universal basis, on which God enters into immediate fellowship with the human soul. Why the perfect religion should have sprung from the bosom of a national faith is a question on which it is idle to speculate. But accepting the fact as we find it, we can see that the final mission of prophecy was to liberate the eternal truths of religion from their temporary national embodiment, and disclose their true foundation in the immutable character of God and the essential nature of man. We shall see how this process culminates in the person of Jeremiah.

It remains, therefore, to indicate in a few sentences the place which Jeremiah occupies in this development. That his life marks a climax and turning-point in the history of prophecy is recognised by all recent students of the religion of Israel, although different estimates have been given of the qualities that distinguish him from his predecessors. Ewald was perhaps the first to characterise his genius in relation to the prophetic movement as a whole; and his diagnosis is true and illuminating so far as it goes. In the judgment of that great critic, Jeremiah stands on the highest level of prophetic achievement, where prophecy becomes conscious at once of its true essence and of its inherent limitations, and reveals a failure of inward force which points to its impending decline. This is seen chiefly in the intrusion of personal emotion into the consciousness of the prophet, which seemed to Ewald a symptom of decay, and a sign that prophecy was no longer able to cope with the degeneracy and confusion of the time, or to guide and master the age as it had done in the strong hands of Isaiah[1]. The merit of supplementing this somewhat negative appreciation of Jeremiah is due mainly to Wellhausen, who in a few incisive paragraphs has emphasised the positive value of this prophet's experience in a way that has profoundly influenced all subsequent exposition. Accepting his view we find that Jeremiah's specific greatness lies in the sphere of personal religion. The strongly marked emotionalism of his temperament is not to be regarded as a weakness or an impediment, but as the endowment of a spirit touched to fine issues, and perhaps a necessary condition of the heart to heart converse with God which

[1] *Die Propheten des alten Bundes*, Band II (1868), 74, 71 f.

unsealed within him the perennial fount of true piety,
—the religious susceptibility of the individual soul[1].
His is the last word of the Old Testament on the
universal essence of religion; and we shall see how, in
speaking it, he breaks through the limitations of the
strictly prophetic consciousness, and moves out into
the larger filial communion with God in which every
child of man may share[2].

Now this discovery of individual fellowship with God
which is Jeremiah's great contribution to the religious
experience of the Jewish Church is also the clue to his
own spiritual biography. The discovery came to him
through the stern discipline of his life, through long
travail of soul, and much contact with the world of men;
but it is the direction in which his life was guided from
the first by the spirit of God, and long before the goal
was consciously realised we catch glimpses of the steps
by which he was led into the secret of personal communion with God. In the chapters which follow I have
sought to present the problems of Jeremiah's life from
this point of view. The selection of material is necessarily
incomplete, and may not be such as will commend
itself to all readers as the best that could be made.
There are important aspects of the work of Jeremiah
besides the central interest to which I have referred,
and I will not shun opportunities of dealing with them
as they come into view. But my main object is to trace
the growth of personal piety in the history of Jeremiah
and, following out the line of thought suggested by
these introductory observations, to elucidate the significance of pre-exilic prophecy as seen through his
mind. 'The book of Jeremiah,' it has been said, 'does
not so much teach religious truths as present a religious
personality. Prophecy had already taught its truths, its

[1] *Israelitische und jüdische Geschichte*, 5th Ed. (1904), pp. 147–150.
[2] See below, pp. 215–222.

last effort was to reveal itself in a life[1].' That life, like every human life, has its incidents, its conflicts and agonies, its heights and depths, its pathos and its tragedy; and in all its varied experiences it is an instructive and fascinating study. But through all its merely human aspects we can see in it the efflorescence of the spiritual principles which are the essence of the prophetic movement in Israel[2].

[1] A. B. Davidson in Hastings' *Dictionary of the Bible*, II, 576.
[2] See especially Chap. XI, below.

CHAPTER II

PREDESTINATION AND VOCATION

FEW travellers in Palestine, Sir George Adam Smith tells us, ever turn aside from Jerusalem to visit the little village of '*Anātā*, which lies about an hour's walk to the north-east. Hidden from the city by intervening ridges, it is visible from the north end of the range of Olivet, and from that point it is described by a recent traveller as a cluster of grey peasant houses, resting on a sloping hillside, and surrounded by green fig-trees and terraces of fruitful fields[1]. If this mean and insignificant hamlet offers few attractions to the casual tourist, to the student of Jeremiah there is, as Dr Smith remarks[2], no more instructive site. For '*Anātā* is of course the ancient '*Anāthôth*, the birthplace of the prophet, and his home till manhood. Its 'wild outlook' northward over the 'stony fields of Benjamin' to the mountains of Ephraim, eastward over a foreground of rough barren hills to the Jordan valley and the heights of Gilead beyond, gives the landscape on which his eyes rested day by day during the impressionable years of his youth, and many pages of his prophecy show how deeply the features of that wide and varied prospect

[1] Dr Hans Schmidt, *Die grossen Propheten und ihre Zeit*, p. 200; in *Die Schriften des alten Testaments in Auswahl...übersetzt* (1914). The modern inhabitants are said (or were said some years ago) to be mostly quarrymen and their families, supplying excellent building stone to Jerusalem. It may have been the same in Jeremiah's time. Were stone-masons from Anathoth among the workmen who were impressed for the building of Jehoiakim's lordly palace, and afterwards defrauded of their hire (xxii. 13 ff.)?

[2] *Jerusalem*, II, 228.

were stamped on his mind. It is significant also that in the records of his life the circumstance is repeatedly mentioned that Anathoth, though included in the kingdom of Judah and so close to its capital, was in the territory of Benjamin (i. 1, xxxii. 8, xxxvii. 12). Ethnologically Benjamin belonged to Israel, and the fact enables us to understand Jeremiah's undying affection for the Rachel-tribes and his longing for the home-bringing of their exiled children (iii. 12 f., xxxi. 4–6, 9, 15–20).

Under the monarchy Anathoth was the residence of a famous priestly family, descended probably from that unfortunate priest, Abiathar, who took the wrong side at the accession of Solomon, and was 'rusticated' in consequence to 'his own fields' at Anathoth (1 Kings ii. 26 f.). Abiathar was the sole survivor of the house of Eli, and his degradation by Solomon involved the permanent exclusion of his line from the service of the central sanctuary at Jerusalem. When we read that Jeremiah was 'the son of Hilkiah of the priests that were in Anathoth,' the natural, though not absolutely certain, inference is that he belonged to this line, thus tracing his ancestry through the priesthood of Shiloh back to the time of Moses and the beginning of Israel's history as a nation. If this be correct there was no family in Israel whose fortunes had been so closely bound up with the national religion as that into which Jeremiah was born. And nowhere would the best traditions and the purest *ethos* of the religion of Yahwe be likely to find a surer repository than in a household whose forbears had for so many generations guarded the most sacred symbol of its imageless worship, the Ark of God.

The probable relation of such a family to the local worship of Anathoth is a much more dubious subject of speculation, but it raises questions of some importance for the biography of Jeremiah. Can we suppose,

for instance, that his father Hilkiah was an officiating
priest at the rural shrine which must have been the
centre of the religious life of the village community[1]?
Or are we to think of him as an adherent of the persecuted prophetic party in the reign of Manasseh, the
party which had already set its mind on the suppression
of the provincial cults and the concentration of the
national worship in the Temple of Jerusalem[2]? We
cannot tell. Cornill decisively rejects the former view
as wholly incredible, mainly on the ground that
Jeremiah's deeply rooted and harmoniously developed
piety must have been the result of parental training, and
his horror of the popular cultus a sentiment which he
must have imbibed through the atmosphere of a devout
home. And it is perhaps not a very likely thing in itself
that the historic house of Abiathar should have sunk to
the level of those parochial Levite-priests whose living
depended on the maintenance of the high places: we
know in fact that the family possessed landed property
(xxxii. 6 ff.). On the other hand, however, we have to
take account of the fact that in later years our prophet's
bitterest foes were they of his own household. His
brethren and his father's house were in full cry after
him (xii. 6) when the men of Anathoth sought his life
because he prophesied in the name of Yahwe. It is clear
therefore that Jeremiah's prophetic convictions were
not shared by the family to which he belonged; and it
is not improbable (as we shall see later) that on the
great practical issue of the time—the law of the One

---

[1] That Anathoth, in spite of its proximity to Jerusalem, had a sanctuary of its own is probable, though it cannot be proved. Conspicuous
among the buildings of the modern *'Anata* is the white tomb of the local
Weli, or patron saint under the Mohammedan regime (H. Schmidt,
l.c.). Considering the tenacity with which the tradition of sacred sites is
preserved in the East, we may suppose that this is the spot where the
'high place' stood in the days before Josiah's reformation.

[2] See below, Chap. VI.

Altar—he and they were on opposite sides. If this were the case Jeremiah's advocacy of the Deuteronomic re-formation would naturally be resented by his brethren as disloyalty to the family interest, and a surrender to the pretensions of the rival house of Zadok, which monopolised the priestly offices in the Temple. The situation is too obscure to admit of positive conclusions, but it is at least doubtful if the higher prophetic ideals were an element in the religious education which Hilkiah imparted to his children. It would not follow that Jeremiah owed nothing to parental instruction or family tradition. There were doubtless many good men in Judah who while lamenting the abuses of the rural sanctuaries nevertheless stood by the old order which sanctioned a multiplicity of altars legitimately used in the worship of Yahwe. Jeremiah's father might be one of these.

We are on firmer ground when we speak of the direct influence of prophecy on the opening mind of Jeremiah. His familiarity with the ideas of the older prophets, especially with those of Hosea, appears so soon after his call, and that call came to him so early in life, that we may safely assume that he had known the prophetic writings and assimilated the principles of their teaching before he had reached the age of manhood. In Hosea he found not only a teacher, but a spirit kindred to his own. Both were men of exceptionally tender and emo-tional temperament, sympathising intensely with the people on which they were constrained to pour out the vials of divine judgment; possibly both were of priestly descent, though neither attached the smallest value to the ceremonial side of the priest's functions. There was an ancestral bond between them inasmuch as Hosea was a native of North Israel from which Jeremiah's family had come, and in whose fate he shows so lively an interest. It was from Hosea that the younger prophet received the religious interpretation of Israel's history which was the framework in which his own message was to be set. What Hosea had learned through the bitter experiences of his home life[1] led Jeremiah early to renounce the hope of marriage, because he felt himself to be like his predecessor the prophet of a nation's dying agony (ch. xvi. 1 ff.). They are the two martyr prophets of the Old Testament, men of sorrows and acquainted with grief, the most deeply exercised in spiritual religion of all the prophets of Israel.

While his religious life was thus nourished from within by contact with great minds of the past, nature without was teaching him lessons which sank deep into his young poetic soul. I have already referred in passing to the impress which nature in her sterner aspect—the wild and desolate scenery on which his native Anathoth looks down—has left on his writings. But that is the least part of the harvest which Jeremiah's quiet eye must have gleaned in youth, not merely from permanent features of the landscape but from the familiar pictures of rural life and the ordinary interests and occupations of men. An astonishing wealth of metaphor and imagery gleams in his pages, embodying his profoundest thoughts of God and man. In this, to be sure, there is nothing peculiar to Jeremiah; for every prophet uses illustrations from the outer world to set forth the truth he desires to convey. Yet I think we may find in Jeremiah's poetry traces of a closer sympathy with the life of nature than in any other prophet. When, for example, he sees in the marvellous instinct of the migratory birds an analogy to the instinct of the human soul for God (viii. 7), he gives expression to the most profound of spiritual truths in a form which only the sympathetic contemplation of nature could have suggested. Again, the striking picture of the eternal snow of Lebanon as an emblem of the

[1] See the first three chapters of his book.

unfailing source of Israel's true religion (xviii. 14) must
have originated in a mind responsive to

> the silence and the calm
> Of mute insensate things.

Such images are more than mere illustrations; they
seem to spring from a sense of a divine order immanent
in nature, not needing to be realised by a violent upheaval of the visible order, but manifesting itself to the
seeing eye in the constitution of the world as it exists—
the living visible garment of the Eternal. This quality
of Jeremiah's poetic genius, more characteristic perhaps
of his later than of his youthful utterances, reveals
itself especially in the tendency of his eschatological
conceptions, which are entirely free from the catastrophic
element which elsewhere bulks so largely in prophetic
representations of the last days[1]. The vision of desolation which frequently rose up before his mind is haunted
by an awful unearthly stillness—a silence unbroken by
the lowing of cattle or the singing of birds (ix. 10, iv. 25).
Nor is it only the world of external nature that appeals
to Jeremiah: 'the still sad music of humanity' also has
its undying echo in his writings. Where can we find
an expression of it more simple and penetrating than
in the repeated lament over the quenching of all the
joys of common life in the coming days when 'the
sound of mirth and the sound of gladness, the voice of
the bridegroom and the voice of the bride, the sound
of the millstones and the light of the lamp' shall be
taken away (xxv. 10; cf. vii. 34, xvi. 9, xxxiii. 11)?

One more element in Jeremiah's preparation for the
work of a prophet must be briefly mentioned. As the
time approached when he had to put away childish
things and enter on the responsibilities of manhood, he
must have become aware of the threatening aspect of

---

[1] See below, pp. 286 f.

public affairs both abroad and at home. The date of
his call (*c.* 626 B.C.) coincides very nearly with the
death of Asshurbanipal, the last of the great Assyrian
monarchs. That event, although Jeremiah could not
have known it at the time, marked a crisis in the history
of Asia. Already there circulated in Judah the rumour
of ominous movements in the north which portended
the break up of the huge empire to which the little
Hebrew kingdom belonged. It was precisely the situation in which the God who doeth nothing without
revealing His secret to His servants the prophets (Amos
iii. 7) was wont to raise up a prophet in Israel. He had
done so recently in the person of Zephaniah, and now
His choice was to light on Jeremiah. In the internal
condition of the country also there was cause for anxiety
and foreboding. Since Jeremiah was a 'lad[1]' at the
time of his call, we may place his birth approximately
in the year 645, towards the close of the long reign of
Manasseh. The religious policy of that king had been
dictated by subservience to Assyria, and involved the
adoption of Assyrian cults alongside of the worship of
Yahwe. The opposition of the prophetic party, which
stood for the pure and exclusive service of Yahwe had
been repressed with a ruthless severity which caused a
later generation to look back on this period as the time
when the doom of the nation was finally sealed (Jer.
xv. 4; 2 Kings xxi. 11, 16, xxiii. 26, xxiv. 3, 4). At his
death in 638, coinciding as it did with the decline of the

---

[1] *na'ar* (i. 6, 7). The word may of course denote any age from
infancy up to the verge of middle life. Commentators are mostly too
afraid of pressing the use of it here in the direction of extreme youth: he
must, they think, have been at least 25 years of age. To render it 'too
young,' in deference to the LXX, seems a needless deviation from the
plain sense of the Hebrew. Considering that Jeremiah was unmarried,
that his renunciation of married life was a consequence of his vocation
(xvi. 1), and that early marriages are the rule among Orientals, it is
quite probable that he was under 20 when the call came to him.

Assyrian power, the smouldering discontent broke out in the flames of party strife, and his son Amon was assassinated after a reign of two years. Jeremiah was old enough to remember this tragic incident, and the accession of Josiah, a boy of his own age, in his eighth year. A good deal has been written about the possible relations between these two young men, growing up within a few miles of one another, and each destined to play an influential part in his country's history. But of personal contact between them at any period of their lives we have no hint whatsoever. We know that Jeremiah had a sincere admiration for the character and administration of his sovereign (xxii. 15 f.), although he was more than critical of the great achievement with which the name of Josiah is associated, the promulgation and enforcement of the law of Deuteronomy[1]. Meanwhile we simply note that the two men had reached the threshold of manhood when Jeremiah passed through the decisive experience that made him a prophet of God. To that event in his history we will now turn our attention.

The call of Jeremiah, as recorded in the first chapter of the book, took the form of a dialogue between himself and Yahwe, through which the consciousness of a life-long vocation to the service of God was impressed on his mind. In *vv.* 4–10 we read:

4 There came to me this word of Yahwe:

5 Before I formed thee in the womb I knew thee,
And before thou camest forth I set thee apart;
A prophet to the nations I ordained thee.

6 And I said:

Ah, Lord Yahwe!
Behold I know not how to speak;
For I am but a lad.

[1] See Chaps. VI, VII.

7 And Yahwe said to me:

> Say not thou art but a lad;
>> For to whomsoever I send thee thou shalt go,
>> And whatsoever I command thee thou shalt speak.

8 Have no fear before them, for I am with thee to succour thee:
'Tis an oracle of Yahwe.

9 Then Yahwe stretched forth His hand and laid it on my mouth, and said:

> Lo, I put My word in thy mouth:
> 10 See, I put thee in charge this day
>> Over the nations and over the kingdoms
>> To pluck up and to pull down, to build and to plant.

The first thing that calls for attention here is the visionary form in which the fundamental experience is cast; but having already said what is necessary on the nature of the prophetic visions in general (pp. 10 ff.), I will only add that the narrative before us is to be explained in the way there indicated. It is worthy of remark, however, that the element of *vision* in the literal sense is here very slight: the prophet is aware of the presence of Yahwe and feels the touch of His hand upon his mouth, but he does not say that he *saw* Him. We are reminded of that 'consciousness of a Presence' which Professor James has described as an 'imperfectly developed hallucination,' and of which he cites examples as occurring to persons of sound intellect in full possession of their waking senses[1]. On the other hand what is sometimes called audition is very prominent: the word of Yahwe comes to the prophet as an audible external voice.

It is instructive from several points of view to compare this inaugural experience of Jeremiah with that of his great predecessor Isaiah. To Isaiah the Lord appeared arrayed in awful splendour and majesty, seated on a high and lofty throne, unapproachable, so that the mortal eye could not gaze on His countenance;

---

[1] *Varieties of Religious Experience*, pp. 58–63.

and the consecrating touch on his lips is given by a ministering seraph. But God meets with Jeremiah on life's common way, standing by his side, and Himself laying His hand on his mouth. His presence inspires no terror or crushing sense of personal guilt, but only a natural shrinking from the greatness of the task allotted to him;—a striking contrast both to the 'Woe is me!' of Isaiah, and his eager 'Here am I.' We cannot but feel that though this may have been Jeremiah's first vision of Yahwe it was not the beginning of his fellowship with Him. It is the consummation of a genuine religious experience, rooted probably in the pieties of home and early life, of a growing self-knowledge and knowledge of God, which now ripens into the consciousness of a special mission.

Accordingly, of the impressions made on Jeremiah at this time the first and fundamental one is just the sense of *personal predestination* to the prophetic office; he realises not merely that he is called to be a prophet *now*, but that he has been destined and fashioned for this calling from his birth. The idea of individual predestination to a great work is not new in the Old Testament (Jud. xiii. 5), but it acquires a peculiar significance in the mind of a prophet. It is not of course a truth suddenly injected into the mind from without— no such process is conceivable—but a conviction formed within, an intuitive perception of the divine ideal and meaning of his existence, of his true place in the divine order of the world, of the work for which he is 'cut out' in the service of God and of His kingdom. In all the higher callings of life there are such moments of self-discovery as are described in the well-known lines of Wordsworth:

> I made no vows, but vows
> Were then made for me; bond unknown to me
> Was given that I should be, else sinning greatly,
> A dedicated spirit:—

moments when the soul yields itself to the guidance of a power higher than its own, when latent capacities of the mind bestir themselves, and far-reaching resolves are made which contain the germ of the best that the man will ever be or achieve. The call of a prophet was this, but it was something more. It was an act not of self-discovery merely, but of self-surrender to a personal Being, who knows even before He is known, and chooses His servants before they choose Him. The sense of predestination in Jeremiah's consciousness means the conviction that the endowments of his whole nature, his physical and moral environment, all the influences of heredity and education that had shaped his life and made him what he was, had worked together under the hand of God to prepare him for the task to which he is now summoned. He is not to be a mere mouthpiece of the word of Yahwe, but a chosen vessel, fitted in every part of his being to be the medium of revelation to his fellow men.

There is, however, another element in Jeremiah's initiation which is at first sight surprising, and difficult to understand. He felt himself called to be a 'prophet *to the nations.*' How, it might be asked, could a young inexperienced individual, unversed in public affairs, have been led to think of himself thus early as presiding over the destinies of powerful empires and great nations? Was it not enough to be a prophet to Israel; and was not his ministry as a matter of fact practically confined to his own people? None of his predecessors, so far as we know, had entertained so exalted an idea of his mission. Both Amos and Isaiah had uttered oracles against foreign nations, and Isaiah had predicted the overthrow of the mightiest empire on earth. Yet to Amos the charge had been simply 'Go, prophesy to my people Israel,' and to Isaiah 'Go, speak to this people.' While Hosea, with whom Jeremiah's affinities are closest, had said nothing about the fate of any foreign people at all. Is it credible that Jeremiah, the most diffident and sensitive of prophets, entered on his public work with this amazing consciousness of the world-wide scope of his commission? Or must we conclude with Duhm that this feature of the call stamps the whole narrative as apocryphal, and that it was only the imagination of later Judaism which transformed the modest young priest of Anathoth into the colossal figure who pulls down and builds up nations and kingdoms, and pours out vials of wrath on the whole world[1]?

Now Duhm suggests a partial answer to his own objections when he points out that a tendency to ascribe to the prophets of Israel a commanding influence over the destinies of foreign states appears already in the popular biographies of Elijah and Elisha preserved in the book of Kings. And that the idea was not strange to Jeremiah's later thinking is seen from the words he addressed to an opponent many years afterwards: 'The prophets that were before me and thee from old time prophesied against many lands and against great kingdoms, of war...' (ch. xxviii. 8),—a passage, by the way, whose authenticity Duhm is at pains to affirm. It would seem, therefore, that the issue is narrowed down to this: whether this conception of the prophetic office is one that could have presented itself to Jeremiah at the moment of his call. I see no reason why it should not. We ought to be very chary of imposing limitations to the insight into his own future which may come to a prophet or man of genius in his first vision of the course his life is to take. And if the current estimate of prophecy

---

[1] It has of course been suggested that the passage expresses a conception of his office which Jeremiah arrived at much later in his career (see ch. xxv. 15 ff.). A few critics have thought to get rid of the difficulty by a slight but utterly unacceptable alteration of the text, reading 'my nation' instead of 'the nations.'

already included a certain cosmopolitan sphere of influence, it is surely conceivable that as soon as Jeremiah knew his place in that goodly fellowship, his thoughts rose instinctively to the height of his calling, and he saw himself put in charge over the nations as the accredited representative of Yahwe the God of hosts.

But the real significance of this aspect of the prophet's consciousness appears more clearly from another point of view. The truth is that the political situation had so changed since the dawn of written prophecy that there was no more room for a merely national prophecy in Israel than for a merely national deity in its religion. Judah was at this time, and had been for more than a century, a dependency of the Assyrian empire. It belonged to an international system so interlocked that the fate of one small kingdom involved the fate of many other States small and great. Moreover, there were ominous signs of a vast impending convulsion which threatened the dissolution of the entire political fabric on which civilisation rested. It was no longer possible that such a judgment as the prophets had foretold could descend on Judah without a general upheaval in which some powers would go down and others be built up. And the true prophet is one who from his watch-tower gives forth the word that rules the storm—the word of the Lord, whose secret is revealed to His servant.

We may here pass at once to consider the import of the two supplementary visions in which these ideas receive a more precise determination—the vision of the almond-branch and of the heated cauldron in *vv.* 11–14. I assume that these belong to the cycle of Jeremiah's initiatory experiences; although the fact that each has a separate introductory formula shows that they are not a part of the original ecstasy, and leaves open the possibility that they date from later periods of his life. These visions have a peculiar psychological

interest. They seem to be instances of a phenomenon
not uncommon in prophecy, viz. the blending of actual
sense impressions with subjective ideas in such a way
that the seer himself is unable to distinguish the two.
The almond-twig and the boiling pot are, I take it, not
hallucinations, like Macbeth's dagger, but real objects
of vision which thrust themselves into the prophet's
cogitations, and become invested with a mystic significance which expresses itself in an oracular utterance,
probably of the nature of an audition.

Thus, it is midwinter, when all nature is asleep, and
Jeremiah's attention is arrested by a solitary almond-
branch bursting into flower. The almond, which blos-
soms in January, was poetically named by the Hebrews
the *wakeful* tree, as the first of all the trees to wake up
at the touch and promise of spring. Looking at it, the
prophet is impelled to pronounce its name: *Shāḳēd*,
'awake.' What does it signify? The answer comes
unbidden: 'I am wakeful (*Shōḳēd*) over My word to
fulfil it.'

Again, in a moment of rapt meditation, his gaze
rests on a pot boiling on the domestic hearth; and he
seems to notice—what he would scarcely have noticed
if his mind had not been preoccupied with the idea—
that its mouth is turned away from the north. The
meaning here lies in two words: 'blown' ('a pot blown
upon'; i.e. fiercely heated by a blast of wind), and
'north'; and they come together in the following oracle:

From the north shall the evil be blown
On all that inhabit the earth.

If I have rightly interpreted the symbolism, we have
here the image of a magic cauldron brewing in the
mysterious north, and sending forth deadly fumes
which will carry ruin and desolation over the world—
an emblem of the sense of calamity which already

haunted Jeremiah's mind, and was to find impassioned expression in his earliest poetic effusions[1].

It is tempting to read into these two visions a fine contrast between the silent upbuilding forces of life and renewal which work slowly and unceasingly for the advancement of mankind, and the destructive agencies which sweep through the world from time to time working out the divine purpose in judgment. That, however, goes beyond the true meaning of the passage. The two images are disparate: one expresses a general principle of prophecy; the other deals with a particular concrete application. The word over which Yahwe is wakeful is the word of threatening as well as the word of promise and hope. On the second vision we need not linger now, because it will occupy our attention fully in the next chapter. But on the first one observation may be made. In early Israel, and even in written prophecy we find occasional traces of a crude conception of the word of God as endowed with an inherent, almost magical, efficacy, in virtue of which it works out its own fulfilment. Traces of that idea occur even in the discourses of Jeremiah; but this vision seems to teach that in principle he had risen above it. The assurance that the word which he will speak in the name of Yahwe will not return to Him void rests on no belief in its self-fulfilling energy, but on the wakefulness of Yahwe—the ever-active, living, personal presence of One who knows the end from the beginning.

[1] Some technical difficulties of this exposition have caused Duhm and others to adopt an entirely different construction of the omen. Reading מִפְּנֵי for מִפְּנֵי, he renders the clause 'with its front (lit. "face") turned towards the north'; and since a pot has no 'face' (!), he takes this to mean that the front of the fireplace was on its northward side, and was fanned by a blast coming from that quarter. This reading creates more difficulties than it solves, and yields a somewhat confused interpretation of the symbol.—In *v.* 14 it is necessary to read with the LXX תֻּפַּח 'shall be blown' for the Hebrew תִּפָּתַח 'shall be opened.'

We may now sum up the impressions which this whole narrative conveys of our prophet's character and individuality. Jeremiah comes before us here in the freshness of his youth, modest and shrinking from publicity, and as one whose days have been 'bound each to each by natural piety.' He knows already something of what it means to be a prophet, and is familiar with the writings and thoughts of Hosea. He is awaking to the consciousness that the times call for another such voice to bring men to a sense of realities. A foreboding of coming doom, a conviction that all is not well between Israel and Yahwe, has taken possession of him and cut him off from the innocent gaieties and pleasures of youth. He is subject to moods of visionary abstraction, in which spiritual things take bodily shape before the inner eye. In one such hour the call of God comes to him with irresistible power; and after a momentary hesitation he yields to its constraint, and is filled with a new inflexible courage which makes him as a wall of brass against all the assaults of an unbelieving world.

In all this we have already an indication of the course which his religious development was to follow. The conviction that he was predestined to be a prophet in itself suggests the consciousness of a broader and more human relation to God than is involved in the call to a special work; and the suggestion is confirmed by his peculiar response to the divine summons. It is as if the sense of vocation appealed only to one side of his nature; there is another side which cries out in protest against it. A personality chosen and moulded from the beginning for the high calling of a prophet: that is Yahwe's estimate of His servant's capacity; and in recognising that it is God's Jeremiah confesses that in the depth of his heart he feels it to be true. But he has his own private estimate of his powers which will not be suppressed, and he exclaims that he is not fit for this task, at least he is not fit for it yet. 'Alas, Lord Yahwe! I cannot speak; I am but a lad.' It is not a rejection of the heavenly vision, but a sincere plea for delay, as if he had said, May I not wait till I can speak with the wisdom and authority that come with years? But the call is inexorable; and Jeremiah's misgivings are overcome by the assurance that the message he is to deliver and the strength to utter it are not his own but the word and power of the Almighty.

Now this incident foreshadows the internal tragedy of Jeremiah's career. The conflict was past for the time; the victory of conscience over inclination, of the spirit over the flesh, of the higher self over the lower, was in principle won. But the brief struggle was the prelude to many others which beset the prophet through life. Again and again he was to experience the opposition between the natural impulses and affections of his human heart and the imperative mandate of the divine word. Of that protracted inward agony there are many poignant expressions in Jeremiah's later poems, and in these we shall find the key to the significance of his personality as the first great exponent of individual and universal religion.

CHAPTER III

THE NORTHERN PERIL

THE vision of the 'seething cauldron' in ch. i. 13 f., which we have already considered, speedily received its historical interpretation in some of Jeremiah's earliest oracles. The fourth chapter of the book contains a selection of short poetic effusions, describing the successive stages of a great wave of barbaric invasion sweeping down from the north, spreading havoc and desolation over the whole civilised world, and discharging Yahwe's wrath against His people. We have now to examine the contents of these poems in the light of the circumstances under which they were composed. A rough translation of the outstanding passages (preserving as far as possible the rhythm of the original) will convey better than any summary an idea of the prophet's state of mind in face of this appalling visitation.

The Watchman's Cry (*vv.* 5*b*–8)

5*b* Let the trumpet be blown in the land;
    Loud be your call:
  'Assemble and let us escape
    To the cities with walls.'

6 Hoist ye the signal for Zion!
    No time for delay!
  For danger comes out of the North,
    And Havoc untold.

7 A lion is roused from his lair,
    A Spoiler of nations;
  He is started,—gone forth from his haunts
    To harry the earth.

8 Gird you with sackcloth for this;
  Lament and wail;
For Yahwe's hot anger lies on us,
  And turns not away.

The gathering storm (vv. 13, 14)

13 Behold, like clouds he comes up,
   His chariots a stormwind!
Swifter than vultures his horses;
  Woe to us! We're undone.

14 O Jerusalem, wash thee from sin
   If thou would'st be saved:
How long shall lodge in thy heart
  Thy dissolute thoughts?

The approaching Foe (vv. 15–17)

15 Hark! a runner from Dan!
   A Herald of Evil from Ephraim's hills:
16 Warn the people: Behold they come!
   Let Jerusalem hear!

From a far land leopards are coming,
  Against Judah's townships they roar;
17 Like sleepless field-watchers they prowl around (?).

*　　*　　*　　*　　*

The Prophet's Anguish (vv. 19–21)

19 My bowels, my bowels! O my pain!
   O walls of my heart!
My soul is in tumult within;
  I cannot keep still,
For the trumpet's din in my ears,
  The alarum of war.

20 Crash upon crash it comes—
   The ruin of all the land.
Of a sudden my tent is ruined,
  In an instant my curtains.
21 How long must I see the signal?
   The blaring trumpet hear?

A Vision of Chaos (vv. 23–26)

23 I looked to the earth—and behold a chaos!
   To the heavens—and their light was gone.
24 I looked to the hills—and lo, they quivered,
   And all the mountains shook.
25 I looked—and behold, no man was there,
   And all the birds of heaven were flown.
26. I looked to the cornland—and lo, a desert,
   And all its cities were razed away.

The Panic of the Invasion (v. 29)

From the noise of horsemen and bowmen
   All the land is in flight:
They crawl into caverns, hide in the thickets[1],
   And scale the crags.
Every town is deserted,
   None dwell therein.

Zion in her Agony (vv. 30, 31)

30 And thou, spoiled one, what doest thou
   Dressing in scarlet,
Flaunting in trinkets of gold,
   And enlarging thine eyes with paint?
In vain thine adorning! The lewd lovers scorn thee,
   They seek thy life.

31 Hark! A shriek like a travailing woman's
   With her first child!
'Tis the voice of the daughter of Zion, gasping,
   Stretching her hands, (and crying)
'Woe is me! For my soul faints away
   At the feet of the slayers.'

Although these poems must have been composed at
intervals, and under many fluctuations of feeling, they
seem to have been carefully selected and artistically

[1] Reading with Erbt, after the LXX: בָּאוּ בַחוּרִים חָבְאוּ בֶּעָבִים

arranged so as to form a complete cycle, beginning
with the first warning blast of the trumpet, and reaching
an overpowering climax in the death-shriek of the
doomed capital, with which the chapter closes. There
might be no great difficulty in supposing that the
selection was the work of Jeremiah himself; but more
probably it was made by an editor, who has supplied
introductory formulae and connecting links (5 a, 9,
11 a, 18) and added certain passages which may be of
later date (10, 22, 27, 28). That it is only a selection
appears from the fact that there are several isolated
poems of precisely the same character and undoubtedly
belonging to the same time, scattered over the succeed-
ing chapters[1]. Those just rendered, however, supply
ample material for a consideration of the phase of
Jeremiah's experience with which we are now concerned.

Our first task is to ascertain how these obviously
idealised descriptions are related to actual facts of history. 'Prophecies,' says Dr Davidson, are usually 'suggested by some great movement among the nations, in
which Jehovah's presence is already felt[2].' The prophet's
mind is the seismograph of providence, vibrating to the
first faint tremors that herald the coming earthquake.
Is this principle verified in the case of Jeremiah? and
if so, to what great movement of peoples can we trace
the presentiment embodied in the vision of the seething
cauldron, and becoming articulate in the poems before
us?

The opening of Jeremiah's ministry, we have seen,
coincides approximately with the death of Asshurbanipal, and therefore with the two earliest attacks of the

---

[1] v. 6 (?), 15–17; vi. 1–5 (6, 7?), 22–26; and, according to some,
viii. 14 ff., and x. 19–22.

[2] *Nahum, Habakkuk and Zephaniah* (in *Cambridge Bible for Schools*),
p. 14; cf. p. 98.

Medes on Nineveh, first under Phraortes and then, shortly afterwards, under his son Cyaxares. Now there is a passage of Herodotus which connects the second of these Median attacks directly with one of those periodic irruptions of northern barbarians which so often deflected the course of ancient history. We read that the Medes had already defeated the Assyrians, and were on the point of capturing Nineveh, when they were routed and driven off by a great host of Scythians, under Madyes, the son of Protothyes, which had come from southern Europe, pursuing the Cimmerians along the north shore of the Euxine, and entering Asia round the east end of the Caucasus. Thereafter the Scythians made a raid towards Egypt, but when they reached the frontier they were induced by the bribes and prayers of Psammetichus to retrace their steps. For 28 years they are said to have lorded it over 'all Asia,' turning things upside down by extortion, rapine and massacre. At last the Medes got rid of them by a treacherous stratagem; and then Cyaxares conquered Nineveh and put an end to the Assyrian empire. In these events, especially the Scythian incursion into Palestine, most critics and historians since Eichhorn have found the suggestion and background of Jeremiah's prophecies of the Foe from the North; and no other theory gives so adequate an explanation of the foreboding with which he entered upon his work. Unfortunately, the vague and misleading statements of Herodotus, and his inaccurate chronology, leave many points obscure; and there is still a difficulty in determining how far Jeremiah's anticipations were influenced or coloured by contemporary historical events.

If we had only the narrative of Herodotus to guide us, it would be natural to suppose that the movement which awoke the prophetic impulse in Jeremiah (and also, we may add, in his older contemporary Zephaniah) was the first appearance of Scythian and Cimmerian nomads in Asia; and that these two prophets had a prevision of the menace that lurked in the teeming populations beyond the Caucasus and the Black Sea. But the Assyrian evidence puts that attractive speculation out of court. The Scythians who relieved Nineveh had been settled on the outskirts of the empire for a century before the death of Asshurbanipal, and had a standing alliance with the Assyrians against the Medes to the east of them and the Cimmerians to the west. Their presence, therefore, must have been known in Palestine when Jeremiah wrote. On the other hand the Scythian raid on Palestine, for which Herodotus is the sole authority, may well have followed the relief of Nineveh about 626; and if we suppose that it took place shortly after that event, it would nearly synchronise with the opening of Jeremiah's ministry. There is thus a good deal to be said for the conjecture that this particular episode of the Scythian invasion was the 'movement among the nations' in which he discerned the signs of coming judgment[1].

[1] See Herodotus i, 103–7; iv, 1. The Σκύθαι of Herodotus are identified by Assyriologists with the Ashguza of the monuments, who as early as the reign of Sargon (722–05), already occupied the district round Lake Urumia, having the Cimmerians to the west of them round Lake Van. Under Esarhaddon (681–68) their king Bartatua (evidently the Πρωτοθύης of Herodotus) sought an alliance with Assyria by offering his daughter in marriage to Esarhaddon. It would seem that the historical perspective is greatly foreshortened in the narrative of Herodotus. He writes as if the Scythians had reached Assyrian territory from Europe just in time to beat off the Medes from Nineveh. Whether that be the course actually followed by the invasion at a much earlier time, or whether Herodotus knew of some more recent migration, is immaterial to our inquiry. The facts seem to be established that the Ashguza-Scythians were allies of the Assyrians, and that their intervention at the crisis of Nineveh's fate was due to this long-standing alliance. See Winckler in *Die Keilinschriften und das alte Testament*, p. 100 ff. It is difficult to know what to make of the obviously exaggerated statement

So far, then, as we can now read the signs of the times from Jeremiah's point of view, there were three elements in the external situation likely to impress the mind of a prophet. There was *first* the known existence of a new group of formidable warlike peoples—Medes, Scythians, Cimmerians—on the northern frontiers of civilisation. *Next* there was the threatened collapse of the Assyrian empire under the pressure of these vigorous races, which meant the dissolution of the whole established system of international relations. *Lastly* there was the dread of an invasion by these barbarians, an invasion whose imagined horrors surpassed all previous experience. How these vague impressions were combined in the mind of the prophet, and in what order they emerged into consciousness, it is of course impossible to discover. We may surmise that at the time of his call he had already gathered from rumours that had reached Palestine a conception of the general character and appearance of the northern peoples—their language, their method of warfare, their predatory habit, and so forth—and that he also foresaw that the empire of Assyria would succumb to their persistent assaults. In these distant troubles that disturbed the north he may even then have discerned the portents of a great political catastrophe, which was to be Yahwe's judgment on the whole earth. At a somewhat later time,

that the Scythians ruled all Asia for 28 years between the first (*c.* 626) and the second (606) assault of Cyaxares on Nineveh. It is quite possible that during that interval they were formidable disturbers of the peace of Asia; and they may have 'ruled' it by predatory excursions; but as an imperial power they cannot have played any part. Lastly, the expedition against Egypt is mentioned by no other authority, and cannot be certainly dated. The silence of the Hebrew historians with regard to any such incident is remarkable; but it does not necessarily discredit the testimony of Herodotus. There is no difficulty in assuming that it happened about the time when Jeremiah was composing his 'Scythian' poems.

when the dreaded invasion became an imminent danger, his foreboding may have found utterance in the 'Scythian poems' now before us.

That Jeremiah's descriptions of the unnamed foe agree *in the main* with what we know of the Scythians and their kinsfolk of later ages—the Gauls, Goths and Vandals—is hardly open to dispute. Exception is taken to one or two details, such as the mention of chariots in iv. 13, and of siege-operations in vi. 3 f., both of which are thought to be inconsistent with Scythian methods of warfare; but these points are too insignificant to neutralise the general impression conveyed by the poems. A wild, primeval, hyperborean race, of uncouth speech, cruel and pitiless, moving on horseback, armed with bow and spear, sweeping like a tornado over the land and leaving desolation in their track, prowling like hungry wolves or howling leopards round the fenced cities where the terrified inhabitants have taken refuge[1] —such is the picture presented in this series of lyrics; and it corresponds with the conception one must form of the character of a Scythian invasion. The correspondence may not be so exact as to exclude absolutely the alternative hypothesis to which some still adhere: viz. that from the first the prophet had in view the Chaldeans, who were the actual instruments of Judah's destruction. But the Chaldeans did not appear in the north of Syria until 20 years after the call of Jeremiah, and it would be contrary to the analogy of prophecy to suppose that a power which had not yet risen on the horizon should convey the first suggestion of Yahwe's final intervention[2].

---

[1] Ch. iv. 5 ff. *passim*; v. 6, 15–19; vi. 1–5, 6, 22–26.

[2] A careful review of the evidence is given by F. Wilke, who comes to the conclusion that the narrative in Herodotus is entirely destitute of historical foundation, and that the poems refer to the Chaldean invasion under Nebuchadnezzar (*Alttestamentliche Studien R. Kittel zum* 60

Now if a Scythian raid in sufficient force to have extorted gifts and prayers from the king of Egypt really took place, the danger to Judah must have been very great. It is usually held that little or no actual damage was done within Jewish territory. The marauders are supposed to have swept past along the coast route and to have returned on their track, leaving the hill country of Judah unmolested. That opinion may be entirely correct. It is consistent with the brief account of Herodotus, who only records the plunder of the temple of Aphrodite at Ashkelon by some stragglers from the main body during the retreat; and what is more important it would account for the silence of Old Testament writers on the episode. The matter is not altogether disposed of by these considerations, and a few scholars have put forward the theory of a more or less protracted occupation of Palestine by the Scythians, under which

Geburtstag dargebracht, 1913, pp. 222 ff.). The objection stated above seems to me decisive so long as we accept the common view that the poems belong to the youthful period of Jeremiah's work. Winckler, abandoning this position, dates the beginning of Jeremiah's prophecy from about 610 onwards, and thinks the dating of his call in the thirteenth year of Josiah was a device of the redactors to make him out to be a forerunner of the Deuteronomic reformation (*Geschichte Israels*, I, pp. 112 f.). That would no doubt make a reference to the Chaldeans plausible; but the suggestion is arbitrary and uncalled for. There is a difference between these passionate and explosive utterances and the later discourses of Jeremiah which is best explained by the difference between youth and age, and points to a considerable interval having elapsed since the 'Scythian' poems were composed. It is true, however, that they were first published about 604, when a Babylonian invasion from northern Syria was threatened; and Jeremiah did then recognise in the new enemy the fulfilment of his early and unshaken presentiment of danger looming in the north. It is therefore possible, though the assumption seems scarcely necessary, that he modified the details of the picture in order to bring it into closer agreement with his altered outlook. On the whole it is a fortunate circumstance that Herodotus has preserved the notice of an incident which seems to throw so much light on Jeremiah's biography as this otherwise unrecorded Scythian invasion.

the kingdom of Judah suffered severely[1]. The question is of some interest for the understanding of Jeremiah's prophecies. If there be any truth in the view just mentioned, the realistic element in the poems before us may be greater than is generally allowed. It is impossible in poetry to distinguish sharply between realism and imagination; and that imagination plays a large part in these poems is of course beyond doubt. Yet as we read these graphic pictures of the consternation and flight of the people, the arrival of messengers in hot haste from the north, the crowding of the rural population into fortified towns, the cutting off of stragglers in the open country, the meditated assault on the capital, it is difficult to suppose that it is all a creation of pure poetic fancy following out the conception of an invasion which was imaginary from first to last. When Jeremiah, for example, warns the country people to seek safety in walled towns and raise the signal for flight to Zion (iv. 5 f.), and afterwards calls on the Benjamites to escape *from* Jerusalem (vi. 1), it is at least a tempting conjecture that his own tribesmen and neighbours had actually taken refuge in Jerusalem and that the city itself was in danger[2]. The conclusion is very uncertain; but we shall lose nothing if we take the Scythian poems to be in the main imaginative anticipations of future calamities, always shooting ahead of the accomplished fact, but at the same time following more or less the development of a grave national crisis which was as real to the prophet's countrymen as it was to himself[3].

[1] See Ewald, *History of Israel* (E.T.), iv, 230 f.; W. Erbt, *Jeremia und seine Zeit*, pp. 208, 211.

[2] Ewald assumes that Josiah was actually besieged for a time in Jerusalem by the Scythians on their return from the Egyptian frontier (*l.c.*, p. 231).

[3] The reading of the situation will depend largely on a difficult section in ch. ii (*vv.* 14–17) in which Israel is spoken of as preyed upon by lions, as having its cities burnt with fire, and its land laid waste. The verses have often been considered an interpolated though genuine

However that may be, it is certain that Jeremiah was left in the end with a considerable margin of unfulfilled prediction on his hands. The crisis passed—how long it lasted we do not know—the nation survived, and years of peace and comparative security followed. How this partial and temporary failure of his prophecies affected the future of Jeremiah's activity, how it reacted on his own conviction of the fundamental truth of his message, are questions which will come up for consideration at later stages of our study.

We now turn from the external circumstances to the subjective aspect of this group of poems: their literary characteristics, their emotional quality, and in general the light they shed on Jeremiah's mind at this early stage of his career. The most noteworthy feature of these oracles is their purely lyrical character. They are,

fragment in ch. ii, composed by Jeremiah at a much later time, and that is perhaps a possible view (see below, p. 56). But if they belong to the early period of his ministry and are connected with the verses which follow, no explanation of them is so satisfying as to suppose they refer to the ravages of a recent Scythian invasion at the beginning of Jeremiah's work. When we find further that they are associated with allusions to a vacillating policy towards Assyria and Egypt (ii. 18; cf. 36 f.), the natural inference is that in the throes of alarm caused by the approach of the Scythians the statesmen of Jerusalem turned for succour first to the one great power and then to the other and were disappointed in both cases. Thus far I am inclined to agree with the somewhat hazardous speculations of Dr Erbt (*l.c.*). But that scholar seems to me to draw too largely on his imagination when he assumes that the rumours of the Scythian depredations were at first received in Jerusalem with grim and eager satisfaction. The prevailing feeling was one of joy and relief that Assyria's hour had come: whatever else might happen, the hated world-empire would perish in this great tumult of the nations (p. 186). Afterwards, when Judah was immediately threatened, help was sought first from Assyria (which was in no condition to give it), and then from Egypt (which was equally powerless and supine); and finally, all other hope being abandoned, negotiations were attempted with the Scythians themselves (iv. 30 f.: p. 200). These precarious combinations afford no help in the interpretation of Jeremiah's writings.

as one critic has said, 'genuine lyrics, the spontaneous outflow in language and imagery of inward experiences and feelings[1].' It may require a little effort to perceive how completely true this is. We note at the outset that they are not the direct word of the Lord to Jeremiah, but the effect of that word on a sensitive human heart, which gives forth its own peculiar tones like the Aeolian harp when its strings are swept by the wind. The speaker is not Yahwe but the prophet himself; the identification of the human *ego* with the divine which is so characteristic of prophetic utterance finds no expression here[2]. Here and there, it is true, they are converted into direct oracles by an inserted heading or phrase (e.g. iv. 9, 12, 17), but the metre generally enables us to recognise these as no part of the original composition. Nor again are they in their first intention a prophetic message to men. The few cases where the people or Jerusalem is addressed are of the nature of poetic apostrophe rather than of prophetic exhortation (iv. 8, 14, 18, 30 f., vi. 1, 8, 26). 'Gird you with sackcloth for this—Lament and wail' is not so much a summons to repentance as a vivid expression of how men would act if they saw the coming danger as the prophet sees it. Like all true lyrics, the poems have their end in themselves, in the artistic utterance of personal emotion; and only in a secondary application do they become a medium of enlightenment or instruction or warning to others.

This lyrical note had never been wholly absent from Hebrew prophecy. Even in Amos and Isaiah, the most severely ethical of Jeremiah's predecessors, it finds occasional expression in the traditional form of the elegy; and Ezekiel, the least sympathetic of his suc-

---

[1] H. Schmidt, *op. cit.* p. 218.

[2] This is true not only of the passages translated from ch. iv, but of the whole series of Scythian poems, with the exception of ch. v. 15–17, which is a direct threat of judgment spoken in the name of Yahwe.

III] THE NORTHERN PERIL

cessors, exhibits a surprising mastery of that form of
expression. In Jeremiah, however, the lyrical gift has a
range and depth of feeling and imagination which give
it a new significance. We cannot speak of him as
'warbling his native wood-notes wild'—his mood is
too sombre for that—but there is a spontaneity in the
outflow of his inmost, most human affections which is
found in no other prophet. Other prophets deliver their
message with no less intensity of personal conviction
than he; but their whole emotional nature goes with the
divine word they utter; and if they have other feelings,
of pity or compunction or depression under the burden
laid upon them, these as a rule are sternly repressed. In
Jeremiah's poetry all this is laid bare to us: the images
that distract and appal him, his mental distress and grief,
and his deep commiseration for the people he loves. In the
Scythian poems especially, this subjective vein so pre-
dominates as almost to conceal the underlying consciousness that they are the inspired word of God to Israel.

But this richly developed subjectivity is not only
interesting as an indication of the bent of Jeremiah's
genius; it is also an important element in his endowment
for the experience of personal religion. There is perhaps
a passing hint of its significance in this respect in an
obscure verse imbedded in ch. iv, which I have omitted
in the translation because the manner of its introduction
makes it doubtful if it belongs to this period of the
prophet's life[1] (iv. 10). The words are:

> Then I said, 'Ah, Lord Yahwe!
> Thou hast simply deceived this people,
> Saying "Ye shall have peace";
> And now the sword has pierced to the life!'

[1] If it does, it can only refer to spurious oracles which had lulled the
people into a false sense of security; and we should have to conclude
that at this early time Jeremiah had not attained to a clear judgment on
the phenomenon of false prophecy (cf. xiv. 13).

Here the prophet's sympathy for his compatriots breaks out in a remonstrance with Yahwe, and a plea in extenuation of their guilt. It is the earliest trace in the book of that reaction of human affection against the constraint of prophetic conviction which contains the germ of the peculiar modification of the prophetic consciousness which comes to light in Jeremiah's later experience.

Erbt makes the observation that Jeremiah was the first to introduce into prophecy this opposition between conscience and feeling, or between the voice of God and the impulse of the heart[1]. In the pages of Hosea, however, we find the struggle between the claims of righteousness and of mercy portrayed with a power which even Jeremiah does not surpass (Hos. vi. 4, vii. 15, xi. 8 ff., etc.). If there be a difference between the two prophets, it is that Hosea reflects the conflict back into the mind of God: it is Yahwe's own heart which is torn by the antagonism of justice and affection: that is to say, the prophet feels that both sides of his nature represent aspects of the mind of Yahwe towards Israel. So far as the idea of God is concerned, that is perhaps the highest truth that the prophetic theology ever reached, and it is exquisitely expressed by Jeremiah himself.

> Is Ephraim a favourite son—
> A darling child,
> That so oft as I speak against him
> I remember him still?
> Therefore my heart is moved for him:
> I have compassion on him[2].

That which is characteristic of Jeremiah is the dialogue of two voices within himself, one known to be divine, and the other consciously his own. As Hegel said of

[1] *Op. cit.* p. 199.
[2] Ch. xxxi. 20; cf. iii. 12, 19, 22, vi. 8, xii. 7, xxxi. 3–5, etc.

himself, he was not one of the combatants, but rather both of the combatants, and also the combat itself. It is possible that in ch. iv. 10, we have an early example of this conflict; but how deeply it was lodged in the consciousness of the prophet is only seen in the solitary wrestling with the mystery of his vocation which marked his riper years.

There is another feature of these poems on which some writers lay stress, as illustrating Jeremiah's mental condition at this time. It is thought that they show traces of having been composed in a state of mind bordering on ecstasy, similar to that in which he experienced the call to be a prophet. The question thus raised is obviously one of peculiar difficulty. The difference between the voluntary exercise of the imagination, which is of the essence of poetry, and the automatic working of it, in which images impress themselves on the senses like realities (as in a dream), is perhaps only a difference of degree. In certain natures there appears to be a point at which under intense feeling the one condition passes into the other; and in literature it must always be a very delicate if not impossible task to discriminate between them. Now most of these Scythian poems would pass without question as ordinary examples of poetic imagination. But there are some which do produce the impression of being a record of real visionary experiences. The strongest case is the passage translated above, beginning 'My bowels, my bowels! I writhe in pain' (iv. 19–21), which has even been characterised as 'among the best descriptions of a vision in the Old Testament, nay in all literature[1].' The excitement under which the prophet labours strains the heart as if it would break; his ears are filled with a medley of horrid sounds, in which are mingled the blare of the trumpet, the shouting of battle, the crash of falling

[1] Schmidt, *op. cit.* p. 205.

towers—the crack of doom: he is in a tent which
suddenly collapses and cannot be raised[1]. And the effect
does not wear off; go where he will, he cannot get rid
of the signal fluttering before his eyes, or the sound of
the trumpet in his ears. Is all this complaint of bodily
pains, this accumulation of incongruous images, merely
a 'nice derangement of metaphors,' or is it a description
of Jeremiah's actual sensations? The answer to that
question is not so clear as Schmidt thinks; but certainly
there are here all the symptoms of a dream-like condition
of mind, in which the perturbation of the prophet's
waking thoughts takes fantastic forms in the 'heat-
oppressed brain.' The following poem, the 'Vision of
Chaos' in vv. 23–26, might be explained in a similar
sense. Jeremiah, walking abroad, is suddenly overpowered by his inward agitation: the familiar landscape
is obliterated from his view; heaven's light is extinguished, and the earth is dissolved into chaos; the hills
become ghostly shapes that reel and totter around him.
Sign or sound of life there is none in all the weird
desolation; no man is there; the singing birds (objects
of special interest to Jeremiah) have flown away. It

---

[1] The image of the falling tent recurs in a still more striking form
in ch. x. 19–22; and relying on that parallel I have in translating
substituted the sing. 'my tent,' for the plu. in the text of iv. 20. In
ch. x, but for one half-verse (19 *b*), it would be natural to explain
the passage allegorically, the speaker being the personified nation, and
the theme the desolation of Exile (see Peake, *ad loc*.). But when Jeremiah
exclaims 'This is a sickness, and I must bear it,' it is clear that he is
speaking of an experience of which he himself is the subject; and we
are driven to interpret it after the analogy of iv. 20. The allusion in
x. 22 to a rumour 'from the land of the north' might suggest that this
poem belongs to the Scythian cycle; but we cannot be sure of that. For
one thing, the connexion of *v*. 22 with the vision is so loose that the
Massoretes commence a new section there. Apart from that, the vision
is one that might recur at any time when the prophet was brooding over
his people's fate, and would bring with it the thought of the northern
terror with which it was originally associated.

would be impossible to determine more precisely to what extent this visionary element pervades the early poetry of Jeremiah, and no good purpose would be served by attempting a minute analysis. It seems a plausible opinion that he was subject to such moods at all periods of his life (the last recorded instance being xxxviii. 21–23), but at no time with such frequency as during the crisis of the Scythian invasion[1]. If this be so, the fact is interesting as a proof of the agitation into which his youthful spirit was thrown by his first vivid presentiment of divine judgment on his nation, and also as a revelation of the psychological process by which his prophetic intuitions took shape in his mind.

I have dwelt at some length on the broad characteristics of this group of poems, partly because I regard them as the very earliest revelation of Jeremiah's genius, but still more because they exhibit tendencies and qualities of mind which are of importance in estimating his contribution to the development of prophecy and of subjective piety. Throughout his life the stream of lyric poetry which we strike here at the fountain head flowed steadily, though perhaps in diminishing volume, enriching the literature of Israel with some of its choicest strains. Through life also his inspiration frequently took the form of vision and audition though he learned that these conditions were not to be identified with standing in the council of the Lord and hearing His word. In Jeremiah the poet and the prophet are combined in a unique degree; and since 'character ripens more slowly than talent' it is not surprising if in his youth the poetic impulse seems to overshadow the prophetic[2]. But a

---

[1] Hölscher (*Die Profeten*, p. 294) gives an incomplete list of instances: iii. 21, iv. 13, 15, 18–21, 23–26, 31, v. 13, 14, vi. 11, viii. 16, 19, 20, x. 22, xxiii. 9. It will be seen that the majority of them are in Scythian poems.

[2] Compare the remarks of Duhm, *Kurzer Hand-commentar*, p. 47.

prophet he was at the core of his being; and as he beat
his music out he realised ever more clearly that his life
was rooted in personal fellowship with the God who
spoke to him and through him in his gift of lyrical
utterance as well as in the direct revelation of His
character and will.

CHAPTER IV

THE TWO RELIGIONS OF ISRAEL

THE message of the pre-exilic prophets rests on two fundamental convictions. One is the certainty or presentiment of an impending historical crisis with disastrous issues for the nation of Israel, and the other the verdict of their conscience on the religious and social disorders of their time. It is an interesting but not very important question which of these was primary, and which was derivative, in the mind of the prophet. Was he first roused by what Amos calls the roar of Yahwe —the premonition of judgment mysteriously awakened within him; and did he then, seeing how unprepared his people were to meet their God, proceed to denounce their sin, and call them to repentance? Or was it the other way about? Was his conscience first stirred by the evidence of abounding iniquity and irreligion, and was he thus led to scan the political horizon for signs of the retribution which, from his faith in the divine righteousness, he knew to be inevitable? These questions mark two opposite tendencies among modern writers on prophecy; but it is doubtful if the prophets themselves could have answered them. The presentiment of coming doom was the result of a variety of subtle impressions borne in upon their minds from many quarters—impressions which they could not have analysed, and of which they may often have been unconscious until they came to them in the form of a vision. A conscience sensitive to the presence of moral evil in the life around them was an essential part of their endowment; but it did not work in isolation from their other faculties, as if its only function had been to find a moral justification for a calamity otherwise foreseen: it was a vital element of the insight which enabled them to discern the signs of the time. Whether in any particular prophet the emphasis was more on the one idea or the other, and which of them came first in the delivery of his public message, are questions of secondary moment. It is the combination of the two, and their convergence on a single aim, which is the distinctive feature of the higher prophecy of the Old Testament.

These two aspects of the prophetic preaching are clearly distinguished in the first six chapters of the book of Jeremiah, the kernel of which consists of oracles dating from the earliest period of his ministry, viz. the five years between his call in 626 and the Deuteronomic reformation in 621. In the Scythian poems of ch. iv we have seen how the foreboding of a great world-convulsion agitated the mind of the prophet, and found expression in the remarkable series of lyrics of which that chapter is mainly composed. We are now to examine an equally striking and homogeneous collection of prophecies in ch. ii, where the ethical note of prophecy is illustrated in a criticism of the *religious* as distinct from *moral*[1] corruptions of the time. In tone and literary character these poems present a significant contrast to those of ch. iv. The Scythian poems are dominated by the apprehension of imminent calamity; allusions to the sin which is the cause of the judgment are few and casual, and some of them are later additions. The prophet speaks in his own name throughout, and expresses his own personal feelings; and there are indications that they were partly composed under ecstatic conditions. In ch. ii all this is reversed. There is first of all a marked change of

[1] The polemic against the *moral* evils of society commences at ch. v, and is dealt with in a later connexion (see Chap. VIII below).

emphasis. Here the main theme is the religious apostasy of the nation and its bitter consequences already experienced; the threat of judgment holds a very subordinate place. Again, the poems of ch. ii are not a lyrical outpouring of private emotion like those of ch. iv, but direct prophetic discourse addressed to the heart and conscience of the people. The speaker is Yahwe, and traces of visionary excitement on the part of the prophet are entirely absent. Now it is difficult to think that these profound differences are due merely to editorial selection and arrangement of oracles issued promiscuously during the same period of Jeremiah's history. The mental strain and agitation which is everywhere visible in ch. iv can hardly have alternated with the quieter reflective mood which is characteristic of ch. ii. It is more natural to suppose that two successive stages of the prophet's activity are represented; and assuming (as we safely may) that both belong to his early years, the only question is whether the stage represented by ch. ii preceded or followed the Scythian poems of ch. iv. It is conceivable, as some critics hold, that the order of the chapters is chronological: that Jeremiah was preoccupied with the corrupt state of public religion, and foresaw the judgment as a moral necessity, before the trumpet-blast smote on his inner ear, and his whole being was convulsed by the portent of 'evil looming in the north and dire destruction.' The obvious objection to that view is the vision of the seething cauldron in i. 13 f.: if that vision belongs to Jeremiah's initiatory experiences, it would be difficult to account for the absence of the foreboding which it expresses from his first prophecies, and its sudden emergence at a somewhat later time. For this and other reasons I prefer the view that the oracles of ch. ii belong mainly to the more tranquil period when the Scythian invasion was past, though

traces of its ravages were still visible as a reminder of
the chastisement which the nation had suffered because
of its ungodliness[1]. Fortunately, however, our understanding of Jeremiah's point of view is not greatly

[1] This opinion is confirmed by *vv.* 14–19 of ch. ii, if they belong
to the group of poems with which we are concerned, and if *vv.* 14–17
be not (as many hold) an interpolated section of later date (see the note
on p. 44 f. above). To that note I here add a few remarks on the historical
setting of these *vv.* Three theories are advanced. (*a*) That the section is
one of the earliest poems of Jeremiah, composed *before* the Scythian
raid. So Duhm, who regards *vv.* 14–17 as the original sequel and
antithesis to the ideal picture of Israel's past in *vv.* 2 *b*, 3. He takes the
verb in *v.* 16 (where I adopt his ingenious reading יְעָרוּךְ for יִרְעוּךְ)
as a future, in distinction from the past tenses of *vv.* 14 f., which refer
to the injuries which the nation had sustained through foreign aggression,
especially from the Assyrians, in the course of its past history. The
expressions of *v.* 15, however, seem to me to point to a more recent
disaster than any Assyrian invasion we know of, and there is a difficulty
in the abrupt introduction of Egypt as a future oppressor. (*b*) Giesebrecht, who assigns the compilation of ch. ii to the reign of Jehoiakim,
holds that the reference in *v.* 16 is to the depredations of the Egyptian
army which defeated Josiah at Megiddo in 608, the verb being rendered
as a frequentative present. This solution fails to give a sufficiently definite
meaning to the language of *vv.* 14 f., where the historic tenses imply a
distinction between the ravages there described and those inflicted by
the Egyptians. Another objection is that the situation it presupposes is
inconsistent with *v.* 18, and therefore requires the detachment of *vv.*
14–17 as an isolated fragment from their context. For if we assume with
G. that *v.* 18 alludes to pro-Egyptian tendencies manifested in Jerusalem
after sufficient time had elapsed for the lesson of Megiddo to be forgotten, we are confronted by the difficulty that by that time Assyria had
ceased to be a formidable world-power, whose alliance would be likely
to be sought by any political party in Judah. (*c*) There remains the
view which I have followed: that *vv.* 14 f. refer to the effects of the
Scythian raids, that the reference to Egypt in *v.* 16 is predictive, and
that *v.* 18 alludes to contemporary approaches to Assyria and Egypt for
help against the Scythians. Cornill, who considers *vv.* 14–17 an interpolation in this chapter, has come at last to the conclusion that only *vv.* 14, 15
are genuine words of Jeremiah, *vv.* 16, 17 being a spurious editorial addition suggested by 18 and 19 (see the Introduction to his commentary,
p. xli *n.*). The translation of the passage will be found on p. 66 below.

affected by this difference of opinion, so long as we see good reason to believe that he is still at the opening of his public career. We may therefore leave that issue in abeyance, and proceed to the exposition of these prophetic reflexions on the practical religion of the average Israelite in the seventh century before Christ.

While every true prophet is in opposition to the religious ideas and tendencies of his age, and in exposing their fallacies and aberrations reveals what religion means to himself, there is no one who has analysed the diverse and successive currents of spiritual influence in the society around him with such penetrating and sympathetic insight as Jeremiah. There is none, either, whose whole thinking is so permeated by the experience of direct personal fellowship with God, which is the ultimate basis and secret of religious life. It is of peculiar interest to ascertain how such a man viewed the common religious beliefs and practices of his contemporaries; and happily we have abundant means of satisfying our desire. In the poems now before us we find a first instalment of this aspect of his teaching: viz. an estimate of the popular religion of Israel from the standpoint of the prophetic theology. Here we have ample material for a study of Jeremiah's early convictions on the nature of religion.

It was a natural consequence of Jeremiah's upbringing in a country village that his first impressions of the religious condition of his people were drawn from the crude notions and half-heathen ritual of the rural population around his home. In the second chapter there is no certain allusion to the capital[1], or the official religion

---

[1] Unless the word נַיְא ('valley') in *v.* 23 denotes the Hinnom valley in the southern outskirts of Jerusalem, which is a possible, but not certain, interpretation (see below). The LXX adds to *v.* 28 a clause from xi. 13 mentioning the 'streets of Jerusalem' in parallelism with the 'cities of Judah'; but it is doubtful if the phrase be original here.

of the Temple, or the tone of religion in the upper ranks of society: what Jeremiah thought on these matters we have to learn from later discourses. We assume that he is still living in his father's house at Anathoth, within sight and hearing of the local sanctuary where the village people and the surrounding peasants and shepherds held their festivals and performed their devotions: with which, we may assume, the priestly traditions of his family had made him familiar. There he would make his first acquaintance with public religion as understood and practised by his neighbours. And he knew that in this respect Anathoth was just a microcosm of the national life. The cultus observed there was in all essentials the same as that which was practised at scores of shrines throughout the land; it was *the* religion of Israel, for it expressed far more truly than the elaborate ritual of the Temple the native bent of the national mind in its effort after contact with the divine. Its monuments were scattered over the face of the country—in altars on every high hill and under every green tree (ii. 20), on the 'bare heights' (iii. 2) whence resounded the 'revelry of the mountains' (iii. 23), the orgies of licentious worship which made day and night hideous to the refined ear of the prophet. And all this was but the visible and outward symbol of the ingrained habit and disposition of the people: the legible record of its sinful propensities (xvii. 1–3).

Now to describe this 'popular religion' of Israel in detail is a task beyond the scope of our present inquiry. But it is important to realise that it was not altogether a chaotic and fortuitous upgrowth of primitive superstitions such as survive beneath the surface of civilisation in all parts of the world. It had a definite historical origin in the circumstances of the settlement in Canaan, and the transition from nomadic to agricultural life; and through all its developments down to the exile it retained a certain continuity of principle impressed upon it at the beginning. Jeremiah had meditated deeply both on its origin and its essence, and it will help us to understand his criticism if we first look at the historic significance of the phenomenon with which he is dealing.

The occupation of Palestine by the Hebrew tribes brought about a peculiar 'polarity' in their religious attitude. They found themselves confronted by a type of religion hitherto unknown, but one which had a strong fascination for the sensuous side of their Semitic nature. This was the nature-religion of the Canaanites, whose manner of life they necessarily adopted, and with whom they largely intermingled. It centred in the worship of the Baals, the local divinities, who were regarded as the bestowers of life, fertility and increase, within the limited sphere of influence which belonged to each. The earliest contact of the Israelites with this type of religion took place, according to the tradition, at Baal-Peor on the east of the Jordan (Num. xxv. 3, xxxi. 16; Deut. iv. 3, etc.); and the prophet Hosea traces the beginning of their apostasy to the readiness with which they succumbed to its immoral attractions (Hos. ix. 10). But what happened at Baal-Peor was repeated with variations at every centre of Canaanite worship after the conquest of western Palestine. The danger of contamination from this impure religion was enhanced by the fact that the desert faith of Israel made no express provision for the devotional exercises suitable to the needs of an agricultural community. Thus it came about that Yahwe was recognised as the God of the nation, whose presence was realised in times of great national enthusiasm; but He was not at first apprehended as the God of the land, and the dispenser of the good gifts of corn and wine and oil which the former owners of the soil had gratefully ascribed to the Baals. Hence when the sentiment of national unity was weakened through the dispersion and isolation of the tribes, and faith in Yahwe burned low, the cult of the local deity seemed to suffice for all the religious wants of which the ordinary Israelite was conscious.

It is probable that the ordinary Israelite in the early stages of the settlement saw no great harm in having 'one religion for times of patriotic exaltation and another for daily life[1],' and abandoned himself to the seductions of Baal-worship with no thought of finally renouncing his national religion. But it was impossible for a permanent rivalry to exist between the God of the conquering race and the gods of the conquered land; and in course of time the two religions coalesced by an unstable compromise, in which Yahwe nominally supplanted the Baals as Lord of Canaan, and the bestower of the fertility of the soil. The change was not wholly for the worse; for in bringing the name of Yahwe into relation with every day concerns it tended to elevate the life of the people by associating its worship with the ethical and social ideals with which the national faith was identified. But this gain was more than neutralised by the degradation of Yahwe to the level of a nature-deity, and by the absorption of the old Canaanite ritual with all its repellent features into the public cultus of Israel. To the prophets, at all events, Baal and Yahwe stand for mutually exclusive principles of religion; and inasmuch as the character of a religion is determined not by the name of its God but by the kind of service in which he is supposed to delight, they do not hesitate to characterise the popular religion of Israel as a worship of Baal under the guise of the worship of Yahwe[2].

[1] W. Robertson Smith, *The Prophets of Israel*, p. 39 (2nd Ed.).

[2] Strictly speaking, perhaps, this applies only to Hosea and Jeremiah, the two prophets who after Elijah emphasise the contrast between the ethical religion of prophecy and the nature-worship into which the

That this is not a fanciful sketch of the origin and spirit of the popular religion of Israel appears most clearly from the analysis of it given in the second chapter of Hosea. Speaking of Israel under the figure of the wife of Yahwe, the prophet describes her actual religion as spiritual adultery with the false deities who had seduced her from her true allegiance. It is enough to quote the few verses in which he exposes the confusion of ideas which had led her astray. 'For she said, "I will go after my lovers (the Baals), the givers of my bread and my water, my wool and my flax, my oil and my drink." Therefore I will hedge up her way with thorns, and wall her up that she find not her paths. And when she pursues her lovers without reaching them, and seeks them without finding them, then she will say, "I will return to my first husband, for better it was with me then than now." But *she knew not that it was I* who gave her the corn and the must and the oil, and bestowed on her much silver and gold' (Hos. ii. 7–10). No words could more clearly express the essentially pagan character of the prevalent worship, or the con-

popular religion had degenerated. Other prophets deal with the evils of the cultus rather as a corruption within the national religion than as a foreign element derived from another religion. The difference is only formal: Amos and Isaiah accept the profession of the people that their worship is addressed to Yahwe, while Hosea and Jeremiah criticise this pretension, and show that it rests on a confusion of the nature of Baal with that of Yahwe. It is worth noting in this connexion that the divine names Baal and Baalim are almost confined to Hosea and Jeremiah among the canonical prophets. They occur about 15 times in the book of Jeremiah (though certainly not all the passages are genuine) and six times in Hosea: elsewhere we have only the solitary mention of the 'remnant of Baal' in Zeph. i. 4. The coincidence may be due to the influence of the older prophet on the younger, but there may be a deeper reason. Anathoth belonged to the tribe of Benjamin, whose affinities were with the then extinct kingdom of Samaria; and it is possible that this type of religion was more characteristic of the genial and fertile central region than of the sterner climate of Judah.

viction that it was a reversion to the Canaanite nature-religion in which it originated.

There is, however, one difference between the popular religion of Jeremiah's time and that of Hosea's, which is symptomatic of a changed religious atmosphere. This is the prevalence of child-sacrifice, which, although of immemorial antiquity in Palestine, and prominent in the Phoenician religion, does not appear to have been adopted by the Israelites till a late period. There is no trace of it in the prophets of the eighth century, nor indeed in the history except in the single case of Ahaz (2 Kings xvi. 3). The impression we get from the pages of Amos and Hosea is that the spirit of the popular worship was one of unrestrained mirth and festivity, untroubled by the morbid fears which impelled a man to give the fruit of his body for the sin of his soul. In Jeremiah (and Ezekiel), on the contrary, references to this custom are explicit and frequent, and they show that like other abominations of Canaanite ritual it had been incorporated in the worship of Yahwe[1]. It may

---

[1] See Jer. vii. 31, xix. 5, xxxii. 35; Ezek. xvi. 20 f., 36, xx. 26, 31, xxiii. 37, 39: cf. Mic. vi. 6–8; and Wellhausen, *Isr. und jüd. Gesch.* (5th Ed.), pp. 134 f. Whether human sacrifice is mentioned in ch. ii of Jer. is a difficult question of exegesis. As already remarked (p. 57 *n.*), the words 'thy way in the valley' in *v.* 23 have been taken to refer to the rites of the Topheth in the valley of Hinnom. This interpretation has with some reason been questioned by Duhm on the ground that the vague expression rather suggests some more widely diffused feature of the prevalent religious apostasy. On the other hand, the same writer holds that *vv.* 33–35 are a description of child-sacrifice, and not (as is commonly supposed) an allusion to executions and judicial murders perpetrated under Manasseh. The verses are obscure and the text uncertain; but whether we follow the Heb. or the LXX form of 33 *b*, the idea of the verse must be that in the search for love (illicit religious satisfaction) Israel had become habituated to flagrantly wicked courses. That is more intelligible as leading up to a denunciation of child-sacrifice than on the supposition that civil bloodshed of any kind is meant. *V.* 34 is ambiguous; but here again it seems more natural to understand the

well have been that the evils of the time, the long-continued Assyrian tyranny, the bloody persecutions of the reign of Manasseh, as well as the persistent propaganda of the prophetic party, had undermined the old joyous confidence in the favour and protection of Yahwe, and produced the mood of superstitious fear which found relief in this hideous form of sacrifice.

Such were the outstanding features of the popular religion of Israel, whose abuses flourished unchecked until Josiah set his hand to the task of reformation in the year 621. It does not appear that the thought of reform has as yet crossed the mind of the young prophet whose impressions of the religious condition of his countrymen are reflected in the passage now before us. Jeremiah's criticism of the prevalent tendencies of the age proceeds on the lines drawn by his predecessor Hosea. It starts from the conception of Yahwe's relation to Israel as analogous to the marriage covenant between husband and wife. The genuine religion of Israel consists in the knowledge of Yahwe her divine Husband and Lord, and a moral fellowship with Him which accords with His holy and righteous character. The actual religion of the people, as expressed in its worship, lacks this ethical element, and is therefore in the judgment of the prophet no true service of Yahwe at all. It is illicit intercourse with the false gods who were personifications of the productive powers of nature. The god whom Israel ignorantly worships is not Yahwe but a Baal, or rather as many Baals as there are images of

blood found on the skirts of the personified nation to be the blood shed in sacrifice than the blood of martyrs or innocent citizens; and if we read אֵלֶּה with the LXX instead of אֵלָּה no other view is tenable.

Finally *v.* 35 as expressing, on Duhm's theory, the atoning effect of the sacrificial rite ('I am absolved') forms a suitable climax to the prophet's indictment; whereas on the other view it must refer to some quite separate ground of assurance.

deity throughout the land. These are the 'lovers' or paramours who have seduced her from her allegiance to her true husband, and transformed the spirit of her religion by substituting a sensuous nature-worship for the 'reasonable service' of heart and life in which Yahwe delights. We can easily see that this circle of conceptions forms the basis of Jeremiah's strictures on the public religion of his day, which we now proceed to examine more closely. The main points of his indictment may be summed up in four words: *Degeneracy, Sensualism, Double-mindedness* and *Unreality*.

1. To Jeremiah the religious history of his people is a record of *Degeneration*—of declension from a pure and lofty origin; and this conviction imparts a peculiar tone of regret to his whole survey of its present degradation. He idealises the wilderness sojourn as a time when Israel's relation to Yahwe was perfect. A relation of tender and beautiful affection, as of a young bride to her husband, a joyous and fearless devotion to her God in the midst of perils and hardships: that was the origin of Israel's national religion. And the memory of that hallowed time is still dear to the heart of Yahwe, and makes him slow to abandon hope of her recovery (ii. 2*b* f.):

> 2*b* I remember the grace of thy youth,
>   Thy love as a bride:
>   How thou followedst Me in the waste,
>   In a land unsown.
>
> 3 Holy was Israel to Yahwe,
>   Firstfruits of His harvest:
>   None who devoured it went scatheless,
>   Evil o'ertook them.

In this idealisation of the desert religion of Israel Jeremiah again follows Hosea (Hos. ix. 10, xi. 1). The essential idea which both prophets mean to convey is that the national religion was then uncontaminated by the corrupting influences of the Canaanite Baalism; and that of course is historically true, though scarcely true to the view of the wilderness period given in the Pentateuchal tradition. It is, for example, almost incredible that either prophet should have written as he does if the incident of the Golden Calf at Sinai had been known to him (Exod. xxxii). Hosea's neglect of it might be explained by the supposition that in his time the tradition was inchoate, and perhaps included little beyond the salient events of the deliverance from Egypt, the Sinaitic Covenant, the sojourn at Kadesh, and the conquest of Canaan. The section on the Golden Calf is usually assigned to a comparatively late stratum of the Elohistic document, which may very well have been added after Hosea's time. Jeremiah's indifference to it is less easily accounted for. It must have been within his lifetime, if not before his day, that a Deuteronomic writer worked the incident into his hortatory review of the history as a warning against the idolatrous propensities that lay in the heart of the people (Deut. ix. 12 ff., etc.); and this suggests that it had already found a place in the older document on which the Deuteronomic narrative is based. The prophet's independence of the tradition is therefore a remarkable and somewhat perplexing fact, which gives rise to critical problems too complex to be entered on here. The simplest solution will be that Jeremiah accepts and amplifies Hosea's view of the religious development, and is at this early period of his life either ignorant of or indifferent to the literary activity which was consolidating the history of the Mosaic age. In any case it is an important fact that Jeremiah, in common (it would seem) with the earlier prophets, looks back to the past as the ideal from which the people has fallen away. Ezekiel is the first prophet who teaches that Israel had been rebellious from the outset.

The contrast to the ideal condition described in *vv.*
1–3 follows in *vv.* 14–19.

> 14 Is Israel a bondman,
>   Or house-born slave?
> Why then is he plundered—
>   His cities burned down[1]?
>
> 15 Young lions against him have roared—
>   Loud lifted their voice,
> And made of his land a waste,
>   None dwelling therein.
>
> 16 Yea the sons of Memphis and Daphnai
>   Shall shave thee bald[2].
> 17 Is not this the result of departing
>   From Yahwe thy God?
>
> 18 And now, why goest thou to Egypt
>   Nile-water to drink?
> And why dost thou go to Assyria
>   To drink of the Stream?
>
> 19 Let thine own misfortune reprove thee!
>   Acknowledge and see
> How bitter it is, thy departing
>   From Yahwe thy God!
> And that fear of Me thou hast none,
>   Saith Yahwe of hosts.

The historical implications of these verses have been
sufficiently discussed on pp. 44 f., 56 *nn.*; and their
didactic significance requires no elucidation. They are
separated from the introductory poem of *vv.* 1–3 by a
passage (*vv.* 4–13) in which we recognise some of the
profoundest and most characteristic of Jeremiah's ideas.
It is in the form of a rhetorical expostulation—a *rîb*

---

[1] Parallelism and rhythm are improved by the transposition of this
line from near the end of the following verse.

[2] יְרָעוּךְ for יְרָעֵךְ , with Duhm.

(*v. 9*)—in which the people are addressed directly and collectively, the personification of the nation being dropped, as the prophet might have spoken to an assembly in the Temple courts. It is an exposition of the causes which have alienated the people from their true national religion. Why has Israel departed from Yahwe, forgotten Him, even ceased to inquire after Him? Did they find Him unfaithful or harsh or unjust? (*v. 5*). How could they so lightly forget Him who had led them safely through the terrible wilderness, and brought them to a goodly land to enjoy its fruits, and its treasures (*vv. 6, 7*)? It was because on their entrance into this land they had met with another god, the Canaanite Baal, and to him they had basely and ungratefully transferred their homage (*vv. 7, 8*). Jeremiah here touches on the historical fact already referred to, that Israel's first contact with the culture of Palestine had transformed both the spirit and the form of its religion by introducing into it a foreign principle which made it no longer a moral fellowship with Yahwe, but a sensuous abandonment to the worship of nature. Such a change seems to the prophet a monstrous and incomprehensible thing. Even among the heathen there is no such thing as wilful exchange of one false national deity for another (*vv. 10, 11*); and for Israel to have exchanged the one Being who is truly God for a fictitious being who 'does not profit' is a thing fit to shock heaven and horrify earth (*v. 12*). It bears witness to some radical depravity in the national character, which perverts every sound religious instinct, and has disappointed Yahwe's expectation of a response to His grace and loving-kindness; *v. 21*:

> Yet with choicest vines did I plant thee,
>> All genuine seed.
> How art thou turned to a nauseous
>> Degenerate plant?

2. The image of the vineyard in *v.* 21 suggests the
transition from the thought of Degeneracy to a second
feature of the popular religion, viz. its gross and revolting *Sensuality*. If a vineyard stocked wholly with
the choicest vines produces degenerate grapes, there
must be something wrong with the soil. So in the soil
of the national disposition Jeremiah discovers the secret
of Israel's amazing apostasy. The true religion was a
'yoke'—a moral discipline (*v.* 20; cf. v. 5), laying a
restraint on the carnal impulses of human nature. But
there was a vein of grossness in the *naturel* of the
Hebrews which broke loose from the control of an
ethical religion, and found in the licentious rites of the
Canaanite worship an irresistible attraction; *v.* 20:

> From of old thou hast broken thy yoke,
> And burst thy thongs;
> And said 'I will not serve':
> While on every high hill,
> And 'neath every green tree,
> Thou sprawledst, a harlot[1].

Now we need not expect in a Hebrew prophet the
easy tolerance of a modern anthropologist in judging
the character of an alien religion; but the prophet's
estimate is likely to be the sounder of the two. The
whole type of ancient religion with which Jeremiah is
here dealing may be said to have rested on a deification
of the sexual instinct. It was an interpretation of nature
by false analogies from the process of physical generation; and it made a persistent appeal to the powerful
impulse in which it originated. Its divinity was conceived as divided into a male and a female principle,

[1] The same idea is still more drastically expressed in the comparison
of the nation to a domestic animal—a young she-camel or a heifer—
running wild in the heat of sexual desire, utterly beyond the control of
her owner, but easily approachable by the males who seek her (*vv.* 23 *b*,
24). The text of these verses is very uncertain, and the combination of
metaphors embarrassing.

whose marriage was the cause of fertility and fecundity and all the blessings which accrued to men from this source. Moreover, it taught its votaries that union with the deity was realised by fleshly intercourse with sacred persons dedicated to this purpose at the sanctuaries. However innocent we may suppose these ideas and practices in their crude primitive *naïveté*, it is obvious that a religion so constituted must act as a leaven of moral corruption in any community that had risen above the level of savagery. Hence the system of religious prostitution in Israel was a social evil infecting the whole life of the nation and undermining the foundations of family morality (Hos. iv. 14). And Jeremiah shows true insight into the nature of religion when he emphasises the essential incongruity between the inherent sensuousness of the false worship to which his people were addicted and the ethical motives of love and trust and gratitude which the right relation of Israel to Yahwe demanded.

3. A third characteristic of the popular religion is what may be described as *Double-mindedness*: i.e. an uneasy consciousness on the part of the people that the god of their habitual worship was somehow distinct from the God they ought to serve; and in consequence a vacillating attitude in their religious professions. We have seen that the nominal identification of Yahwe with the Baals could not altogether obscure the knowledge that they stood for irreconcileable principles; and it is plain from this chapter that even so late as the time of Jeremiah a dim perception of the antithesis existed in the mind of the people. They followed the Baal religion from inclination, but with a bad conscience, and with a sense that it did not suffice for all their needs as a nation (*vv.* 26, 27):

As a thief is ashamed when he is caught
So is Israel's house ashamed;

Who say to a tree 'Thou'rt my father,'
    And to a stone 'Thou hast brought me forth.'
For their back they have turned to Me,
    And not their face;
But in time of their trouble they'll say
    'Arise, Thou, and save us.'

That is to say, at ordinary times they buried their faith
in Yahwe beneath a mass of grovelling superstitions;
but in times of national distress, such as drought or
famine or the threat of invasion, they sought Him
consciously, and with some apprehension of His true
character. Their demeanour under the censure of the
prophets was a strange mixture or alternation of self-
deception, defiance and despair. When taxed with defection from the national religion, and with having
forfeited all right to be considered Yahwe's people,
they would say 'I have not sinned' (*v.* 35), or 'I have
not gone after the Baals' (*v.* 23), meaning 'I have not
forsaken the worship of Yahwe[1].' When confronted with
the moral requirements of Yahwe they would have none
of Him: 'We roam at large; we come no more to Thee'

[1] Duhm argues acutely for the omission of the words 'I have not
gone' in *v.* 23 as metrically superfluous, and as expressing a sentiment
which the people could not possibly entertain: they knew well enough
that they had gone after the Baals, but what they deny is that they are
thereby disqualified for the worship of Yahwe. The distinction is perhaps
too subtle. The omission of the words yields at the best an ambiguous
pregnant construction: 'I have not defiled myself (by going) after the
Baals'; which may mean either (1) 'I have not so far defiled myself as
to go after the Baals,' or (2), as Duhm interprets, 'My going after the
Baals has not defiled me.' But surely from the standpoint of ancient
religion the conscious recognition in worship of other gods *must* have
implied infidelity to Yahwe? The real difference between the people
and the prophet is that they 'emphasised the destination, he the quality
of their worship' (Peake). It is quite true that in *v.* 25 they announce
their determination to go after strangers; but that confession falls into
line with *v.* 31, and expresses a mood which cannot by any possibility
be reconciled with that of *vv.* 22, 23.

(*v.* 31). Most pathetic of all is their despairing answer
to His gracious invitation to return ere it be too late:
'It is hopeless! No! for I have loved strangers and after
them I must go' (*v.* 25). No doubt these inconsistent
utterances express dramatically Jeremiah's own view of
the people's state of mind; but none the less they reflect
conflicting aspects of that 'halting between two opinions'
(1 Kings xviii. 21) which had marked the popular
religion through all its history. Jeremiah would end it
by stripping it of all pretension to be the religion of
Israel: 'Where are thy gods whom thou hast made for
thyself? Let them arise, if they can save thee in thy
time of trouble!' (*v.* 28).

4. Lastly the prophet characterises the prevailing
religion as an *Unreality*. As ostensible worship of Yahwe
it is unreal, because it establishes no contact with Him
as a moral Being; as Baal-worship it is unreal, because
the Baals are not real deities, but figments of the
imagination. Israel has foolishly 'exchanged its glory
for that which does not profit' (*v.* 11). And where the
object of religion is unreal the subject becomes unreal
also: 'They followed after vanity and became vain'
(*v.* 5). They neither worshipped a real God, nor
worshipped with their real selves. That is the most
distinctive point in Jeremiah's analysis of religious experience. The principle that the worshipper is assimilated
to that which he worships had been enunciated by
Hosea in a more obvious fashion when he wrote 'They
became an abomination, like that which they loved'
(Hos. ix. 10). Jeremiah's thought goes deeper. The
Baals are not merely abominations but nonentities, and
'they that trust in them are like to them' (Ps. cxv. 8,
cxxxv. 18), because a life devoted to such service receives
no reinforcement from the one real and unfailing Source
of spiritual succour and energy. This conviction of the
unreality of all religions save one, of all gods but Yahwe

finds its classical expression in one of the most memorable of all Jeremiah's utterances (*v.* 13):

> Two evils have My people committed:
>   Me they have forsaken, a fount of living water,
> To hew for themselves cisterns—
>   Broken cisterns, that hold no water.

I cannot leave this subject without a word on the
allegorical framework in which the argument is cast.
Plainly, the maxim that you cannot draw an indictment
against a nation finds no countenance here. It is precisely to a nation, and to individuals only as members
of that nation, that Jeremiah's remonstrance is addressed.
The truth underlying this representation is one that is
difficult to state without exaggeration on one side or
another. The treatment of Israel as a unity, personified
as an individual mind, capable in relation to God of
all the wealth of personal thought and emotion, is
unfamiliar to our individualistic manner of thinking.
The idea is often expressed by saying that in the prophetic theology the 'religious unit' is not the individual
soul but the community; and that is undoubtedly true
so far as it goes. The object of Yahwe's love and care
is the nation of Israel; the great revealing acts through
which His character is known are His providential
dealings with the people as a whole. But this is not to
say that all religion is resolved into acts of corporate
worship, that there was no such thing as personal piety,
nor any belief in a divine providence watching over the
individual life. It means simply that to the Israelite the
consciousness of his nationality was an integral element
of his faith in God, and that every act of personal
devotion was sustained by the sense of 'solidarity' with
the people which Yahwe had made His own. Thus far
the personification of Israel as the *object* of Yahwe's
regard is intelligible. It is when we turn to the *subjective*

side of the relationship that the inadequacy of the conception begins to be felt. For the response to Yahwe's love could only come from the hearts of individuals, and the rejection of Him was equally an attitude of the individual mind. The nation, in short, was not like Wordsworth's cloud, that 'moveth altogether if it move at all'; the unity of the national consciousness existed only in the poetic imagination of the prophet and the antique mind in general. The personification of the nation as an ideal personality thus involves an ambiguity which was incidental to a transition stage of religious experience. It may be regarded as an attempt to express personal religion in terms of national religion. Jeremiah (like Hosea before him) virtually, though perhaps not consciously, transcends the common level of the Old Testament religion. It is his own personal knowledge of God which he reads into the relation between Israel and Yahwe, and is the standard by which he judges the actual religion of his people.

CHAPTER V

THE CALL TO NATIONAL REPENTANCE

AT the point we have now reached in the examination of Jeremiah's early prophecies there arises a question of great importance for the understanding of the spirit and aim with which he entered upon his work. Was he sustained at this time by the hope that by his preaching the people would be turned from their evil ways, and that the judgment which he announced might be averted by an act of national repentance? Or was he from the first possessed by the conviction, which he certainly felt in later years, that the breach between Yahwe and Israel was irreconcileable, and that the doom of the nation was inevitable? In the searching criticism of the popular religion which we have just considered there seems to be nothing which points decisively to one of these conclusions rather than the other. The threat of punishment is there; but it is expressed with a certain forbearance, and in a tone which does not exclude the hope of a national conversion. That possibility is discussed in the third chapter of the book; and there, if anywhere, we may expect to find an answer to the question which has just been stated.

The question, however, concerns not Jeremiah alone, but all the prophets. It is one of those general problems of prophecy which have always been a subject of controversy, and on which extreme views are maintained by the advocates of opposing tendencies. It may be well, therefore, before proceeding to the consideration of Jeremiah's earlier attitude, to look at the broader issue which is implicit in the nature of Old Testament prophecy as a whole.

I

The general problem arises on the question whether the prophets' announcements of doom were made conditionally or absolutely. It is clear that the prophets were not mere soothsayers, uttering Cassandra-like auguries of impending disaster; they were preachers of righteousness, and the burden of their preaching was a summons to public repentance and reformation. So much is admitted on all hands. But does not this imply that their predictions of judgment were relative to the response which the people might make to their appeal? For what purpose could the threat of punishment be introduced into a call to conversion if not to point out the consequences that would follow persistent rebellion? Must it not be essentially the presentation of an alternative: 'if ye be willing and obedient ye shall eat the good of the land, but if ye refuse and rebel ye shall be devoured by the sword' (Isa. i. 19 f.)? It would thus appear that the prophet's certainty of the event could not be a mathematical certainty, like that of an astronomer predicting an eclipse, but a moral certainty of Yahwe's purpose in relation to the present state of the people, qualified by the conviction that if the people would turn, Yahwe would change His purpose from judgment to mercy. But then, on the other hand, if the incidence of the judgment depends on human freedom, what becomes of the prediction? 'A hypothetical prediction,' says Smend, 'is a contradiction in terms, as if one should speak of "wooden iron"[1].' And does it not belong to the essence of prophecy to survey the future with a vision from which contingency is excluded, and to declare a divine purpose which is fixed and irreversible? 'I have spoken and will not repent: I have purposed and will not turn from it' (Jer. iv. 28).

The conflict of opinion on this matter is very pro-

[1] *Alttestamentliche Religionsgeschichte*, p. 191.

nounced; and it goes back to a difference of emphasis on the two aspects of the prophetic consciousness which were distinguished at the beginning of the previous chapter. If we suppose that the prophet's certainty of an impending crisis came to him as an immediate presentiment of the trend of events, we should naturally hold that it would not be affected by any change in the mind of the people, and his prediction would be absolute and unconditional. If on the other hand the announcement of judgment rested entirely on moral grounds we might conclude that the prophet's outlook would vary with the religious attitude of the people, and that he would labour to bring them to repentance with the hope of averting the judgment. We find accordingly that on one side it is maintained that the pre-exilic prophets always looked forward to the catastrophe as inevitable. Their prevision of calamity was an immediate presentiment of the fact itself, and not an inference from the law of retribution; hence the certainty of their predictions is unaffected by the popular reception of their message. The call to repentance was not seriously meant[1]. No doubt the prophets believed that if the nation were to repent Yahwe would stay His avenging hand; but they were convinced in their hearts that the people would not and could not repent, and the mere theoretic possibility of such a change did not in the least disturb their inward confidence that the fate of the nation was sealed. On the other side it is argued, with perhaps less rigour, that however confidently the prophets may at times express themselves—however unqualified their predictions may be in form—the element of contingency is always present in intention, the very object of the predictions being to bring about the change of heart which would render the judgment unnecessary.

[1] Smend, *l.c.*

Of these opposite theories it may be truly, if tritely, said that each is right in what it affirms but wrong in what it denies. It is true that the prophets utter unqualified predictions of the doom of their nation, and it is also true that they hold out the hope of salvation on condition of genuine repentance. But it is arbitrary to assert that either of these attitudes represents their real mind, and that the other is merely a rhetorical expression of passing reflexions which do not belong to the substance of their message. Of the two extreme views that which insists on the categorical nature of prediction seems to err most widely in this respect. Although there is an absolute element in prophecy, we have no right to identify the prophetic consciousness with this side of their teaching exclusively, and maintain (as is done by Smend) that the note of warning and the call to repentance lie outside the strictly prophetic function, and are an irrelevant outflow of purely human feeling, or a way of bringing home to the people their responsibility for the doom which is irreversibly decreed against them. But it is equally illegitimate to hold that the absolute element can be eliminated from prophecy, as if its only meaning were to frighten the people into a sense of the danger that threatened them because of their sins. It may be, as Dr Davidson said, 'a very delicate operation to strike the balance...between the moral element which introduced contingency into the prophecy, and the absolute element which lay in it as a prediction[1].' But at least we must recognise that both elements exist side by side in the prophetic writings, though we may not be able to see how the two were combined in the minds of the prophets themselves. We may easily be mistaken in framing rigid generalisations on the phenomenon of prophecy, forgetting that the name prophecy is but an abstraction from the activity of the men whom we call

[1] *Old Testament Prophecy*, p. 251.

the prophets, and that each prophet has his own individual character and point of view. We should be
prepared to find, not only that one prophet differs from
another in the emphasis which he lays on the two
aspects of his mission, but also that the same prophet
may vary his attitude at different periods of his life.
The only safe procedure is to examine the oracles of
each prophet separately, and try to determine whether
at a particular time he did or did not entertain the hope
that the threatened judgment might be averted. And
our present concern is with Jeremiah [1].

Now, Jeremiah's later attitude on this matter presents
difficulties which we are not yet in a position to consider.
We find many utterances which suggest that he regarded
the doom of the nation as inevitable. We find other
passages which appear to imply that the aim of all his
work was to turn the people from their evil ways, so
that Yahwe's wrath might be averted from them (see
vii. 5–7, xxv. 5, 6, xxvi. 3, xxxvi. 2–7, etc.; and cf.
xviii. 7–12). It is noteworthy, however, that in passages
of this kind there is nothing that amounts to a positive
expectation that the result will be such as his heart
desired; and hence we might conclude that his fundamental attitude was one of resignation to the irrevocable
decree of God. The question now before us is whether

---

[1] The questions touched upon in the above paragraphs are fully discussed by Giesebrecht (*Berufsbegabung*, pp. 79–89, 113 ff.), who while
admitting that prediction is essentially 'apodictic,' protests strongly
against the one-sided disparagement of the ethical element in prophecy
by Smend. On the other side see Buttenwieser (*The Prophets, etc.*, pp.
176 ff.), whose view appears to be that the prophets were so confident
of the final triumph of righteousness and so sure of the subservience of
present events to this great end that they did not trouble themselves
about the effect of their words on their immediate hearers, but announced
the doom of Israel simply as a necessary step towards the realisation of
their ideal. It would be more intelligible if this had been said of the
invitations to repentance!

this was his attitude from the outset, or whether he entered upon his work with a real and confident hope that the people would respond to his message and repent before judgment came on them to the uttermost. And for an answer to that question we must turn, as I have said, to an analysis of the third chapter of the book.

II

Unfortunately the composition of this chapter is one of the most intricate of the many critical problems which the book of Jeremiah presents, and no analysis that has been given is completely satisfying. It deals throughout with the possibility and the conditions of a reconciliation between Israel and Yahwe, but the subject is looked at from varying points of view, and there are many evidences of discontinuity of treatment and differences of date. Taking the chapter as it stands, we can distinguish four main sections; and the general sequence of thought is as follows.

i. In *vv.* 1–5 the question of a possible reunion of Israel and Yahwe is raised in the most direct and explicit fashion. Judged by human analogies it must appear an utter impossibility. Israel is the divorced wife of Yahwe, she has gone astray after many lovers, and if law and custom forbid remarriage to a woman who has been united to a second husband, how much less can Yahwe receive back one whose shame has been published on the hill-tops and by the wayside! No hypocritical phrases of endearment can atone for such infamous conduct. That is the gist of the section. To what conclusion does it point? Is it that the human analogy holds good and is decisive—that there can be no reunion between Yahwe and Israel: or is it that this thing which is impossible with men is possible with God and in His great mercy may be realised? On the former alternative the argument is closed and the passage requires no sequel; on the latter a sequel is necessary, and the question is where we are to find it.

ii. The next section, *vv.* 6–13, is obviously not the original continuation of *vv.* 1–5. It is marked off by a separate heading from what precedes; it is in prose style; and the allusions make it clear that if written by Jeremiah at all it belongs to the post-Deuteronomic period of his ministry. It is almost certain that it has been inserted in this place by an editor because of an accidental coincidence of subject with *vv.* 1–5. In any case it starts a new train of thought, contrasting Yahwe's relations and feelings towards the sister kingdoms of Israel and Judah, both married to Yahwe, but the one already banished for her infidelity, the other, though the more sinful of the two, still in His house. Thus the ideal unity of Israel, which is maintained throughout ch. ii, is conceived as broken up, and in the closing invitation (*vv.* 12, 13) the hope of restoration is held out to the northern Israelites alone (but see the notes on pp. 81, 83 below).

iii. In *vv.* 14–18 we have a section which is now universally recognised by scholars as foreign to the context. It consists of a series of detached oracles loosely strung together, and inserted here because of affinity of subject with the main theme of the chapter. It has a certain editorial fitness in its present position inasmuch as it speaks of a restoration of both Israel and Judah from captivity, and brings the whole nation once more within the scope of the promise of forgiveness which follows. But that is evidently a post-exilic point of view, and it is doubtful if the section contains any genuine words of Jeremiah at all. These verses must therefore be left out of account when we seek to recover the original connexions of thought in ch. iii.

iv. The chapter reaches a magnificent climax in *vv.* 19–25. From the bare heights which had been the scenes of their idolatrous worship, the prophet hears the bitter weeping of the children of Israel, convinced at last of their sin in forsaking the Lord their God. He hears the voice of Yahwe inviting them to return, and assuring them of His readiness to heal their backslidings. The appeal finds an immediate response in the heart of the people: 'Yea, we come to Thee, for Thou art our God.' Renouncing the vain religion of Baal which had brought them to ruin, they cast themselves in penitence and shame upon the mercy of Him who is the Saviour of Israel.

Now the question on which the attention of recent commentators has mostly been concentrated is whether, after the removal of *vv.* 14–18, *vv.* 19 ff. are the continuation of *vv.* 6–13 or (omitting 6–18) of *vv.* 1–5. If the former view be correct, the last section simply expands in a highly dramatic form the invitation to the northern Israel already expressed in *vv.* 12, 13. If on the other hand the connexion goes back to *v.* 5, we have here the answer to the question propounded in the opening section of the chapter: viz. the possibility of a reconciliation of the whole nation of Israel to its divine Husband[1].

A good deal can be said on both sides of this question, and much acute reasoning on opposite sides will be found in the commentaries of Giesebrecht and Cornill; but the result is indecisive. As regards suitability of connexion there is little to choose between the three

---

[1] The sequence of thought is not greatly affected by Duhm's retention of 12 *b*, 13, as the original transition from *v.* 5 to *v.* 19. He holds that the allegory of *vv.* 6–11 is a spurious interpolation, and that 12 *a* was inserted by a redactor under the false impression that in what follows Israel means North Israel. Erbt, while agreeing in the main, argues that by the excision of this clause—'Go and proclaim these words *northward*' —Duhm removes the very thing that misled the redactor into thinking that North Israel is addressed in what follows; but his own explanation is so unnatural as to deprive his objection of all practical value.

views: that *vv*. 19–25 are the sequel to *vv*. 1–5, that
they continue *vv*. 6–13, or that *v*. 5 is linked to 19 ff.
by 12 *b*, 13. No theory yields an unexceptionable
sequence. In favour of a reference to North Israel is the
circumstance that Jeremiah's hope for the future seems
always to attach itself to that part of the nation which
had passed through the fire of judgment. It was so at
a later time when he contrasted the bright future in
store for the exiles in Babylon with the fate of the
remnant left in Palestine (see pp. 251f. below); and again
still later when for a brief space he cherished the dream
that the poverty-stricken settlement at Mizpah would
prove the nucleus of the new people of God (pp. 276f.).
Now in his early years the northern kingdom had
suffered the calamity which the prophets had foretold;
and it would harmonise with Jeremiah's interpretation
of the ways of God that he should have a message of
immediate consolation for the exiled Israel from which
Judah was as yet excluded. There is, however, nothing
to suggest that this distinction was in the prophet's
mind except the problematical connexion of *vv*. [12 *b*,
13], 19–25 with *vv*. 6–11, which involves the equally
doubtful assumption that *vv*. 6–11 were written by
Jeremiah. If this passage be genuine it clearly belongs
to a time subsequent to the Deuteronomic reformation
(see *v*. 10); and reflexion on the issue of that movement
might naturally have suggested the contrast between
the open profligacy of Israel and the feigned loyalty of
Judah. But the allegorical treatment of the theme, and
the whole style of the passage are very unlike Jeremiah;
and the resemblances to Ezekiel (xvi. 44 ff., xxiii.) are
sufficiently striking to warrant a conjecture that the
working up of the idea is due to an editor, who wrote
the verses as an introduction to oracles which seemed
to contemplate a return of the northern tribes from
captivity. And even if Jeremiah composed the allegory,

its connexion with the promises that follow can hardly
be original. It is difficult to conceive that with his profound insight into the nature of religion he could have
seen any ground of hope for the restoration of Israel in
the more aggravated guilt of Judah.

Apart from *vv*. 6–11, or 6–13, it would probably
never have occurred to any modern reader that *vv*.
19–25 refer to North Israel exclusively. Some have
argued that the consistent use of the name 'Israel[1]'
lends support to this view; but that impression does
not appear to be borne out by the usage of Jeremiah.
There is no difficulty in supposing that the name is
used, as throughout ch. ii, of Israel as a whole,
with perhaps a contemporary application to Judah as
the residuary legatee of the national inheritance. Similarly, the 'lovely land' of *v*. 19 is more naturally under-

---

[1] Cf. 'Israel,' iii. [12] 23, [iv. 1]; 'sons of Israel,' iii. 21; 'house of
Israel,' iii. 20. It is difficult to make out Jeremiah's own usage of these
terms from the mass of editorial matter which is spread over the book,
but for our present purpose it is sufficiently illustrated by the following
facts. Confining ourselves to passages which may reasonably be ascribed
to him, and whose text is fairly certain, we find (1) that the expression
'sons of Israel' is not elsewhere used by Jeremiah himself (except *possibly*
in xvi. 14 [= xxiii. 7], where it describes the people as a whole); so that
no inference can be drawn from its isolated occurrence in iii. 21.
(2) 'House of Israel' is generally coupled with 'house of Judah,' in
which case of course it denotes North Israel (v. 11, xi. 10, 17, xiii. 11,
xxxi. 31); standing alone it is never used of North Israel exclusively, but
either of all Israel (ii. 4, ix. 25, xxxi. 33) or with special reference to
Judah (ii. 26, v. 15, xviii. 6). (3) 'Israel' means North Israel in vii. 12,
xxiii. 13 (and of course in iii. 6–11); it means the whole nation in the
very frequent title 'God of Israel,' and in ii. 3, xii. 14, xiv. 8, xvii. 13,
xxix. 23: in ii. 14, vi. 9, xviii. 13 it is applied to Judah as the surviving
representative of the historic nation. In xxxi. 2, 4, 9, 21, which I assign to a
late period of Jeremiah's life (see Ch. XVI), 'Israel' undoubtedly includes
the northern tribes; but that it refers to them alone is not clear: these poems
seem to contemplate a return of the whole family from exile. The evidence therefore does not seem to establish even a presumption in favour
of the theory that *vv*. 19–25 speak of the conversion of the Ten Tribes.

stood of Canaan as a whole than of either division of
it[1]. And the allusions to the 'bare heights' in *v.* 21 and
the 'revelry of the mountains' in *v.* 23 presuppose a
people resident in the land and praying to Yahwe from
the sites of their former idolatrous worship (cf. ii. 20,
iii. 2, 6). The most probable conclusion is that *vv.* 21–25
are an independent poem, having no literary connexion
with either iii. 1–5 or 6–11, but dealing with the same
situation as the second chapter, and belonging like it
to the early period when Jeremiah's thinking was
strongly coloured by the influence of Hosea.

If these conclusions be right, the closing verses of
ch. iii must be read as a confession put into the
mouth of Israel in its ideal unity, as the unfaithful
spouse of Yahwe, convinced at last of her guilt and
folly. On any view the description is an ideal one; for
we may be sure that no such spontaneous cry of penitence as is described in the following lines ascended
from the high places of Judah in the lifetime of Jeremiah
(*vv.* 12, 13, 21–25):

> [12aβ]'Return, thou truant Israel,
>   To Me,' saith Yahwe;
> 'I will not frown on you,
> [12b]For gracious am I,
>   I grudge not alway.

[1] It might be urged that the promise of the land assumes that the
people addressed was deprived of its land, which was true of North
Israel but not of Judah in the time of Jeremiah. But the only thoroughly
natural reference of *v.* 19 is either to the Exodus period, before Israel
had obtained possession of Canaan, or the Exile after it had lost it. If
the first suggestion be admissible we might find an appropriate place
for the verse after ch. ii. 1–3. Apart from metrical irregularities
(which are not irremediable) it would form a suitable third stanza to the
poem with which that chapter opens (p. 64 above). It must have been
inserted here because of the phraseological resemblance to iii. 4, which
is an additional reason for relegating *vv.* 6–18 to a later stage of the
redaction. *V.* 20, with the 2nd pers. plu., is another isolated fragment;
and both these verses must be removed from their connexion with 21 ff.

13 'Only acknowledge thy guilt,
  Thy revolting from Yahwe thy God,
  In yielding thyself to strangers
  Under every green tree[1].'

21 Hark! from the bare heights is heard
  The wailing of Israel's sons;
  For on crooked ways they have gone,
  And forgotten Yahwe their God.

22 'Return, O wayward children;
  I will heal your waywardness.'
'Lo, we come to Thee,
  For Thou art our God.

23 'Surely the hills are a fraud—
  The noise on the mountains;
  Surely in Yahwe our God
  Is Israel's succour.

24 'But the Baal has devoured
  Our fathers' substance—
  Their flocks and their herds,
  Their sons and daughters.

25 'We will lie down in our shame,
  Our disgrace shall enfold us;
  For against our God we have sinned
  From our youth until now.'

The whole tone of these verses is opposed to the idea
that they represent one of those sporadic fits of shallow
repentance and unreal conversion which were characteristic of the popular religion of Israel in times of public
distress (ii. 27). It has been suggested, however, that
Jeremiah here adopts the form of the Temple liturgy
used on such occasions, in order to impress on his
hearers the necessity for a sincere confession of guilt

---

[1] For דְּרָכַיִךְ Du. reads בְּרְכַּיִךְ 'thy knees.' The last clause of the
v. is omitted.

and renunciation of Baal-worship, as conditions of a true reconciliation with Yahwe[1]. The theory does justice to the seriousness of the prophet's appeal; but it is difficult to see why one with Jeremiah's gifts of imagination and poetic expression should resort to so conventional a method of conveying his message. An analogy from Hosea suggests a more attractive explanation. The book of Hosea closes in ch. xiv with an address to Israel which has a close resemblance to the passage before us. In both we have the invitation to repentance; in both the requirement of confession and the offer of pardon; and in both, dramatically expressed, the response of the nation to Yahwe's appeal: the phrase 'I will heal [their] your backsliding[s]' occurs almost *verbatim* in both. Is it too bold a conjecture that Jeremiah was familiar with this chapter of Hosea, and that his faith in the restoration of his people took its direction from the words of his predecessor? To whom, then, does Hosea hold out the promise of reconciliation? Not to a people already in exile; for it is practically certain that he did not live to see the captivity of the northern kingdom. On the other hand it cannot have been to his contemporaries in the expectation that their

---

[1] Erbt, *Jeremia und seine Zeit*, pp. 133 f.; similarly Schmidt, *Die grossen Propheten und ihre Zeit*, pp. 229 f. Both these writers find the divine answer to the people's confession in iv. 1 (Erbt) or iv. 1, 2 (Schmidt); and it has been a common opinion that these two verses, in whole or in part, form the necessary or appropriate conclusion to ch. iii. I think it more probable that the connexion is redactional. That Jeremiah wrote *v.* 2 in either the Massoretic or the LXX recension is hardly possible; and yet the only natural construction of *v.* 1 is that which takes it along with 2 *a* as the protasis to 2 *b*. To treat *v.* 1 as a complete and independent sentence—'If thou wilt turn, Israel, saith Yahwe, to Me thou mayest turn; and if thou wilt remove thy abominations from before Me, then thou need'st not wander,' or some such rendering—has been shown by Cornill to be objectionable on both formal and material grounds. He is thoroughly justified in rejecting both verses.

doom might be averted; for to Hosea the discipline of exile was a clearly foreseen step in the process by which Israel was to be brought to a knowledge of the things that belonged to her peace (see Hos. ii. 14 ff., iii.). We must conclude that in the Epilogue of the book he is looking beyond the judgment, or rather that he is thinking of the nation as one through all the vicissitudes of its history, indestructible by any political catastrophe, ever living to the thought and love of Yahwe. It may be the same with Jeremiah. The subjects of the repentance delineated in ch. iii are neither Israel nor Judah as separate political entities, but the sons of the ideal Israel, once Yahwe's true and loyal bride, and destined to be reunited to Him when she repents of her sin and casts herself in shame and sorrow on His infinite mercy.

It would thus appear that in ch. iii we find no direct answer to the question with which we started. The result we arrive at is consistent with the supposition that Jeremiah in his early years hoped that the final destruction of Israel would be averted by the penitence of the men of Judah; but it is also consistent with the view that from the first he saw the ruin of the State to be inevitable. Strictly speaking that question was not before his mind when he wrote this poem. We are led to regard it as an ideal picture of national conversion, setting forth the condition of restoration to Yahwe's favour as a change of heart expressing itself in a corporate act of confession in which the whole nation is conceived as taking part. As such it is one of Jeremiah's profoundest contributions to the theology of grace and redemption. His thought still moves on the plane of national religion. His whole view of the divine love and tenderness and compassion is bound up with the conception of Israel as the object of Yahwe's regard; his gospel is one not for the individual but for the nation

as a whole. It is probable that he had not yet begun to
reflect on the difficulty or impossibility of a decisive
change in the national mind without the mysterious
operation of divine power on the human will (see ch.
xxiv. 7); but the conviction remained with him to
the end that only by the salvation of Israel could
Yahwe's character be fully revealed, and His purpose
accomplished. And at no time of his life could he have
written a finer description of a truly penitent nation
than is contained in the verses on which our attention
has been concentrated.

CHAPTER VI

JEREMIAH AND DEUTERONOMY

THE Scythian terror which had overshadowed the opening years of Jeremiah's ministry vanished as suddenly as it had appeared; and the country settled down to peaceful pursuits, with a fairer prospect of prosperity than it had known since the days of Uzziah and Jeroboam. But in the highest quarters of the land a new spirit was at work, which was resolved that the lesson of the late crisis should not be lost, and that the national life should be purged, by force if need were, from the religious and social abuses which had provoked the anger of Yahwe. This movement took effect in a series of drastic reforms enacted and enforced by Josiah in the eighteenth year of his reign.

It may help us to realise something of the perturbation caused by this revolutionary measure if we transport ourselves in imagination to Anathoth, where we assume that Jeremiah was still living, in comparative obscurity, in the year 621 B.C. First of all, in the spring of that year, a rumour reaches the village of the discovery in the Temple of an ancient law-book, said to be that of Moses, which had caused the gravest concern to the king because of the glaring disparity between its requirements and the existing state of things in matters religious and moral. This is speedily followed by a summons to the local elders to a great national convention at Jerusalem at the approaching Passover season. When the delegates return they have a thrilling story to tell—of a Passover such as had never been observed in Israel before, of a Solemn League and Covenant

entered into by the king and the heads of the people to
make the newly found law the basis of public religion,
and to extirpate everything inconsistent with it, of a
cleansing of the Temple from idolatrous emblems, the
ejection of sacred prostitutes and the whole crew of
diviners, astrologers and wizards from the Temple
precincts, and many other startling demonstrations of
reforming and iconoclastic zeal. Enough already to
rouse the misgivings of all lovers of the old order in
Anathoth! By and by the village is visited by a royal
commission with sufficient force to overpower resistance;
the edict proclaiming the new covenant is read, and
then the work of destruction is done on the local *Bāmā*
or 'high place,' where sacrifice to Yahwe is no longer
to be permitted. Something like this must have taken
place at every township throughout the country in that
memorable year; and we can faintly imagine the resentment and dismay of the populace when they saw their
holy places wrecked and profaned, their priests reduced
to beggary, and themselves denied the privilege of
access to Yahwe after the manner of their fathers. It
was a blow at the very life of the popular religion;
but though it felled the tree to the ground it could
not tear up the roots of custom and hallowed association which had struck deep into the heart of the
people.

What was Jeremiah's attitude in this time of tension
and violent change? That is the most difficult problem
of his biography, and one on which his modern bio-
graphers are sharply divided. It is necessary to deal
with the question somewhat fully, if not with much
hope of settling it, at least with a view to gaining a
truer appreciation of his character and work from a
consideration of the complex data which enter into the
problem. But in the first place we must try to understand the spirit and aim of the reforming movement,

the motives which inspired it, and the forces which
carried it to a successful issue.

Three indisputable (though not quite undisputed)
facts form the starting-point of this inquiry: *first*, that
a radical reform of public worship was initiated in the
eighteenth year of Josiah (*c.* 621); *second*, that the programme of the reform was a law-book alleged to have
been found in the Temple, and *third* that this law-book
is preserved in substance in the book of Deuteronomy.
Beyond these positions, which I must here assume as
established, we are in the region of more or less reasonable conjecture. Uncertainty begins when we ask how
much of the present Deuteronomy belongs to the
original law-book which was the basis of the reform,
and how much was added afterwards. In my opinion
the most probable, though not the most prevalent, view
is that the original law-book consisted of what is called
the 'legislative kernel' of Deuteronomy (chs. xii–
xxvi, apart from editorial expansions); that after the
reformation this was published for popular use in successive editions, which were amalgamated and supplemented by later writers; until in the course of one or
two generations the book assumed substantially the
form in which we now possess it[1]. One result of this
theory is that it enables us to regard Deuteronomy as
the record of a great contemporary movement of thought
of the age in which Jeremiah lived. The new law, whatever be the date of its composition, fell like seed into
prepared soil; it crystallised ideals and convictions
which profoundly influenced the best mind of the
nation; it created a literature and a literary school which
dominated the theological development of the ensuing
century, which gave Judaism its first Bible, and made
its adherents once and for all a 'People of the Book.'
And it is with these contemporary influences quite as

---

[1] See Steuernagel, *Einleitung in das alte. Test.*, pp. 183 ff.

much as with the original code itself that we have to do when we discuss Jeremiah's relation to the Deuteronomic movement as a whole.

A much more vital question is that of the *bona fides* of the parties more immediately responsible for the promulgation of the law, especially Hilkiah the priest and Shaphan the chancellor. Did Hilkiah really discover an old book in some recess of the Temple, or did he connive at a pious fraud in order to secure the more ready acceptance of its authority? To put it otherwise: was the Law-book of 621 drawn up in the time of Josiah by a band of reformers who sought in this way to obtain legislative sanction for the ideal they had set before them; or was the reformation wholly controlled by the prescriptions of an ancient document which had unexpectedly come to light? Here again I can only express an opinion that the truth lies between two extremes. The reformation of Josiah was not brought about by the dead hand of written authority apart from the living aspirations of the age; nor was the book a contemporary production of the reform movement of the reign of Josiah. A prophetic reforming party had existed in the State since the days of Isaiah, and among its cherished objects was a centralisation of cultus such as had been attempted by Hezekiah. It would be an interesting link in the history of this party if, as has been surmised, the nucleus of Deuteronomy was the programme of Hezekiah's reform, or even the royal edict which set it in motion[1]. It would be easy to suppose that this document was preserved in the Temple archives, was afterwards expanded, and then lost sight of till it was discovered in the course of Josiah's repairs to the fabric. Although there are difficulties in that precise hypothesis, there is none in believing that the kernel of the book was composed by an adherent of the

[1] Steuernagel, *Die Entstehung des deut. Gesetzes* (1896), pp. 100, 112.

prophetic party, and was concealed in the Temple until an opportunity should present itself to put it in force. Some such hypothesis would enable us to understand the immediate rally of the prophetic party to the newly discovered law, without attributing deliberate dishonesty to the principal personages in the transaction. I cannot enter further on a discussion of the date of Deuteronomy or of the suggestion that its public reception was due to a pious fraud. It would not have been necessary to say so much, were it not that some support for the theory has been sought in the words of Jeremiah himself.

The general aim of Deuteronomy, as we see from the circumstances of its introduction, was to secure the continuance and prosperity of the Jewish State by an effort to bring the national life into harmony with those moral and religious conditions on which the favour of Yahwe depended. To such an effort a variety of interests lent their support in the age of Josiah. The reviving spirit of nationality, due to the decline of the Assyrian power and the hope of recovering political independence, welcomed the restoration of religion on a distinctively national basis, as opposed to the cosmopolitan and syncretistic tendencies which had marked the period of Assyrian domination. Another contributory influence was the demand for just and humane treatment of the poor and defenceless, which is so characteristic of Hebrew legislation, and is strongly in evidence in the law of Deuteronomy. But after all we cannot doubt that the central impulse of the reformation was a genuine interest in the religious life of the nation, and a desire to realise the ideal of righteousness contained in the teaching of the great prophets. The warnings and denunciations of the prophets had so far penetrated the conscience of the people as to produce a conviction that many things in the life of Judah had to be changed before it could rely on the protection of Yahwe. The prophetic conceptions of God as a perfectly righteous and holy Being, and of religion as obedience to his moral will, found inadequate, but still sincere, expression under the form of the Covenant, with its conditional promises and threats, which is the embodiment of the Deuteronomic idea. And that a profoundly religious motive lay at the heart of the movement is shown by the impressive inculcation in the book of whole-hearted loyalty to Yahwe, the only God whom Israel may serve, whose love to the fathers had called the people into existence, and whose gracious providence had endowed it with privileges such as no other nation enjoyed.

Of the practical measures adopted by the reformers, the most conspicuous, and the most far-reaching in its consequences, was the centralisation of worship in Jerusalem, with its negative counterpart in the suppression of the provincial sanctuaries. It is very important for the understanding of Jeremiah's possible attitude to the movement to observe that in the view of the Deuteronomists the centralisation of worship was not an end in itself, but only a means to a higher end, namely the purification of public religion from its heathenish excesses, and the assertion of Yahwe's sole claim to the nation's homage. The sacrificial and ceremonial legislation of Deuteronomy, which many modern critics find so obnoxious, is really a subordinate element, amounting to little more than a regulation of ancient usages too deeply bound up with the life and thought of the people to be swept away by legal enactment. It is sufficient to show that the promoters of the reformation did not as practical men rise to the high ethical conception of the prophets; but it is doing these men an injustice to say that their whole view of religion was vitiated by this compromise with existing customs and ideas[1]. We must note, however, that two parties were interested in the promotion of this particular reform. One was the Temple priesthood, which with all its lapses from the pure service of Yahwe had been distinguished by a certain fidelity to the national religious institutions and had already carried through important measures of reform. The other was, as we have seen, the prophetic party, which had kept alive the ideals of Isaiah, and had never ceased to cherish the hope of seeing Hezekiah's scheme of centralisation brought to a successful issue. The goodwill of the priesthood is demonstrated by the action of Hilkiah in giving publicity to the new law-book; and the support of the prophetic party may be inferred from the answer of the prophetess Huldah to the king's anxious inquiry (2 Kings xxii. 15–20). How far the co-operation rested on a common basis of principle may be doubtful. Even if such a union existed prior to the reformation, it carried the seeds of dissolution in its bosom. The priesthood was interested chiefly in the positive idea of centralisation, and was exposed to the temptation to emphasise the ritual element of the law, to the neglect of its moral requirements. The prophetically minded were more concerned with the negative aspect, the abolition of local cults, and could not acquiesce in any undue exaggeration of ceremonial. But there was another latent danger, to which men of both parties were exposed, and which marked a line of cleavage

[1] 'The code of Deuteronomy...starts from the observation that it is impossible to get rid of Canaanite elements of worship until sacrifice and ritual observances are confined to one sanctuary....From one point of view the law of the single sanctuary seems a poor outcome for the great work of Isaiah, and yet when it was construed in the way set forth in Deuteronomy it implied a real step towards the spiritualisation of all the service of God, and the emancipation of religion from its connection with the land and holy places of Canaan.' W. Robertson Smith, *The Prophets of Israel*, pp. 368 f.

soon to emerge: the tendency to rest on the formal fact of the covenant transaction as a sufficient pledge of Yahwe's favour, while its ethical content was ignored. And closely connected with this was the still more insidious error of regarding external obedience to the law, irrespective of the inner disposition of the heart, as a satisfactory response to the will of Yahwe. The germ of hypocrisy is latent in every legal religion; and in the often quoted words of Dr Davidson, 'Pharisaism and Deuteronomy came into the world the same day.' All this has to be borne in mind as we now proceed to consider the relation of Jeremiah to this many sided movement.

The first fact that strikes us is that Jeremiah's name does not appear among the active promoters of the reformation. To infer from this, or from the other fact that he was not even consulted as to the authority of the Law-book, that he was unsympathetic or hostile is to stretch the argument from silence much too far. In all probability he was still living in Anathoth, and his influence did not extend beyond his native town. He was not consulted simply because no one thought of him as a person to be consulted. The tidings of what had transpired in Jerusalem came upon him, as upon all his neighbours, like a thunderclap. But we may be sure that the event did not leave him unmoved. He might approve the measures that had been taken, or he might condemn them: a neutral onlooker he could not be. This was the biggest effort that had ever been made to bring the life of Israel into conformity with the will of God; it dealt with evils which he himself had denounced; and he could not avoid asking himself whether the thing was of the Lord or of man. The question what his judgment was covers many possibilities. Did he accept the new Law as of divine authority, or did he regard it as the work of well-meaning but mistaken scribes? Did he maintain a consistent position on this matter throughout his life, or did his early support of the movement give place, under the teaching of experience, to an attitude of distrust and aversion? And if the latter was the fact, was his opposition directed merely against the evil consequences which he perceived to follow from the formal observance of the Covenant, or against the whole idea of a covenant based on a written code? Or, finally, did he sympathise with the aim of the reformers, but object to the violent methods by which they sought to attain it?

The answers to these questions naturally depend largely on *a priori* considerations drawn from the character of Jeremiah and the leading principles of his teaching. But while it is impossible to exclude arguments of that nature, it is an obvious dictate of sound criticism to start from those utterances of Jeremiah which have a direct bearing on the problem. The presumption for or against his having supported the Deuteronomists can never be so strong as to bar *a limine* examination of any passage which seems to yield evidence on the one side or the other. Now there are just two passages in the book in which it is thought that clear and direct reference to Deuteronomy can be discovered: ch. xi. 1–8 and ch. viii. 8.

1. The former passage (xi. 1–8) contains two things: *first*, a curse on the man who will not observe a certain covenant (*vv.* 1–5), and *secondly* an injunction to Jeremiah to preach this covenant in the capital and provinces (*vv.* 6–8). That the reference in both is to Josiah's Covenant is an opinion so firmly rooted, and on the surface so plausible, that to the majority of recent critics the only point worth discussing is whether the verses are authentic words of Jeremiah or a legend of later date. But when we examine the context closely the reference to Deuteronomy is by no means so

certain as is commonly assumed. Let us look first at
vv. 1–5.

The introduction (1–3 *a*) is a clumsy and unintelligible
piece of writing, and is evidently the result of repeated
and careless editing. Clearing up the text as best we
can, we may read as follows:

The word which came to me from Yahwe: 'Cursed is he
who will not hear the words of *this Covenant* [which I enjoined
on your fathers at the time when I brought them out of the
land of Egypt, from the iron furnace, *saying* "Obey my voice,
and do according to all that I command you, and ye shall be to
me a people, and I will be to you a God; that I may confirm
the oath which I swore to your fathers, to give them a land
flowing with milk and honey," as at this day¹]. And I answered
and said 'Amen, Yahwe!'

The initial difficulty here is the indefiniteness of the
expression 'this covenant.' What covenant? 'Undoubtedly,' say the commentators, 'Josiah's covenant!
There was no other of which the prophet or his hearers
could be thinking².' But that does not meet the point.

¹ The words in square brackets are made up of characteristic phrases
of Deuteronomy, and are in all probability a later expansion of the text.
See below.

² It is absurd to suppose that in the current language of the time
Josiah's law-book was always referred to as 'this covenant,' so that
wherever the phrase is used we are to understand that Deuteronomy is
meant. Nor is any support for this view to be found in the fact that in
2 Kings xxiii. 3 (cf. Deut. xxix. 8 [9]) the contents of the new law-book
are described in terms identical with those here employed: 'the words
of this covenant' (*vv.* 2, 3, 6, 8). For in the historical narrative the
reference of the demonstrative pronoun is clearly determined by the
full description of the document in the previous verse: 'all the words of
the book of the covenant which was found in the house of Yahwe';
whereas here it is precisely the absence of any antecedent which is the
cause of obscurity. The explanation is quite inadequate on the supposition that Jeremiah is the author, and even more so if we have to do with
the work of a late and ill-informed writer, whose *Tendenz* must have
led him to put Jeremiah's connexion with Deuteronomy beyond a

Even if we grant that as a matter of fact Deuteronomy is meant, we still require an explanation of the manner in which it is introduced as '*this* covenant.' There are two directions in which a solution may be sought.

(*a*) The most obvious solution is to discard the reference to Deuteronomy, and take 'this covenant' to mean the covenant defined by the relative clauses which follow: 'this covenant which I enjoined on your fathers ...*namely*, "Obey my voice, etc."' Some such idea appears to have been in Dr Davidson's mind (although

doubt. There is another point of some importance which is overlooked by those who are satisfied with this interpretation of the phrase. The original Deuteronomy did not give itself out as the basis of a covenant made in the days of Moses. The only place in the book where this idea explicitly occurs is xxviii. 69 [E.V. xxix. 1] where a distinction is drawn between a covenant in the land of Moab (which is of course Deuteronomic) and the covenant at Horeb. But ch. xxix is no part of the original Deuteronomy; it appears to be the framework of a late separate edition of the Law, and at all events was not written till after the Exile (see A. F. Puukko, *Das Deuteronomium*, pp. 216–20). The early Deuteronomists know of only one Mosaic covenant, the covenant made at Horeb, of which the basis was the Decalogue (Deut. v. 2 ff., ix. 9 ff.). Deuteronomy itself is ostensibly a speech of Moses at the end of the desert sojourn (i. 5, iv. 1, 45 and *passim*), in which he expounds certain ordinances delivered to him privately on the mount (v. 31); and the only covenant ever based on it is the national covenant in the eighteenth year of Josiah. Bertholet has put forward the ingenious conjecture that in xxvi. 16–19 we have the *ipsissima verba* of the ratifying formula recited on that occasion (*Kurzer Hand-Commentar*, pp. xxiv, 82); but even if that suggestion be regarded as too subtle, the verses do not warrant the inference that a covenant transaction took place in the land of Moab. Now the covenant spoken of in Jer. xi is one made with Israel at the time of the Exodus from Egypt. To suppose, therefore, that Deuteronomy is meant is to assume a departure from the proper Deuteronomic point of view which we cannot readily attribute to a contemporary like Jeremiah. The argument of course does not hold against the opinion that the verses are spurious in whole or in part, for a late writer would naturally adopt the view of Deut. xxviii. 69. But if we accept the passage as genuine it becomes very difficult to think that Deuteronomy would be described in the way here employed.

he has not worked it out exegetically) when he wrote:
'Jeremiah may have sought to impress on men the
general idea of Deuteronomy, that of the covenant
between Yahwe and Israel, for this was his own idea in
another form; but a formal championship of Deuteronomy would have been very unlike him[1].' That is to
say, what Jeremiah means by covenant is just the
fundamental principle of Old Testament religion, that
Yahwe is Israel's God and Israel Yahwe's people, and
that this relation is maintained on the condition of
obedience to the will of Yahwe in whatever way it may
be revealed. The conception might have been suggested
by Josiah's covenant; but here he abstracts from the
concrete instance, and sums up the essence of the
covenant relation in the words I have quoted. If this be
the right interpretation, the passage is not only no proof
that Jeremiah supported Deuteronomy, but may even
be regarded as a strong polemic against it[2]. But if we
accept this view it will be difficult to ascribe the passage
to Jeremiah at all. The accumulation of distinctively
Deuteronomic phrases and ideas in *vv.* 4, 5, implies a
dependence on that book which savours strongly of
editorial workmanship.

(*b*) The other solution is one proposed by Erbt. It
starts from the reconstruction of a 'definite historical
situation' as the background of the oracle. A suitable
occasion would be the solemn scene in Jerusalem
described in 2 Kings xxiii. 1 ff.—the ratification of the
National Covenant, at which we may imagine that
Jeremiah was present; or the first proclamation of the
new law in the village of Anathoth. The young prophet
is stirred to the depths of his spirit by this great public

[1] Hastings' *Dictionary of the Bible*, ii, 570 *b*.
[2] So König, who holds that Jeremiah here asserts the validity of the
Sinai-covenant (with the Decalogue) in opposition to Deuteronomy
(*Geschichte der Alttestamentlichen Religion*, pp. 376 f.).

act of repentance and conversion to the pure service of
Yahwe as taught by the prophets. The conviction that
it was the will of God comes to him as an inward voice:
'Cursed be he who will not hear the words of this
covenant!' and the response of his conscience utters
itself in the audible exclamation, 'Amen, Yahwe!' On
this view we should omit the nearer specification of the
covenant in *vv.* 4, 5, as a Deuteronomistic amplification,
and let the 'this' refer to the law just read. The verses
would thus record a vivid momentary experience of the
prophet, in which he stands revealed as wholly in
sympathy with the aim of the Deuteronomic reformers.

The same method of excision is also applied by Erbt
to the following section, *vv.* 6–8; but here he has the
partial support of the LXX, which omits the whole of
vv. 7 and 8 with the exception of the words 'and they
did not' at the end. With this abbreviated text the
passage reads: 'And Yahwe said to me, "Proclaim all
these words in the cities of Judah and the streets of
Jerusalem, saying, Hear ye the words of this covenant
and do them"; But they did them not[1].' From these
verses it has often been inferred that Jeremiah's zeal in
the cause of reform led him to undertake an itinerant
mission round the cities of Judah to recommend
acceptance of the new law. Dr Davidson expresses the
opinion of many scholars when he pronounces such an
idea to be 'most improbable'; but short of denying the
authenticity of the entire passage, I do not see how it
can be got rid of, at least in the general sense of an
active public advocacy of the principles of the reformation. For the explanation of 'this covenant' (*vv.* 6, 8)
as meaning simply the formal idea of the covenant
without special reference to Deuteronomy (which might
suffice for *vv.* 3–5) cannot be applied to *vv.* 6–8. It is

---

[1] The connexion is not altogether natural; and it is doubtful if in this
case the shorter text of the LXX is older than the Hebrew.

true that in *v*. 7 the covenant idea appears to be viewed
as a continuous principle running through the whole
history of the nation, demanding obedience to a continuous revelation of the will of God through prophecy
(cf. vii. 25). But in *v*. 8 the clause 'I brought upon
them all the words of *this covenant*' must refer to a
particular document containing specific threats against
breaches of the covenant; and this could hardly be
anything else than the book of Deuteronomy. And since
v. 8 presupposes the exile, we must either delete it,
with *v*. 7, as a later addition, or reject the whole section
as spurious.

It is thus not easy to reach a positive conclusion as
to the real bearing of ch. xi on Jeremiah's relation
to Deuteronomy. So far as I can judge, it is only by
adopting some such theory as Erbt's that we can maintain the fundamental historicity of the narrative. Recent
critics have been far too ready to dismiss it as the baseless fabrication of a later age, invoking the authority of
a great prophet in support of the book of Deuteronomy.
That view has very little probability. We have seen that
the language is too ambiguous to be effective for that
purpose; and besides we know of no circumstances in
which the authority of Deuteronomy was so much in
question as to call for any such expedient. There is no
doubt that the collected prophecies of Jeremiah passed
through the hands of the Deuteronomic school, and
were freely edited by them. His discourses have been
interpolated, amplified, in some instances rewritten. But
the deliberate invention of an incident which had no
point of contact in the authentic record of his life is a
procedure to which no assured parallel is found in the
book. We must at least believe that a trustworthy
tradition lies behind the passage in ch. xi; and the conclusion to which it naturally points is that Jeremiah was
at first strongly in favour of the law of Deuteronomy,

and lent his moral support to the reformation of Josiah.

2. A much deeper issue is raised by the second passage, ch. viii. 8—a remarkable verse, standing in a remarkable connexion. The prophet has been deploring the people's propensity to evil courses; and in the preceding verse he has traced it to a deadening of the religious instinct, that knowledge of God's will which at an earlier time he had hoped to find at least among the educated classes (v. 5): 'My people know not the *ethic* of Yahwe' (viii. 7). Then he proceeds:

> How can you say, 'We are wise,
> And the *Tôrā* of Yahwe is with us'?
> Why, mark you! it has been turned to falsehood
> By the false pen of scribes[1]!

The suggestion that the verse expresses Jeremiah's antipathy to Deuteronomy was first made by Prof. Marti in 1889[2], and it has received the *imprimatur* of some of the foremost names in O.T. scholarship. This is not surprising. In Jeremiah's time Deuteronomy was the only written law which we can readily imagine to have been the object of such religious confidence as is described in the first half of the verse; and that *Tôrā* here means written law is so much the most natural view that we need hardly consider possible alternatives. It is noteworthy, too, that the peculiar claim to 'wisdom' in virtue of the possession of the law finds an echo in the book of Deuteronomy itself: 'For this is your

---

[1] The last sentence might also be rendered 'The false pen of scribes has made it in falsehood,' or even 'has wrought falsely,' or 'in vain' (1 Sam. xxv. 21). It is difficult to render the exact force of the combination אָכֵן הִנֵּה. אָכֵן expresses, as often, the reality, in contrast to what is wrongly supposed: 'But lo! the fact is, etc.' (see Brown, Driver, Briggs, *Heb. Lex.*, *s.v.*).

[2] *Der Prophet Jeremia* (not seen!). Also in his *Geschichte der Israelitischen Religion* (1897), p. 166.

wisdom and discernment in the eyes of the peoples, who shall hear of all these ordinances, and shall say, Surely a wise and discerning people is this great nation' (Deut. iv. 6). Nor is it in the abstract impossible that Jeremiah should have challenged its divine authority. In short, that Marti's view *can* be read into the passage is undeniable; and the only question is whether this be the only admissible interpretation. Now, the second half of *v.* 8, being the answer to the first, might mean *either* that the people had *not* the true *Tôrā* of Yahwe (in which case Deuteronomy is stigmatised as a fraud), *or* that having it they are none the better, because it had been so overlaid by scribal additions as to have lost all value as an ethical standard. Hence several writers hold that the reference is to tentative legislative essays in the direction of the later Priestly Code, whose tendency was to emphasise the ceremonial element in religion, and enhance the prestige of the Temple and the power of the priesthood. There are turns of expression in 8 *b* which favour this explanation. It might be argued that the law in question is only said to have been *made into* falsehood, not that it was false *ab origine*; and again the indefiniteness of the phrase '(many) a false pen of scribes[1]' points rather to a multifarious literary activity than to the production of a single document.

At all events the evidence of deep-seated hostility to Deuteronomy in viii. 8 is not so clear as to neutralise the opposite impression we have derived from ch. xi. And two additional considerations have to be borne in mind. (1) Ch. viii. 8 represents a later—probably much later—estimate of the movement than xi. 1–8. However radical Jeremiah's opposition at the later date may have been, it will not follow that he had never held a different view. It can only show that he was dis-

---

[1] See König, *op. cit.* p. 325; and in *Studien und Kritiken*, 1906, pp. 384 ff.

appointed with the spiritual fruits of the reformation, and was led to revise his judgment on the instrument by which it was effected. (2) Jeremiah is here concerned, not directly with the contents of the law, but with its indirect effect on the mind of the nation. 'The law is good if a man use it lawfully.' He had looked on Deuteronomy as setting forth a high ideal of national life, and a means of accomplishing much-needed reforms: in that sense it was to him a word of God; and he could say 'Amen' to the curse on him who refused to obey it. But to the people it became a fetish, and its possession a substitute for the inward knowledge of God which then and always was to Jeremiah the essence of religion. This is the error he is concerned to expose; and to do so it was not necessary that he should denounce the law root and branch as a product of human deceit and imposture. It was enough to assert that it had fallen into the hands of a professional class, whose interest it was to 'develope' its teaching in a direction which was foreign to its original spirit and purpose.

This brings us to the heart of the subject. The disinclination to admit even a temporary co-operation of Jeremiah with the Deuteronomists rests less on the exegesis of particular texts than on the broad ground that his insight into the nature of religion makes it inconceivable that he could ever have had any sympathy with an attempt to convert the nation by a forcible change in its forms of worship. He must have been aware of the essential discordance between the spirit of law and the spirit of prophecy,—between the ideals of the Deuteronomists and his own. Now, that is doubtless true of the later Jeremiah. But is it necessary to suppose that it was all clear to him from the outset? Had he nothing to learn in the course of his life about the inherent defects of a national religion, and the impossibility of bringing about a national conversion by an exercise of the authority of the State? The difference of principle was always there implicitly; but just as a woman has sometimes to be engaged to a man before she knows that she cannot marry him, so Jeremiah may have had to go some way with the Deuteronomists in order to discover that he was of a different spirit from theirs. It does not detract from the greatness of the prophet to think that his knowledge of religion was acquired gradually as a result of the experience and discipline of his life; and to my mind his mental development is more intelligible if we assign an important place in that experience to reflexion on the working of the Deuteronomic covenant.

To sum up briefly our conclusions as to Jeremiah's relation to Deuteronomy: Josiah's reformation found him still a young, little known prophet, living quietly at Anathoth. At first he espoused the cause of reform with a zeal which drew down on him the deadly hatred of his townsmen (see pp. 109 ff. below). At this time Deuteronomy was to him simply the programme of a great and beneficent reform; and while accepting it as such he may not have given much thought to the conception of religion which lay behind it. But very soon its defects became apparent: its superficiality, its inability to cope with prevalent immorality, and the surviving tendencies to polytheism and superstition; and Jeremiah began to suspect the inherent impotence of the legal method of dealing with national sin. At a later time he detected a worse evil in the new-born spirit of self-righteousness based on a formal acceptance of the Covenant and an outward compliance with its demands. Against this spirit Jeremiah protested in the way we have seen. He saw that the door was opened to a new class of professional religionists, the scribes, in whose hands religion was divorced from the essential and the

spiritual, and resolved into a routine of sumptuous
ritual and priestly ceremony.

But we need not suppose that Jeremiah, any more
than Jesus and Paul, repudiated the law which was the
occasion of this evil, as in itself of no authority. And in
spite of differences there are close affinities between the
school of Deuteronomy and the teaching of Jeremiah.
The mere fact that the prophecies of Jeremiah were
edited by the Deuteronomic school shows that there
was no consciousness of antagonism between them.
Deuteronomy as well as Jeremiah insists on the need of
a circumcision of the heart (Jer. iv. 4; Deut. x. 16,
xxx. 6); and the author of the principal edition of
Deuteronomy—the writer who more than any other
has stamped his individuality on the book—inculcates
so earnestly the inwardness of true obedience as springing from love to God, that we can almost think of him
as a disciple of the prophet, or a Melancthon to his
Luther. Moreover the stedfast loyalty of the family of
Shaphan till the end of Jeremiah's life suggests that
he never broke openly with the reforming party[1], and
certainly makes it extremely improbable that he had
ever denounced them as a clique of forgers and de-
ceivers. Inwardly, no doubt, he felt himself isolated
from them. He was driven in upon himself and back
upon God. He perceived ever more clearly that neither
law nor prophecy could reach the obdurate heart of the
people, or cure the 'perpetual backsliding' which made
a return to 'the ancient paths, the way of good' a moral
impossibility.

[1] See p. 278 below.

CHAPTER VII

IN THE WAKE OF THE REFORM

WE have now entered upon the second period of Jeremiah's career. The promulgation of the Deuteronomic law in 621 was an event which could not fail to change the character of his ministry whatever his original attitude to that transaction may have been. From that time till the tragic death of Josiah in 608 we may assume that an effort was made to carry out the legislative provisions of the Covenant; and Jeremiah must have watched with deep concern the effect of the new order of things on the religious temper of the nation. Soon after the death of Josiah the threatening aspect of foreign affairs made Jeremiah a prominent actor on the stage of history, and he continued to work in the full blaze of publicity till near the end of his life. Between these dates there is an interval of about thirteen years during which our knowledge of the prophet's activity is certainly very imperfect. It has been a common opinion among his commentators that so far as extant prophecies are concerned this interval is an almost complete blank in his history. The fact is sometimes explained by the assumption that the conduct of public affairs was very much in harmony with Jeremiah's ideals and gave him no occasion to intervene; sometimes by the suggestion that he had been reduced to silence by the failure of his early Scythian predictions. Neither of these considerations has much plausibility in itself, and the fact which they are put forward to explain is at least incapable of proof. When Jeremiah says (xxv. 3) that he had exercised an unremitting ministry of three and twenty years from the thirteenth year of Josiah to the fourth of Jehoiakim, it would be surprising if more than the half of that period had left no literary remains. The theory is intelligible on the assumption that the prophecies are in the main chronologically arranged. It would follow from that assumption that in passing from ch. vi to ch. vii we step at once from pre-Deuteronomic days to the beginning of Jehoiakim's reign, and that all the prophecies from ch. vii onwards are of still later date. But if in accordance with the tendency of recent criticism we abandon entirely the hypothesis of chronological order there is nothing to justify the improbable view that we have so long an interruption in the record of Jeremiah's activity. It may be true that no discourse can *certainly* be dated from the second half of Josiah's reign—certain dates are hard to find in the writings of Jeremiah—but there are a considerable number of utterances which on internal evidence may be more naturally assigned to this period than to any other. It will therefore be convenient at this point to devote a chapter to the examination of some miscellaneous poems, illustrating different aspects of Jeremiah's experience in the obscure middle section of his life, but more especially his reflexions on the result of the Deuteronomic reformation.

I

We will look first at two passages of extraordinary biographical interest in which we can perhaps detect the earliest repercussion of the reform movement on the fortunes of Jeremiah: ch. xi. 18–23 and xii. 1–6. That his removal from Anathoth to Jerusalem was a consequence of his advocacy of the Deuteronomic covenant is a view which has commended itself to many writers. We may admit at once that it cannot be proved to be true. It is suggested by the proximity of the passages to the account of the prophet's championship of

Deuteronomy in the earlier part of ch. xi; but that might
be purely accidental, and it is easy to imagine equally
probable occasions which might have called forth such
utterances as those before us. Still, no occasion is *more*
probable than this; and in considering a passage of uncertain *provenance* there can be no objection to placing it
at what may be called the point of maximum illumination.

In ch. xi. 18, 19, then, Jeremiah tells indirectly the
story of a plot against his life by the men of Anathoth,
who had been stirred to a frenzy of hatred by his
prophesying in the name of Yahwe (*v.* 21). Now
an attack on the life of a prophet because of his prophesying must have been a very rare thing in Israel.
There must have been in Jeremiah's preaching some
peculiar provocation to the prejudices of his neighbours;
and nothing is more likely to have excited their fury
than an open approval of the desecration of the local
shrine under royal authority. For a time he was all
unconscious of the ill-will he had provoked. He could
not understand the dark looks and muttered maledic-
tions which he encountered as he went peaceably out
and in amongst his acquaintances. But at last, by a
sudden illumination which he ascribed to divine inspiration, he saw into their hearts, and knew that they were
resolved on murder.

> 18 But Yahwe made me know, and I knew:
>   Their ill deeds I saw;
> 19 While I like a tame pet-lamb
>   That is led to the shambles
> Knew not that for my undoing
>   They hatched a plot:
> 'Let us kill the tree in its sap,—
>   Cut him off from the land of the living,
>   That his name be remembered no more.'

Full of resentment against these treacherous men,
the prophet rolls his cause on Yahwe with a prayer for

vengeance, and receives in answer a revelation of the terrible fate in store for his persecutors (*vv.* 20–23).

If the following passage (xii. 1–3, 5, 6) refers to the same incident, which again is not certain, though probable, we have a still more instructive revelation of Jeremiah's mind in this crisis of his history. Reflexion on the experience through which he had just passed seems to have raised the general question of the rectitude of Yahwe's providence: that great problem of retribution which so exercised the minds of later Hebrew thinkers was perhaps first formulated by Jeremiah.

> 1 Thou art in the right, O Yahwe,
>   Should I dispute with Thee;
>   Yet of matters of right
>   Would I speak with Thee.
>
>   Why is the way of the wicked so smooth,
>   And all treacherous men at ease?
> 2 Thou plantest them: they also strike root,
>   Beget[1] and bear fruit.
>   Near art Thou in their mouth,
>   But how far from their heart!
> 3 But Thou, O Yahwe, hast known me,
>   Hast tried how my heart is with Thee.
>   Drag them forth like sheep to the shambles,
>   For a day of slaughter devote them!

The answer to this expostulation is given in *v.* 5 (*v.* 4 is plainly an insertion):

> 5 With footmen thou hast run and art weary,
>   Then how wilt thou vie with horses?
>   In a land of peace thou art not at ease,
>   Then how wilt thou fare in Jordan's brake[2]?

---

[1] So LXX.

[2] The 'Pride of Jordan' (xlix. 19, l. 44; Zech. xi. 3) is not the swelling of the agitated waters of the river, but the luxuriant growth of cane, willows, etc., which clothes its margin, and was a haunt of lions in ancient times and even as late as the Crusades.

Thus the answer which Jeremiah receives to his wistful questioning of Yahwe's dealings with men is a stern summons to a more heroic and strenuous conflict with the forces arrayed against the truth. But is not this a strange admonition to a man who has just narrowly escaped assassination at the hands of treacherous townsmen? Therein lies a real difficulty in connecting this passage with xi. 18–23, or with a flight from Anathoth. For xii. 6 is usually taken to imply that the greater trial ahead of him is the enmity of his own family, and that would certainly be something of an anti-climax to an attempt on his life. But that is perhaps not a necessary implication (see below). No interpretation of xii. 5 seems to me half so probable as the old view which reads in it a contrast between the trials of the prophet's youthful ministry in Anathoth and the more formidable opposition which he must encounter in Jerusalem[1]. The warning must therefore have come to him at that point of his life when he was driven from his native village to find a refuge in the crowded streets of the capital. And if we may suppose that xii. 1–6 is a retrospective meditation written in the safety of his retreat in Jerusalem, it is not inconceivable that in spite of the frightful danger which he had escaped he should thus contrast the comparatively tranquil life he had left behind for ever with the stormy career which awaited him in the great city[2].

[1] See Cheyne, *Jeremiah: his life and times*, pp. 122 f.

[2] Cornill (who assigns the incident to a late period of Jeremiah's life) seeks to harmonise the two sections by reversing their order, taking xii. 1, 2, 5, 6, as the prelude to xi. 18 ff. He conceives Jeremiah as brooding over the abstract problem of God's dealings with individuals (xii. 1, 2), when he is suddenly shaken out of his reverie by the challenge of *v.* 5, which tells him in effect that these theoretical perplexities are but as child's play compared with the life and death struggle in which he will speedily be involved. The nature of that conflict is indicated by *v.* 6: it is the enmity and treachery of his father's house that will try his

faith and courage to the uttermost. And this is the divine warning referred to in xi. 18 which discloses to him the danger to which he is exposed. From the clouds of abstract speculation he is thus brought sharply down to the realities of practical life; and he realises that beside the trials that lie before him his wrestling with the inequalities of providence was as a race with footmen compared to a contest with horses. This ingenious theory is at first sight very attractive, but on examination it proves to be vulnerable at several points. It necessitates the rejection of *v*. 3; for if that verse be retained it was clearly no speculative theological problem that troubled the prophet, but the prosperous lot of particular men whose treachery (*v*. 1) was well known to him. A more serious objection lies in the sense given to *v*. 5. It does not seem a natural application of the figures there used to take them as denoting the contrast between theoretical perplexities and a desperate fight with human foes: the difference suggested is one not of kind but of degree. But the weakest point of the theory is what Cornill regards as its chief recommendation, viz. the identification of the revelation contained in xii. 6 with that of xi. 18. That is inadmissible for two reasons. In the first place they refer to two quite separate things; for we have no right to assume that the plot to murder Jeremiah was instigated by members of his own family. And in the second place we cannot identify the two without robbing xi. 18 of its proper and obvious meaning. It plainly means that by a sudden flash of God-given insight the prophet discovered the peril of his situation; and the idea that he was falling back on a previous divine communication is suggested by nothing in the narrative. Ch. xi. 18 ff. is in short perfectly intelligible by itself, and the only question is whether xii. 1 ff. can be understood as a sequel, or must be referred to some totally unrelated incident. Since it is hardly likely that an event of this kind occurred twice in Jeremiah's life, I have ventured in the text above to hazard an explanation which might enable us to combine them without sacrificing what appears the most satisfying interpretation of xii. 5. Two objections, however, must be frankly faced. (1) xii. 6 can no longer be taken as explanatory of *v*. 5; and the thrice repeated ‫בֹּגְדוּ‬ must be understood as emphasising a circumstance of Jeremiah's recent experience which made a return to the old conditions impossible. (2) The last clause of *v*. 6 appears to imply that Jeremiah was still in touch with his family, and liable to be deceived by their fair words. But Cornill has pointed out the contradiction between this clause and the preceding ('even they are after thee in full cry'), and rejects the latter as spurious. It would be just as easy to reject the other; if, indeed, it would not be better to omit the whole verse as a mistaken commentary on *v*. 5.

These two passages are interesting in another respect. They are the first of a unique series of devotional poems commonly known as the 'Confessions of Jeremiah,' which unfold the secret of his best life, the converse of his soul with God through which the true nature of religion was disclosed to him. In all probability the sections we have just considered mark the opening of that well-spring of inward devotion which sustained him through life. It would throw great light on his spiritual history if we could ascertain that this strain of subjective piety dates from the crisis in his life when he first tasted the bitterness of the man whose foes are they of his own household[1].

II

If the account of Jeremiah's original attitude to Deuteronomy given in the last chapter be in the main correct, we might expect to find among his prophecies some indication of his growing alienation from the spirit and aims of the party of reform. We need not be surprised if the evidence on this subject is scanty and ambiguous. For it is not probable that Jeremiah remained long a supporter of the accomplished reformation. The new law must have passed immediately into the control of the priesthood, in whose hands it developed tendencies which more than neutralised any good that the movement ever contained. Jeremiah must have been quick to detect this soul of evil in things good; and there is abundant proof that he protested against the formalism, the wrong emphasis on cultus, and the false religious confidence engendered by the Law, with all his might. The difficulty is to determine how far such utterances express disillusionment or change of attitude on his part, or whether they are consistent with

[1] See Chap. XI below.

an earlier advocacy of the Deuteronomic covenant.
Cornill maintains that the entire absence of favourable
references to Deuteronomy (apart from xi. 1–8) shows
that at no time could the prophet have been in sympathy
with the reformation, or hopeful that any good could
result from it. It might be argued with equal force that
if he had been from the first opposed to it, he must
have denounced it in far more unsparing terms than we
find anywhere in the book. The truth is that explicit
and unmistakable allusions to Deuteronomy are fewer
than we should have anticipated on any view of Jeremiah's judgment on its merits. The really significant
fact is that while he relentlessly exposes the evil effects
of the formal acceptance of Deuteronomy, he never
(with the disputed exception of viii. 8) directly assails
the Law itself, or the men who were responsible for
first putting it in force.

With this question in mind, the first passage which
arrests our attention is the striking oracle of ch. vi.
16–20, in which one writer[1] thinks we can discover the
earliest evidence of Jeremiah's opposition to the spirit
of Deuteronomy:

16 Thus said Yahwe:

> 'Stand by the ways and see,
>   And inquire for the ancient paths,
> Which is the way of good, and walk in it,
>   And find rest to your soul.'
>   And they said, 'We will not walk.'

> 17 And I set watchmen over them,
>   [2]*   *   *   *   *   *
> *   *   *   *   *   *   *
>
> 'Give heed to the trumpet's sound.'
> And they said, 'We will not heed.'

---

[1] Schmidt, *op. cit.* p. 252.   [2] Two lines perhaps omitted.

18 Therefore hear, ye peoples, ye shepherds of flocks[1]!
19 Hear, thou earth!

Behold, I bring evil on this people,
The fruit of their falling away[2];
For to My word they gave no heed,
And My law they contemned.

20 What is incense from Sheba to Me,
Or calamus fine from a distant land?
Your holocausts find no favour;
Your sacrifices delight not Me.

Few of Jeremiah's utterances present a more interesting exegetical problem than these verses. They describe the failure of the discipline by which Yahwe had sought to bring Israel to a right mind. Two methods He had tried in vain. He had appealed to the conservative principle which is essential to a sound religious development. He had called the people to pause and consider the diverse religious tendencies of their age, and to follow that which was in harmony with the historic faith of Israel. The 'old paths' are the genuine ethical principles of the Mosaic revelation embodied in the traditional Tôrā or teaching of Yahwe (v. 19). These are contrasted with new-fangled costly refinements in cultus—'frankincense that comes from Sheba' and 'fine calamus from a far off land' (v. 20)—through which their new spiritual guides held out the delusive promise of peace of mind. Only by renouncing these expedients, and returning to the 'way of good' marked out by all the best teaching of the past, could they find the rest for which their soul pined and which they had not got. The second method was 'the sound of the trumpet,'— the warnings of providence interpreted by prophecy. To both appeals the people had turned a deaf ear, and

---

[1] Following the text of the LXX.
[2] LXX.

their refusal is accepted as final: judgment can no longer be averted (*vv.* 18 f.).

Such is the general sense of the passage. That it belongs to the post-Deuteronomic period of Jeremiah's ministry is almost certain. It deals with the spirit of shallow and half-hearted optimism which the self-constituted guardians of the covenant endeavoured to instil into the mind of the people. 'They (the priests and prophets) heal the hurt of my people lightly, saying, "Peace! Peace!" when there is no peace' (vi. 14)[1]. Jeremiah knew that this official propaganda of optimism had failed to allay the feeling of unrest which troubled the public mind, and could only be removed by a return to the old paths of morality and true religion. The rest of soul here spoken of is not to be identified with the inward spiritual satisfaction which Jesus promises to the weary and heavy laden[2]; and yet there is more than verbal agreement between these two great sayings. From the lips of the prophet it means the deep peace of mind in face of threatening national dangers which comes through a life ordered in accordance with the eternal laws of the divine government of the universe; in the mouth of Jesus it is the higher blessedness of the individual who in meekness and humility accepts the yoke of Christ and knows that nothing can separate him from the love of God in Christ Jesus his Lord.

---

[1] Kraetschmar (*Die Bundesvorstellung im A.T.*, p. 48) has pointed out that 'peace' (שלום) is the word technically used for the relation between two parties which results from the ratification of a covenant. In any case there can be little doubt that the ground of confidence on which these soothing assurances were based was the renewal of the covenant between Yahwe and the nation. To Kraetschmar also I owe the observation that שלום, in the sense of peace with God, is first found in Jeremiah (p. 149).

[2] Matt. xi. 29: καὶ εὑρήσετε ἀνάπαυσιν ταῖς ψυχαῖς ὑμῶν.

The question now is, What is meant by the summons
to seek for the old paths? Does it refer to a single event,
or is it a general exhortation such as a prophet might
have addressed to his contemporaries at any period of
the later history? Has it, in short, anything to do with
Deuteronomy? Now if the prophet is here dealing with
the religious temper induced by the covenant, he must
have had Deuteronomy in his mind; and his criticism
of the results of the reformation must involve a certain
estimate of the instrument of that reformation—the
Deuteronomic code. And this might take three directions. (1) The promulgation of the Law might itself
be the divine call to walk in the old way revealed amid
the thunders of Sinai. On that interpretation Jeremiah
still believed in Deuteronomy as an expression of the
true religion of Israel, and the sin with which he charges
the people is their refusal to observe the covenant in its
essential ethical requirements (cf. xi. 10). (2) The idea
may be that Deuteronomy stands opposed to the fundamental principles of the religion of Yahwe, and the
prophet calls on the people to renounce their trust in a
written code, and live in the spirit of the faith once
committed to their fathers. (3) He may mean that they
are to *test Deuteronomy itself* by the fundamental principles
of the national religion, and discover how far the
tendencies which it fostered were in accordance with
the revelation of Yahwe's will. It seems to me that the
last view enables us to harmonise the conflicting indications of the prophet's estimate of Deuteronomy. No
doubt it implies a critical attitude towards a movement
of which he had once been an ardent supporter; but
such a change is intelligible, and was in the circumstances inevitable. We know that the emphasis on the
ceremonial side of religion was to Jeremiah the dead
fly in the ointment of the apothecary. Now in Deuteronomy the ritual element, though present, is subordi-

nated to the higher purpose of purifying the national
worship; and it is clearly a much more advanced phase
of ceremonialism that is contemplated here. Deuteronomy says nothing about frankincense and calamus—
these belong to the more sumptuous ritual of the
Priestly Code—but since they were evidently in use
we may be sure that the 'false pen of scribes' (viii. 8)
was already at work investing them with legal sanction.
We can understand that Jeremiah might accept the
moderate ritualism of Deuteronomy for the sake of the
moral demand which the code laid on the conscience of
the nation. But when he sees the whole reform movement degenerating into a superstitious trust in the
Temple and its worship he falls back on a principle;
and he asserts that principle absolutely ($v.$ 20 b),
although logically it sweeps away as irrelevant the
sacrificial element in Deuteronomy itself.

We here touch on the question of the prophetic view
of cultus in general; but that is a subject which demands
fuller treatment in another place[1]. We may note, however, the peculiar significance of Jeremiah's teaching
in regard to this matter. It lies in the fact that he himself
stood in a sense at the parting of the ways, at a time
when much that was good in the life of Israel was
passing into legal and ritual moulds; and that standing
there, the last great exponent of prophetic theology, he
uncompromisingly affirmed its fundamental doctrine,
that in religion nothing counts but for a man 'to do
justly, and love mercy, and to walk humbly with his
God' (Micah vi. 8).

We turn next to the exquisite monologue of ch.
viii. 4–8, the last verse of which we have already discussed in its bearing on Jeremiah's opinion of the Law-
book of Josiah. The whole passage shows more clearly
than any other utterance of Jeremiah how his insight

[1] Chap. IX.

into the nature of religion was cleared and deepened by meditation on the effect of Deuteronomy on the spirit of the nation[1]. It reads as follows:

> 4 Do men fall and never rise up?
> Or turn and not return?
> 5 Why falleth this people away
> Unceasingly backward?
> They cling to deceit,
> Refusing to turn.
>
> 6 I have hearkened and heard;
> They speak not the truth.
> Not one repents of his evil,
> Saying, What have I done?
> Each rushes along in his course
> Like a horse in the battle.
>
> 7 Yea the stork in the heavens
> Knoweth her season,
> And the turtle and swallow
> The time of their coming;
> But My people—they know not
> The manner[2] of Yahwe.
>
> 8 How can ye say, 'We are wise,
> And the Tôrā of Yahwe is with us'?
> Lo! surely, 'tis written in falsehood
> By a false pen of scribes!

The contrast between the religion of the letter and the religion of the spirit could not be more finely described than in these lines. The prophet is lost in amazement at the persistent impenitence of his people. When a man falls the next thing is he rises again; if he turn aside in his way he will turn back; but Israel seems to have learned the secret of perpetual relapse. The prophet has listened in vain for any sign of misgiving

---

[1] pp. 105 ff.

[2] On the sense of מִשְׁפַּט here, see p. 139 *n*. below.

or better thoughts: No man repents of his wickedness, saying, What have I done? Their headlong career of wickedness is like the impetuous rush of a horse in battle, reckless of obstacles and consequences. Then follows the contrast of the migratory birds, those denizens of a purer air, which far as they wander are compelled by a mysterious law of their nature to return at the appointed season. Such is religion as Jeremiah conceived and experienced it. It is the instinct of the human soul for the divine,—an instinct which responds to the laws of the spiritual universe, and, unless perverted by evil habit (xiii. 23), guides it unerringly to its true home in God. In this fine image Jeremiah anticipates the great word of Augustine: *Quia fecisti nos ad te, et inquietum est cor nostrum donec requiescat in te*[1]. The people pride themselves on their possession of a written law; and when the prophet charges them with having no religion in their hearts, they retort that they have what is better, —they have it in a book! It is this illusion of infallibility and finality attaching to the written word, as if it were superior to the living voice of prophecy or the dictates of the religious sense, that Jeremiah seeks to dispel by the sweeping declaration that the true *Tôrā* of Yahwe has been falsified by the mischievous activity of the scribes.

Religion is an instinct: in the sense that it is implanted in human nature—not, of course, in the sense that it is unintelligent. In a repeated phrase of Jeremiah it is 'knowledge of Yahwe' (ix. 2, 5 [3, 6], xxii. 16). To know God is to be likeminded with God, to have a sympathetic understanding of His will and character. And the mind of God is declared in a couple of verses which, whether written by Jeremiah or not, sum up his conception of what religion is: 'Let not the wise man glory in his wisdom, nor the strong man in his might, nor the rich man in his wealth. But let him that will glory glory in

[1] *Conf.* I, i.

this: in having discernment to know Me, that I am
Yahwe who work kindness, justice, and righteousness
in the earth; for in these things I delight, saith Yahwe'
(ix. 22 f. [23 f.]; cf. xxii. 16). Hence if we ask in what
religion consists the answer is, negatively, not in anything external: not in the possession of a written book, or
the observance of traditional rules, or the performance
of actions outwardly right such as the reformation of
king Josiah. Religion has its seat in the heart, which in
Hebrew includes the reason and the moral sense (iv.
3, 4). Here we must guard against misconception.
Jeremiah does not teach that the heart can of itself
generate the true knowledge of Yahwe. The fact of
revelation is to him axiomatic: Yahwe takes the
initiative in making Himself known. The revelation
takes the form of *Tôrā* (direction), or *mishpāṭ* (right
custom) embodied in the religious institutions of the
nation; and the personal inspiration of the prophets.
But these fail of their effect except in so far as they find
a response in the heart and conscience of the individual.
Jeremiah came to realise that there was an inherent
inadequacy in the method of revelation hitherto imparted to the chosen people (xxxi. 31 ff.). We cannot
tell at what time that truth dawned upon him; but we
see a preparation for it in the profound thought which
is expressed in the verses we have considered.

> But I have always had one lode star,—now,
> As I look back, I see that I have halted
> Or hastened as I looked towards that star,—
> A need, a trust, a yearning after God.

III

Another series of oracles, which it is impossible to
date precisely, shows that the *foreboding of doom* was
never far from Jeremiah's thoughts during the obscure middle period of his ministry. To this period we

may assign the gloomy utterance of ch. xvi. 1–9, in which he discloses the reason of his remaining unmarried and childless, and holding aloof from all occasions of neighbourly intercourse whether of a festive or a funereal character. Erbt[1] remarks rightly enough on the extraordinary strength of individuality which such defiance of custom implied in the ancient world; but it is still more remarkable as a proof of the deep hold which the foreboding of his people's fate had taken of the prophet's mind. He sees the children born in that time destined to agonising deaths (whether by sword, famine or pestilence does not appear)[2], and the ground littered with their unburied corpses; all mourning rites suspended because of the magnitude of the calamity, and all the joy of human life—'the sound of mirth and the sound of gladness, the voice of the bridegroom and the voice of the bride'—quenched in universal gloom. He seems at one time to have been haunted by the spectacle of fields covered by the bodies of the slain, and cities crowded with the emaciated victims of famine: 'When I go out to the fields, lo, there the slain with the sword; and if I enter the city, lo, there the horrors of famine' (xiv. 18; cf. ix. 21 [22] below). The difficulty of understanding such passages is to know whether they are descriptions of actual experiences or imaginative or visionary pictures of calamities still future. That Judah suffered severely from famine in the reign of Josiah is almost certain (see on ch. xiv below); but on the whole the visionary explanation is perhaps to be preferred; and on this assumption we can have little hesitation in dating the oracles from the later years of Josiah.

[1] *Op. cit.* pp. 154 f.

[2] Vague references to sword and famine (and pestilence) as instruments of the judgment are frequent, although all the passages may not be genuine; cf. v. 12 f., xi. 22, xiv. 12 ff., xv. 2, 3, etc.

With regard to another poem it is more doubtful whether it depicts a definite historical situation, or a prophetic vision of impending woe; but it may be quoted here as the culminating expression of the mood we have just characterised. It is perhaps the most brilliant example of the prophetic elegy which the Old Testament contains, and it would be hard to find anywhere a more vivid and pregnant poetic image than the figure of the Reaper Death with which it closes (ch. ix. 16, 17, 19–21):

> [16]Call for the mourning women to come;
> Send for the wise ones [17]in haste;
> Let them raise a coronach o'er us.
> Let our eyes dissolve in weeping,
> And our eyelids gush forth tears[1].

> [19]Yea, hear, ye women the word of Yahwe,
> Lend your ear to the word of His mouth!
> And every one teach her daughter a plaint,
> And her friend a dirge:

> [20]*Death has come up through our windows—*
> *Has entered our halls,*
> *Cutting off the child from the street—*
> *The youths from the square.*

> [21]*And the corpses of men lie prone*
> *On the open field,*
> *Like sheaves behind the reaper,*
> *With none to gather.*

The next passage calls for closer examination on account of its doubtful unity, its complex dramatic structure, and its stronger suggestion of a distinct historic background: ch. viii. 14–23 [ix. 1]. By several critics it is broken up into short disjointed sections of various dates; but that seems unnecessary; or if there

---

[1] *V.* 18, which breaks the connexion, seems to have been inserted here because of similarity of subject, and the catchword נֶּהִי in *v.* 17.

be discontinuity the separate poems may still form a
cycle emanating from a single situation.

14 Ah, wherefore sit we still?
    Assemble and let us go in
  To the fenced towns, and there meet our doom;
    For Yahwe our God has doomed us,
  And drugged us with poison draughts;
    For against Him we have sinned.

15 We waited and waited for peace,
    But good came not:
  For a time of healing,
    And lo, Destruction!

16 The snort of his horses was heard from Dan,
    From the loud neighing of his stallions the whole land quaked;
  And they came and devoured the land and its fulness,—
    The city and them that dwell therein[1].

18 Incurable is my sorrow;
    My heart within me is sick.

19 Hark! my people's cry of distress
    From the land far and near:
  'Is Yahwe not in Zion?
    Is no King there?
20 Past is the harvest, ended the fruit-time,
    And we are not saved.'

21 For the ruin of my people I mourn,
    Horror hath seized me.
22 Is there no balsam in Gilead?
    No healer there?
  Why then does no healing come
    For my people's hurt?

---

[1] I omit the prosaic verse 17, which, as a threat of future punishment,
and introducing direct speech of Yahwe, is entirely unsuitable in its
present position. _V._ 19 _b_, also spoken by Yahwe, reads like an editorial
interpolation in the middle of the people's complaint.

²³O that my head were waters,
    And my eyes a fountain of tears!
That day and night I might weep.
O'er my people's slain.

Assuming that the passage is a unity, it falls naturally
into two parts: *vv.* 14–16 describe the collapse of the
national spirit under some overwhelming disaster, and
vv. 18–23 the effect on the prophet's mind. In both
sections there are striking resemblances to the Scythian
poems of chs. iv–vi. The second line of *v.* 14 is
verbally identical with the last of iv. 5; *v.* 16 is a close
parallel to iv. 15; and the prophet's anguish in *vv.* 18 ff.
recalls the agitation expressed in iv. 19 ff. These coin-
cidences seem at first sight to justify the opinion of
Erbt and others that the poem takes us back to the
early years of Jeremiah's work. But Cornill well points
out that this view overlooks a very important difference
of tone between this poem and the undoubted Scythian
oracles. 'There nervous unrest, vehement excitement;
here dull resignation, utter despair.' And it is easy to
conceive that the ideas and images of the earlier period
should have been revived under the pressure of a new
and still more formidable calamity. Certainly the hopeless dejection here depicted is a mood into which the
nation could hardly have been brought by the Scythians,
unless their devastations had been much more extensive
than we have any reason to suppose. A feeling of
stupefaction and despondency has taken possession of
the people, as if some deadly narcotic had been adminis-
tered to them, depriving them of energy and thought
(*v.* 14). The long anxious vigil of hope deferred has
been ended by a sudden and desolating stroke (*v.* 15),
and they resign themselves to a miserable death. Yet
it does not seem to be the final catastrophe which is
described. There is still the apprehension of danger
from the North (16); still a wistful looking to Zion;

still the cry of distress rises from all quarters of the
land (19). And to this corresponds, point for point, the
prophet's state of mind as revealed in the second half
of the poem. He is broken with the breach of his people,
which he knows to be irretrievable (*v.* 21); his sorrow
like their wound is incurable (18). Deliverance would
now come too late, for the season which might have
brought forth the fruits of righteousness has been
suffered to pass unimproved (*v.* 20). But with what
reluctance Jeremiah abandons the hope of recovery, and
realises that for him nothing remains but ceaseless
unavailing tears, we see from the last two pathetic
stanzas (*vv.* 22, 23).

It is no doubt hazardous to fix down a passage like
this to a definite background. There is but one situation
known to us which would enable us in some measure to
combine its varied allusions; and that is the time of
consternation and dismay which must have followed
the disastrous battle of Megiddo. It closed the period
of mingled optimism and anxiety which had been
initiated by the Deuteronomic covenant, and lasted till
the death of Josiah. It shattered the illusory hopes based
on the formal acceptance of the Covenant, and must
have plunged the nation into the depth of gloom which
is the ground-note of these verses. The only serious
obstacle to this theory is the reference to a northern
enemy in *v.* 16, which (since it cannot apply to the
Scythians) is most naturally understood of Jeremiah's
later foe from the North, the Chaldeans. We are told,
however, that after the battle Pharaoh Necho took up
his headquarters at Riblah on the Orontes (2 Kings
xxiii. 33); and it is just possible that for once the northern
foe is the Egyptian army encamped there, obsessing
the mind of the people with the dread of an invasion
from that quarter. It is not a very convincing suggestion,
though it seems the only one consistent with an inter-

pretation of the poem which on other grounds has
much to recommend it[1].

The passage we have just considered shows Jeremiah's sympathy with a people crushed in spirit by an
appalling catastrophe; we turn next to one which will
reveal his attitude in an emergency that brought him
into conflict with the prevalent religious tendencies of
the time.

IV

The fourteenth chapter of Jeremiah is a mixed collection of oracles purporting to have been uttered
'concerning the drought' (v. 1). Although the connexion of some parts of the chapter with such a visitation
is extremely problematical, it is quite certain that the
drought did not exist merely in the imagination of the
redactors; and we shall not go far astray if we date it
in the later years of Josiah's reign. The series opens
with a picturesque description of the calamity under
which land and city are suffering: vv. 2–6:

> 2 Judah laments, and her gates do languish;
>> They sit mourning on the ground;
>> While a cry goes up from Jerusalem.

1 The only support I have found for this conjecture is in Steuernagel's
Einleitung, p. 546: 'Worte wie viii. 21 ff., ix. 16 ff. dürfen das Ungluck
des Jahres 607 zur Voraussetzung haben.' Apart from the difficulty in
v. 16 the theory would in my opinion be greatly strengthened by
extending it to the whole of this passage. As for the inclusion of ix. 16 ff.,
I am now more sceptical, though there is something to be said for
assigning it to the same situation. There are two other poems which
might be considered in this connexion. Ch. xiv. 17, 18, has some
affinities with viii. 18–23 in the mention of a 'great breach' and an
'incurable wound' (מכה, שבר), and the prophet's continuous weeping
over the slain. But this seems rather a presentiment of future calamity
than a record of real experience (see on v. 18, p. 123). Again, in xiv.
19–22 the last couplet of v. 19 is almost word for word identical with
viii. 15; and in spite of its place in ch. xiv might, if we detach v. 22
as a later interpolation, refer to a great disaster in the field rather than to
the slow misery of a drought. To deny the genuineness of the whole
passage (Cornill, etc.) seems uncalled for.

3 The nobles have sent their menials for water,
   They came to the cisterns but water they found not;
 They returned with empty pitchers.

4 The tillers of the soil are dismayed,
   For no rain has fallen:
 The husbandmen are ashamed, and cover their heads.

5 Yea the hind in the field forsakes her young,
   For there is no grass;
6 And wild asses stand on the knolls,
   Gasping for breath, with glazing eyes;
   For there is no herbage.

In the following verses we have two prayers of the people called forth by this judgment (*vv.* 7–9, 19–22), with the divine answer in each case (xiv. 10, xv. 1–4). In substance the two prayers are nearly identical; and we will here confine our attention to the first (*vv.* 7–9) with the answer in *v.* 10.

7 If our offences witness against us, Yahwe,
   Act for Thine own name's sake!
 For many are our backslidings before Thee;
   Against Thee have we sinned.

8 Thou Hope of Israel, Yahwe!
   Its Saviour in time of need!
 Why be like a guest in the land—
   As a traveller spending a night?

9 Why be like a man asleep,
   As one unable to save?
 For Thou'rt in our midst, O Yahwe!
   By Thy name are we called.
   Forsake us not quite!

10 Thus saith Yahwe to this people:
 'Even thus do they love to waver;
   They restrain not their feet.'
 Yahwe has no pleasure in them;
   Now He'll remember their guilt.

This prayer is uttered in the name of the people; and the remarkable thing about it is that it contains nothing which rises above the popular religion of the time. We find in it a general confession of sin without specification of offences or promise of amendment, a profession of trust in Yahwe as the Saviour of Israel, a strongly anthropomorphic appeal to Him to show Himself neither too unconcerned nor too weak to deliver; and finally an expression of the nation's claim on Him as its patron Deity, involving as it does the honour of His name. Now Jeremiah was aware that a sense of ultimate dependence on Yahwe was latent in the religious consciousness of the nation, and apt to come to the surface when all other help failed (ii. 27). If that vague conviction of a claim on Yahwe's succour existed under the unreformed religion of the prophet's early ministry, it must have been greatly strengthened by the renewal of the national covenant under Josiah[1]; and the question arises how far such a prayer expresses Jeremiah's own feeling. It is difficult to believe that it is an intercession in which he identifies himself with the people in their acute distress; for it represents neither his conception of the divine character, nor his view of the relation between Israel and Yahwe. Is it then, as Duhm thinks, an ironical exposure of their crude idea of Yahwe as a placable, good-natured, but capricious deity; or even a mocking parody of public prayers actually offered in the Temple[2]? That is almost inconceivable. Jeremiah would not have thrown so much warmth and poetic imagination into the composition if he had meant it as a caricature of a type of devotion which he merely despised (Cornill). It is far easier to suppose that he simply wrote down the words as he had heard them

[1] The second prayer (*v.* 21) contains an express appeal to the covenant.

[2] So Erbt, p. 264.

sung by the Temple choir; and that the psalmists of the
pre-exilic Temple were capable of writing a hymn as
full of poetic feeling and imagination as this, we have
no right to deny. But whether we take that view or hold
that Jeremiah himself is the author, there is no doubt
that his final and deepest conviction is expressed in the
stern sentence of rejection in *v.* 10 *a*. This return to
Yahwe is but a phase of the chronic vacillation and
halting between two opinions which marked the religious
history of Israel: they love swaying hither and thither:
now they run after the Baals; then, in trouble, after
Yahwe; and their present mood of contrition is 'as the
morning cloud, and the dew that early passes away'
(cf. Hos. v. 15–vi. 4)[1].

V

We have seen (pp. 122 f.) that Jeremiah was isolated
from the social life around him because the shadow of
impending calamity lay heavy on his heart and made
him a misunderstood and lonely man. But another
thing that drove him into solitude was his sensitive
recoil from the wickedness—especially the deceit and
treachery—which seemed to pollute the air he breathed

---

[1] The rest of ch. xiv has no bearing on our present subject. *Vv.*
11, 12 are evidently inserted here under the impression that *vv.* 7–9
are Jeremiah's own intercession for the people; and if that impression
be mistaken they are misleading in their present position. Their substantial genuineness, however, is not to be questioned. The idea recurs
too frequently in the book (vii. 16, xi. 14) not to have some basis in
Jeremiah's experience; and that he actually interceded for the people is
asserted in passages of undoubted originality (xv. 11, xviii. 20, etc.).
Similarly we must recognise a genuine element in *vv.* 13–16, which
have nothing to do with the drought, but have found a place here
because they begin with a palliation of the guilt of the common people
which seems to have struck the editors as another form of intercession
on their behalf. The passage belongs to a series of oracles against false
prophecy which will be considered in a later chapter. The two remaining
sections (17, 18 and 19–22) have been dealt with in other connexions
(pp. 123, 128*n.*).

in the company of his fellow men. Under this sense of
social estrangement he wrote a poem whose haunting
melancholy was to find an echo in the kindred spirit of
William Cowper[1]. Although it might have been composed at any time of Jeremiah's later life, a certain
resemblance to the opening of ch. v tempts one to
assign it to the early days of his residence in Jerusalem
(see pp. 138 ff. below). It is found in ch. ix. 1–8 [2–9]:

> 1 O that I had in the desert
>   A wayfarer's lodge!
> For fain would I leave my people,
>   And go clean away.
> For adulterers are they all,
>   A concourse of traitors!
> 2 Falsehood and not good faith
>   Succeeds in the land;
> They hasten from evil to evil;
>   And 'Me they know not,'
>   Saith Yahwe.
>
> 3 Beware each man of his friend,
>   Let none trust a brother!
> For a brother will cheat like Jacob,
>   And every friend will slander.
> 4 Each one deceives his neighbour;
>   They speak not the truth;
> They have trained their tongue to lies;
>   They are weary in wrong-doing (?)
> 5 Crime follows on crime, deceit on deceit:
>   'They *will* not know Me,'
>   Saith Yahwe.

1 Oh for a lodge in some vast wilderness,
Some boundless contiguity of shade,
Where rumour of oppression and deceit,
Of unsuccessful or successful war,
Might never reach me more! My ear is pained,
My soul is sick, with every day's report
Of wrong and outrage with which earth is filled.

6 Behold I will smelt them and try them;
  For how can I look on my people[1]?
7 Their tongue is a deadly arrow,
  The words of their mouth deceit.
A man will speak peace to his neighbour,
  While at heart he lies in wait.

8 'Shall I not visit for these things?'
  Is Yahwe's word,
'Or on such a people as this
  My soul not take vengeance?'

VI

One more poem, of unknown date but quite possibly from the reign of Josiah, may be quoted here as an illustration of Jeremiah's perception of the analogy between the natural and spiritual worlds (ch. xviii. 13–17):

13 Inquire among the nations:
  Who hath heard such a thing?
A thing appalling hath she done—
  The Virgin of Israel.

14 Dissolves from Sirion's crest
  The spotless snow?
Or cease the mountain streams
  Their ice-cold flow?

15 But Me have My people forgotten;
  They serve the Unreal!
They have come to grief in their ways—
  The tracks of yore,
Walking in paths 'uneven'—
  A road unpaved;

---

[1] Duhm reads for אֶעֱשֶׂה, אֶשְׁעֶה strictly = 'look away from'; and inserts 'evil' with the LXX.

16 To make their land desolation—
   A scoff for all time.
   All who pass by are shocked,
   They shake their heads.

17 Like an east wind I will disperse them
   Before their foes;
   My back, not My face, I will show them
   In their day of distress.

The gem of these somewhat unequal lines is the image of *v.* 14, and it is peculiarly unfortunate that the point of the comparison is entirely obscured by the uncertainty of the text and interpretation[1]. Whether we have two distinct and independent images, or one image in two parts; whether they are merely a picturesque illustration of the unchanging in nature as a contrast to Israel's fickleness in religion, or have a deeper content and significance, it is impossible to say. One may venture on the suggestion that to Jeremiah the eternal snow of Lebanon (or Hermon), with the cold perennial streams which it sends down to the plains, combine to form an emblem of the unfailing

---

[1] In the first half of *v.* 14 I have adopted, for the sake of a smooth English rendering, an emendation of Cornill which has commended itself to many subsequent writers. He reads for שָׂדַי of the Hebrew שִׂרְיוֹן (the Phoenician name of Mount Hermon: Deut. iii. 9; cf. Ps. xxix. 6), and changes לבנון at the end to לבן 'white.' The two changes support each other, and it all looks plausible enough. But it is not clear that any emendation is really necessary. צוּר שָׂדַי might mean the 'native rock,' or even (from its Babylonian ancestry: see Burney, *Judges*, pp. 111 f.) the 'mountain rock'; or if these be considered improbable, צוּר שַׁדַי 'eternal rock' would be sufficient (so Rothstein).

The second half of the verse is untranslatable as it stands; and here I have followed Rothstein, who reads מֵימֵי הָרִים for the unintelligible מים זרים. The other conjectures are nothing but desperate *tours de force*.

source of national vitality which the true religion would
have been to Israel, had it not given itself over to the
unreal worship that had sapped its energies, and would
reduce its land to an arid waste.

To Jeremiah, as we shall learn in the next chapter,
sin, whether national or individual, was a strange
unnatural thing. It comes from the perversion of an
original instinct for God in the human soul, producing
a hardening of heart[1] caused by evil habit in the
individual and evil custom in the community. Expressions of pain and wonder often break from his lips at
the thought of the blindness and infatuation of Israel
in forsaking the true God to worship unreal beings
that cannot profit. This was one of his earliest reflexions
on the popular religion of Israel (ii. 4–13), and here it
meets us again towards the close.

The oracles discussed on the above pages have many
features in common. They were probably all composed
in the wake of the Deuteronomic reformation; and
though direct references to that event are few and
uncertain they reveal more or less clearly the prophet's
reflexions on the issues of the movement. They are
for the most part lyrical monologues,—outpourings of
personal emotion like the Scythian poems of ch. iv,
but pervaded by a profound sadness of which these
youthful effusions showed little trace. There is something more akin to it in the other group of early
poems in ch. ii, dealing with the corruptions of the
popular religion. But nowhere in the pre-Deuteronomic
utterances of Jeremiah do we find an approach to the
sombre and melancholy mood which breathes through
these later poems. They are like glimpses into a 'huge,
motionless, interior lake of sorrow[2]' in the breast of the

[1] שרירות לב.

[2] The phrase is used by Carlyle in describing the last years of
Frederick the Great—a very different person from Jeremiah, to be sure!

prophet, reflecting nothing from its leaden surface but his hopeless grief over the waywardness of his country-men, and the terrible retribution in store for them. If these passages had been delivered in public Jeremiah might have had to complain, with better reason than Ezekiel, that he was listened to 'as a troubadour with a pleasant voice, and skilled in playing an instrument' (Ezek. xxxiii. 32). But that is a trial to which he does not appear to have been exposed. There are some indications that his ministry at this time was mainly of a semi-private kind[1]; and it is probable that prior to their literary publication in 604 his poetic oracles were known only within the limited circle of his personal friends and sympathisers. However that may be, it is in these intimate impassioned utterances that we find the purest expression of Jeremiah's mature genius. They reveal a nature sensitive to the whole range of human feeling, unrelenting towards every form of falsehood in religion, but responsive to the appeal of distress, and capable of utter self-identification with the fate of the people he mourned. To say of Jeremiah that 'dans ses quarante années de prophétisme, il a prêché, il a agi, il a maudit, *il a peu pleuré*[2]' is a more one-sided exaggeration than the popular view to which he is *par excellence* the 'weeping prophet.' No doubt his versatile emotional temperament reacts variously to the prospect of ruin which he clearly foresaw; but we have seen enough to show that there were times when his overcharged sorrow could find no expression save in bitter and solitary weeping. The causes of that sorrow and isolation are revealed in the poems before us: the painful weaning of his affections from all that makes human life dear, his resolute refusal to be

[1] See pp. 209 f. below.

[2] Darmesteter, *Les Prophètes d'Israël*, p. 67—the italics of course are mine.

blinded to the realities of his position, and his uncompromising opposition to the men who were striving by superficial reform to save the State from the doom which he alone saw to be inevitable. In a future chapter we shall learn how in this valley of Baca[1] wells of spiritual refreshment were opened to him; how through tribulation and inward desolation he came to know that in his personal fellowship with God he possessed the secret of religion and the victory that overcomes the world.

[1] Ps. lxxxiv. 7 [6].

CHAPTER VIII

THE PROPHET AS MORAL ANALYST

THE fifth chapter of Jeremiah opens with a poem which introduces us to a new phase of the prophet's activity, and possibly to an important event in his life (ch. v. 1–5):

> 1 Roam through Jerusalem's streets,
>> And see for yourselves;
>> And seek in her market-places
>> If a man you can find—
>> If one there be practising right,
>> Or mindful of truth.
> 2 Nay, when they say 'As Yahwe lives,'
>> They swear to a lie.
>
> 3 Hast Thou eyes, then, O Yahwe, for fraud,
>> And not for good faith?
>> Thou hast smitten them sore, but they winced not;
>> They took not reproof;
>> They have hardened their faces like flint,
>> Refusing to turn.
>
> 4 I bethought me: 'These are the poor,
>> The ignorant folk,
>> Who know not the way of Yahwe,
>> The manner of their God.
>
> 5 'I will go to the men of high station;
>> With them I will talk;
>> For *they* know the way of Yahwe,
>> The manner of their God.'
>> But *they* have quite broken the yoke,
>> And burst the thongs.

It is an interesting conjecture of Duhm that in these verses we have a transcript of Jeremiah's first impressions of social conditions in Jerusalem just after he had taken up his abode there. Duhm draws a somewhat fanciful picture of the young prophet, fresh from his provincial home, moving about in the lanes and bazaars of the capital, keenly observant of the manners of the people, but bewildered and distressed by the meanness, the depravity, and the utter lack of religious principle which he found everywhere. How he was overreached in a bargain by an unscrupulous dealer, who had backed up his voluble falsehoods with an oath by the name of Yahwe: how this same dealer suffered divine chastisement in the shape of a fractured limb, but felt not the least compunction for his offence, nor recognised the hand of God in his misfortune (*v.* 3)! This description no doubt oversteps the limits of sober exposition; but the passage does at least suggest a very definite and impressive personal experience. It is certainly a significant feature that Jeremiah is represented as making his first acquaintance with the life of a great town through contact with the lower orders. It almost seems as if he had struck on a stratum of society with which he was previously unacquainted, and whose moral degradation surprised and revolted him—the uneducated populace, whose souls no man regarded. 'These are but common people—stupid; they know not the way of Yahwe, the *ethic*[1] of their God.' So he resolves

---

[1] The word מִשְׁפָּט ('judgment,' 'custom,' etc.) in *vv.* 4 and 5 (cf. viii. 7) is probably to be understood, with Duhm, of the manner of life which Yahwe requires of His worshippers. As each earthly court has its peculiar etiquette which must be learned and observed by those who move in the highest circles, so in antiquity every religion had its own code of morals, its own ceremonial, on the knowledge of which intercourse with the deity depended. Thus the foreign population settled in Samaria by the Assyrian kings 'knew not the *manner* of the

to try the more enlightened upper circles, the nobles, the priests, the leaders of thought and opinion, in whom the fruits of true religion must surely be found. But here a still more appalling discovery awaits him. If these men have taken away the key of knowledge from the classes beneath them, they have made no good use of it for themselves. Their immoralities are so flagrant that he sums them up in one sweeping sentence of condemnation: 'These men,' he says, 'have all broken the yoke outright, have burst the thongs,' i.e. have thrown off all moral and religious restraints. It is an experience of complete disillusionment, which Duhm compares with the effect of Luther's memorable visit to Rome in 1510.

Duhm holds that the genuine poems of Jeremiah stand in the book very nearly in chronological order: and accordingly he assigns this incident to a very early period in the prophet's career, before the time of Josiah's reformation. The question arises, however, whether it be possible to combine his interpretation with the view advanced in the last chapter: that Jeremiah's migration to Jerusalem was caused by the enmity which he had incurred through his zealous advocacy of the Deuteronomic covenant. Apart from the literary question of the arrangement of the prophecies (on which I will say something presently), the supposition presents no inherent difficulty. In 620 Jeremiah would still be a young man, probably not more than 25 years of age. Driven from his home for his adhesion to the cause of reform, he would naturally seek refuge in Jerusalem, where he could find protection from his persecutors, and live in the congenial atmosphere of the prophetic revival, which had so suddenly captured the court, the priesthood, and the influential classes in

god of the land,' and had to be instructed in it by a priest of Yahwe (2 Kings xvii. 26).

the metropolis. He is hardly settled there when his disillusionment begins. We can fancy him a friendless stranger, living in a mean street, acquiring a first-hand knowledge of city manners among the people at his door. The result we have already described. And when he betakes himself to the upper class, the men who sat in Moses' seat, and had put the new law in operation, he is shocked to find that their private lives are honeycombed with vice, and their zeal for public religion a hypocritical pretence. For the first time, perhaps, he fully realised the extent of his people's depravity, and the magnitude of the task which lay before him as a prophet of Yahwe.

If this be the true setting of the passage we have been considering, it would undoubtedly possess an importance for the understanding of Jeremiah's spiritual history which it would not have at an earlier period in his career. It would simplify our conception of the progress of his mind to suppose that his work as a moral censor dates from his settlement in Jerusalem, and began in disappointment with the fruits of the Deuteronomic reformation. We might believe that up to this time he had been occupied with the problems of national religion, as we find it treated in the second and third chapters of the book: that he thought of Israel as a moral unity, of its sin as national apostasy, and its eventual restoration as brought about by an act of repentance on the part of the people as a whole. It would even be conceivable that he accepted the Deuteronomic covenant as such an act of repentance, and at least a partial realisation of his hopes for the salvation of the 'remnant of Israel.' It was only when he began to test the results of the movement on men's lives and characters, and saw how unreal and superficial was the amendment which it had produced, and what new insidious forms of self-deception it engendered,

that his thoughts were turned towards the vital question
of the nature of religion as a relation between the
individual soul and God. The experience recorded in
the beginning of ch. v, and the new form of prophetic
activity which it introduced, would mark the transition
from the one point of view to the other; and if it took
place at this critical juncture of the prophet's life, it would
acquire an enhanced interest from the association.

The question whether this particular poem belongs
to the pre-Deuteronomic or the post-Deuteronomic
period of Jeremiah's life can never be absolutely settled,
and is not in itself of supreme importance. It is not
certain that it presupposes a protracted residence in
Jerusalem, nor can we be sure that Jeremiah's removal
thither was subsequent to the promulgation of Deuteronomy. A casual visit to the capital at any time would
account for such an experience as is here recorded, if
indeed it be necessary to refer it to any definite incident
at all. We must therefore recognise the possibility that
the passage dates from the first stage of his career,
and that the prophetic function which he here dis-
charges ran parallel with his criticism of the popular
religion in ch. ii, or his announcement of evil from
the north in ch. iv. What is of importance, however,
is that the poem does represent a distinct phase of
Jeremiah's activity, which we have not yet considered.
It introduces a mixed assortment of prophecies dealing
mainly with moral and social evils in Jerusalem, just as
ch. ii has dealt with the religious abuses of the time
as exhibited at the rural sanctuaries. In this fact we
seem to have a clue to the composition of chs. v
and vi; and a glance at the contents of these chapters
shows that chronological order is completely disre-
garded: that pre-Deuteronomic utterances alternate
with others which belong to the middle part of Jeremiah's work commencing with the reformation.

We find, for instance, a few sections which clearly belong to the cycle of Scythian poems represented by ch. iv, and were undoubtedly composed at the same time (v. 15–18, vi. 1–5, 22–26; cf. v. 6, 10, vi. 6). It is this fact more than anything else which gives plausibility to the common opinion that chs. ii–vi are a summary of Jeremiah's activity prior to the reformation. In reality these sections owe their position to a fixed practice of the redactors, to make the threat of judgment follow on the denunciation of sin: they have done so on a large scale in placing ch. iv after chs. ii and iii; and they have applied the method in detail to the arrangement of chs. v and vi. With the exception of the 'Scythian' poems there is perhaps no passage which can be positively assigned to the early years of Jeremiah; and there are a good many that suggest a later date. The Scythian terror seems to have passed, and men give themselves to their selfish and lawless pursuits with a feeling of security: 'Thou hast smitten them and they felt no pain, [hast consumed them but] they refuse to accept correction' (v. 3; cf. vi. 13). The people are being lulled by promises of prosperity into a false confidence (vi. 14). They have learned to deride the prophecies of doom which once caused them to tremble: 'The prophets are for the wind and the word is not in them' (v. 13). It is a time for reflexion and deliberate search for the old and good paths in which soul-rest is to be found (vi. 16 f.). We note further that the prophet's language has almost lost the accent of mournful expostulation which frequently appears in chs. ii and iii, and changed to one of stern indignation against flagrant social vices and moral delinquencies. All this confirms the impression that in these two chapters we have crossed the Deuteronomic watershed, and find ourselves in the religious atmosphere produced by the reform movement. For the redactors it can be said that they have shown a fine sense of fitness in opening this subdivision of the book with the striking poem of ch. v. 1–5, and closing it with the not less remarkable utterance of vi. 26–30.

In the present chapter, accordingly, we are to deal not with a *period* but (as I have said) with a *phase* of Jeremiah's activity: a phase which is more particularly illustrated in chs. v and vi, but which is characteristic of the whole of his later ministry, and comes to light in many other passages of the book. Our subject is Jeremiah's conception of sin; and this we may look at from two points of view: *first* as revealing his own character and individuality, and *secondly* as influencing his consciousness of his prophetic mission.

I

To our conventional habit of reading the Old Testament it may seem a matter of course that a prophet should denounce sin. It was certainly a prominent part of his message. Micah had laid it down as an essential mark of the true prophet that his voice is raised in unsparing protest against the prevailing iniquities of his time. 'But I am filled with might and rectitude and courage to declare to Jacob his transgression, and to Israel his sin' (Micah iii. 8); and all the prophets had acted on this view of their mission. But we are not to suppose that any true prophet took up the task from a mere sense of professional duty. No man can denounce sin with power and sincerity without revealing what manner of man he is; nor, further, without a reflex influence of his preaching on his own character and his relation to God. Of all the great prophets Jeremiah is least open to the suspicion of perfunctoriness in the discharge of this function. It is experience of life, actual contact with the vices which stain the hearts and lives

of the men around him, that excites his indignation
and calls forth his complaint. He is quite convinced
that the divine sentence of condemnation is reproduced
in his own ethical perception of right and wrong.
Yahwe appeals to his own observation and moral judgment on the evils around him: '*Seest thou not* what they
do in the cities of Judah and the streets of Jerusalem?'
(vii. 17). And it is not simply the verdict of his conscience that finds expression in his writings; it is even
more the torture of a sensitive human spirit in the
presence of moral evil. Just as in his earlier days the
religious degeneracy of his countrymen came home to
him in the tumultuous revelry and licentious orgies of
the rural sanctuaries, which grated on his innate sense
of reverence and purity, so in later years it is the
pollution of the whole social atmosphere, acting on a
mind of acute susceptibility, that reveals to him what
sin is, and what God must think of it.

Now, to Jeremiah, as to the prophets in general, sin
is primarily a national or at least a social fact. To say
this of course does not mean that a prophet had no
sense of personal demerit before God. When Isaiah
was overpowered by the sudden vision of the divine
holiness, his first exclamation was 'Woe to me! I am
undone; for I am a man of unclean lips'; and only in
the second place does he reflect on the state of his
nation: 'I dwell in the midst of a people of unclean
lips.' But it follows from the Old Testament idea of the
nation as the subject of religion, and from the conception of prophecy as the organ of Yahwe's intercourse
with the nation, that the evils with which the prophets
had to deal were those which can be described as
national, either in the sense that they were due to the
action of the State through its constituted authorities,
or that they were so prevalent in the community as to
give tone and character to the corporate life. Hence

the prophets' consciousness of personal sin lay in a sense outside the sphere of their official commission: in Isaiah's case it preceded it. We do not find in their writings confessions of individual guilt or prayers for individual forgiveness, such as are frequent in the Psalms; or if a partial exception has to be made in the case of Jeremiah, we shall see (in another chapter[1]) that it is the exception which proves the rule. In so far as feelings of this kind entered into their consciousness, it was in the way of sympathy with the people whom they were obliged to condemn; and that certainly is very prominent in the utterances of Jeremiah. But as prophets they were the mouth of Yahwe to Israel; and what they had to declare was His judgment, which was also the judgment of their own conscience, on the moral condition of the nation as a whole.

It would appear, however, that Jeremiah's criticism of the moral condition of his people was from the first more intimate and individual than that of his predecessors. The outstanding social abuses which called forth the denunciation of the earlier prophets—oppression of the poor, corrupt administration of justice, inhumanity, greed, and ostentatious luxury among the rich, and such like—were still rampant in his time, and did not escape their meed of censure at his hands. Dr Hugo Winckler, who sees in Jeremiah a 'theocratic ideologue,' finds his views on this subject 'lame and shallow' as compared with those of Isaiah. 'Nothing here,' he says, 'of the conviction so powerfully expressed by Isaiah that the well-being of the community is the first condition of a stable political order! In Jeremiah we meet for the first time that hypertrophy (*Ueberwucherung*) of the theocratic perversion of the world-order which later gained the ascendancy in Judaism, and in many periods of the Christian Church, according

[1] Chap. xi below.

to which humanity exists for the sake of the ecclesiastical organisation[1].' It would be difficult to put into words a more utter misrepresentation of Jeremiah's position than this statement, which is based on Winckler's erroneous estimate of the attitude of Jeremiah to the Deuteronomic movement. There is no obvious lack of vigour or conviction in the following oracle in ch. v. 26–29:

> [26] Yea, rogues are found in my people,
>   Who set snares to do for men.
> [27] As a cage is full of birds
>   So their houses of unjust gain.
>   Hence they are grown great and rich
> [28]   They are fat and stout.
>   They espouse not the cause of the orphan;
>   Nor defend the right of the widow.
> [29] 'Shall I not visit for these things?'
>   Saith Yahwe's voice;
>   'Or on such a nation as this
>   My soul not take vengeance?'

If such passages are rare in the writings of Jeremiah, the reason is not that given by Winckler, but precisely the reverse. It is not doctrinaire abstraction from the realities of public life, but a vivid interest in human character and motive, that is distinctive of Jeremiah's ethical teaching. His indignation at social wrong was shown not in word only but in deed, and at the risk of his life, on more occasions than one. His zeal for public justice is finely expressed in his eulogy of the kingly character of Josiah (xxii. 15, 16); his democratic sympathies come out in a scathing philippic against Jehoiakim in the same connexion (xxii. 13 f., 17); and also in his firm protest against the re-enslavement of the Hebrew bondmen who had been emancipated during the last siege of Jerusalem (xxxiv. 8 ff.).

[1] *Geschichte Israel's*, i, pp. 110 f.

What is characteristic of Jeremiah is that, following the bent of his own nature, he carries the searchlight of the prophetic conscience into the region of private morals. It is true he is not the only prophet who does this; but unless all the indications are misleading, no one else had the same sense of sin as introduced into the common life by the acts and dispositions of individuals, and working through the whole with disintegrating and debasing power. Two evils in particular are persistently denounced as evidence of the deep-seated corruption that infected society and rendered judgment inevitable: *untruthfulness*, with its hateful brood of treachery and slander; and *sexual profligacy*. The former is a theme of frequent and poignant complaint: Jeremiah marvels that Yahwe's truth-loving eyes can endure the sight of it (v. 3, quoted above). There is no finer trait in Jeremiah's personality than his feeling of the priceless worth of truth between man and man. This is on one side the reflexion of the inward sincerity which was the basis of his own religious life: being true to the God whom he could not see, he could not be false to the men whom he saw. On the other side it was the expression of a sensitive and affectionate nature, craving for human sympathy and friendship, and longing to dwell in harmony and goodwill with his neighbours. It was his bitterest experience to be cut off from this solace by the universal suspicion and disregard of good faith which sapped the foundations of social life, and made mutual confidence impossible[1].

Of the other outstanding social vice we have a lurid picture in a verse near the beginning of ch. v; where the men are charged with frequenting houses of ill fame, and compared to lustful stallions each neighing after his neighbour's wife (*vv.* 7 f.). It seems plain that this refers to the morals of the upper class in the

[1] See Chap. vii, pp. 131 f. above.

capital; indeed it is probable that these verses are the mutilated sequel to *v.* 5, continuing the indictment of the aristocrats, though the connexion is broken by the insertion of a fragment of a Scythian poem. It is remarkable that the accusation of adultery is a prominent item in Jeremiah's polemic against the professional prophets of his day[1].

We have already seen that it was Jerusalem that first opened the prophet's eyes to the depth of the people's depravity, and its ripeness for judgment. As the centre of the nation's life she had drawn to herself all that was worst in the narrow Judah of Josiah's reign; and Jeremiah sees nothing in her worthy to live. In a striking apostrophe he likens the city to one of those underground reservoirs on which the inhabitants depended for their water-supply, where the water was carefully preserved from evaporation, and kept fresh and ready for use (vi. 6, 7):

> 6 Ah, thou deceitful city!
> All extortion within!
> 7 As a cistern keeps cool its waters,
> So she her evils.
> Rapine and outrage are heard in her;
> Before Me are evermore sickness and wounds.

Now, it is obvious that this view of social immorality must lead to a more profound conviction of the power of evil than had previously been entertained. So long as national sin was seen in such acts of state as introducing a heathen cult, or forming alliance with a foreign power, it was possible to seek a remedy, as Elisha and the Rechabites did, in political revolution. And even when the evil was seen to lie deeper, in oppression and injustice and violation of personal rights, there was still room for hope that legislative measures might put things

---

[1] See below, pp. 191 f.

straight. But where it is perceived that sin is not national merely but social—a disease that spreads through every fibre of the body politic, and vitiates the relations of each individual to his fellows—it becomes difficult to think that health can be restored by any political surgery. It must be remembered that Jeremiah's conceptions were matured in the wake of the greatest effort at legal reformation that had ever been made in the history of Israel. Whether he expected much or nothing from the enforcement of the law of Deuteronomy, he was under no illusion as to the result. At one time it might have appeared to him that a return to the fountain-head of the national religion would work a saving change in every part of the people's life. But the experiment had been tried; and whoever was deceived as to its success, Jeremiah certainly was not. Of what avail was it to have suppressed by force the licensed prostitution of the local sanctuaries, when the very same vice was prevalent among the upper ten in Jerusalem? What law could reach it there? and what law could infuse into men's minds the spirit of respect for human personality, of piety and justice and truthfulness, the want of which made the society of his fellows intolerable to Jeremiah? It must have been under the influence of such feelings as these that he exclaimed, in words which now stand inappropriately as the introduction to the Scythian poems: 'Plough up your fallow ground! Sow not among thorns: Circumcise yourselves to Yahwe, and remove the foreskin of your hearts, men of Judah and citizens of Jerusalem, lest My wrath go forth like fire, and burn inextinguishably' (iv. 3, 4).

It would be rash to affirm either that Jeremiah was the first to discover the necessity of a radical change of heart in order to bring forth fruits meet for repentance, or that it was the failure of Josiah's reformation which taught him the lesson. It is a universal assumption of the prophets that national repentance to be of any avail must be sincere; that it must proceed from a genuine love of righteousness, and an inward sympathy with the mind of God both in His judgment on sin and in His demand for ethical holiness. At the same time there can be no doubt that Jeremiah's perception of the truth had reactions in his experience which gave it a new significance. This is due partly to the moral sensitiveness of his nature, but partly also to the conditions of the age in which he lived. Although, therefore, the sentences I have quoted might have been uttered at any time of his life, or indeed by any true prophet at any period of the history, there was no time at which they could have carried the same weight of meaning as in the age which witnessed the enforcement of the Deuteronomic Covenant. And there is a profound significance in the metaphors by which the prophet expresses his judgment on the situation. The 'fallow ground' is the national character, formed by generations of evil living and neglect of moral and religious ideals: the 'thorns' are the spontaneous product of unregenerate human nature—untruthfulness, avarice, inhumanity, profligacy, and licentious worship;—and it was vain to think that righteousness and true religion could flourish alongside of these. The Deuteronomists had tried to cut down the thorns, or the worst of them; but the movement had wrought no such stirring of the nation's conscience as would have made a true response to the will of Yahwe possible. Unless by some divine husbandry the roots could be extirpated and a new heart formed (Ezek. xviii. 31) there could be no real conversion to God, and no amendment acceptable in His sight. It is more difficult to ascertain the precise idea which underlies the figure of uncircumcision of the heart; but the general conception is the same. Circumcision to the Israelite was a rite of initiation into

the worship of Yahwe—an act of dedication signifying
the removal of the impurity inherent in the state of
nature[1], through which the individual becomes a member
of the religious community. Jeremiah's teaching is that
the reality thus symbolised is a change of heart: 'Put
away the impurity, the propensity to evil, which clings
to your natural disposition; only thus, and not by any
fleshly ceremony can you be worshippers of Yahwe in
spirit and in truth.' We see how he is led to trace sin to
its seat in the perverted individual will. All those transgressions which in their sum constitute national guilt are
acts of individuals, revealing the heart of the individual.
And the heart of man—though it was in his own heart
that Jeremiah made this discovery—'is more inscrutable
than anything, and incurably diseased' (xvii. 9). Sin, in
a recurrent phrase of his, is 'induration of heart[2]'—
the deadness to religious influences of minds enveloped
in an atmosphere of ungodliness which cuts them off
from Him who is the one source of spiritual life.

With all this, it is doubtful if Jeremiah's view of sin
is strictly individualistic. It marks a long advance in
that direction; but it is not so clear that the goal is
reached. In the end he may have looked forward to a
time when 'every one that eats the sour grapes shall
have his own teeth set on edge' (xxxi. 30); but that is
under a new dispensation of religion, when the truth
of man's relation to God will be more adequately
revealed than under the forms of the Mosaic Covenant.
In his judgment on the present he does not seem to
isolate the individual from his social environment. He

---

[1] Cf. Lev. xix. 23, the 'uncircumcision' of a fruit tree during the
first three years of its growth.

[2] שרירות לב. Cf. iii. 17, vii. 24, ix. 13, etc. Apart from Deut.
xxix. 18 [E.V. 19], Ps. lxxxi. 13 [E.V. 12], the word is confined to
the book of Jeremiah (eight times), but many of the passages are not
genuine.

still views Israel as an organism; but an organism every member of which is contaminated by the sin which pervades the national life. It was the great perplexity of his work to know that sin is rooted in the individual soul, and yet as a prophet to have no message except to the nation. The effect appears to have been to strengthen the conviction that national regeneration was impossible, and that nothing could save the existing political organisation from final dissolution. The most characteristic expression of his later judgment is the isolated sentence in which he asserts the fatal force of custom over the human will: 'Can the Ethiopian change his skin, or the panther his stripes? Then may you do good who have become habituated to do evil' (xiii. 23). Jeremiah stops short of a doctrine of human depravity, which holds that evil is man's first nature. But in that slavery of habit which we call second nature, and in the *nexus* of habits which form a realm of sin around the individual life he recognised a tremendous power of evil which neither the will of the sinful individual nor the corporate action of the State was able to break.

II

Now here we may pass to the second point of view from which we were to consider Jeremiah's view of sin: viz. its reflex influence on his prophetic consciousness.

Among the symptoms of 'obduracy of heart' which he observed he makes frequent mention of sceptical and scornful reception of the word of God. 'They have denied Yahwe, and said "Not He!" And the prophets are a mere wind; and the Word is not in them' (v. 12 f.). 'To whom should I speak and testify, in hope that they might hear? Lo, their ear is uncircumcised, and they cannot give heed; the word of Yahwe is to them a scoff; they have no respect for it' (vi. 10). 'And I set over you watchers (who said), "Hearken to the trumpet's sound"; but they said "We will not listen"' (vi. 17). These are but a few expressions from chs. v and vi of a prevailing temper of mind which Jeremiah recognised as the greatest obstacle to his teaching, and the most alarming symptom of the people's spiritual condition. It was an exhibition of that 'sin of insensibility or indifference to the voice of God in times of moral crisis' which Dr Denney has spoken of as one of those which tend to make forgiveness doubtful and even desperate.

There is abundant evidence of the effect produced by this callous and unbelieving attitude of his hearers on the mind of Jeremiah. At times it appears to drive him back on the primitive idea of the self-fulfilling power of the divine word, the belief that the prophet not only foretells the future, but in a sense actually creates it, by the power of his inspired announcement. In his opening vision he had seemed to rise above this crude notion of prophecy (see Chap. II); but undoubtedly he comes very near it in one or two of his utterances. He derives support from the conviction that the word which he speaks is charged with a destructive energy which will destroy his opponents; nay, that he is filled with the very wrath of Yahwe finding vent in human speech. 'Thus saith Yahwe of Hosts, Because they have spoken this (unbelieving) word, behold I make My word in thy mouth a fire, and this people wood; and it shall consume them' (v. 14; cf. xxiii. 29). And again, 'But with the wrath of Yahwe I am filled; I am weary with holding in; I must pour it out on the child in the street, and on the gathering of the young men' (vi. 11; cf. xv. 17, xx. 9). It is difficult to say whether there is here an intrusion of human feeling into the discharge of his commission which Jeremiah afterwards saw to be unworthy of his calling, and a disturbance of his fellowship with God (xv. 19; see Chap. xi below).

But in Jeremiah's reflexions on the apparent fruit-lessness of his mission another idea emerges which is startling in its seemingly fatalistic implications. The primary aim of his preaching, as of all prophetic exhortation, we must hold to have been the conversion of the people he addressed. Now we have seen that Jeremiah recognised more and more clearly as life went on that his work in that aspect was doomed to failure; and it might have appeared as if this involved the defeat of God's purpose in calling him to His service. That is a conclusion in which no true prophet could possibly acquiesce. The sense of vocation was too deeply rooted in the experience of the prophet to be shaken by out-ward failure or success; it sprang from the inward illumination and constraint of the word of God which cannot return to Him void, but shall accomplish that which He pleases. He knows himself to be the instru-ment of a will which is omnipotent, and a purpose which will reach its ends even through the failure and frustra-tion of the direct object of his work. The prophetic commission is thus like a two-sided shield; one side represents the moral element which is contingent on the attitude of the people, and the other the absolute element which belongs to it as a declaration of the immutable counsel of God. And when the motto on what we may call the positive side becomes invisible through human disobedience and indifference, the prophet turns to the reverse side and discerns a divine purpose in his very failure to move the people to repentance.

Although we cannot trace the growth of this con-viction in the mind of Jeremiah, it finds expression in several utterances of unknown date, but of undoubted genuineness. He speaks of himself as commissioned by

Yahwe to demonstrate the incapacity of the nation to produce works meet for repentance. In ch. vi. 9 he compares his work with that of the grape-gleaner passing his hand for a final trial over the barren branches and finding no fruit; and the following verse shows that the test lies in the resultlessness of his own preaching: 'Before whom should I speak and testify that they might hear? Behold, uncircumcised is their ear, and they cannot give heed; behold the word of Yahwe has become a scoff to them, they have no delight in it' (vi. 10). Similarly in ch. viii. 13 we read: 'Would I gather their harvest, there are no grapes on the vine, and no figs on the fig-tree, and the leaves are withered.' But the most striking and suggestive expression of the idea is under a very different figure. It occurs at the close of the first great division of the book, and is obviously a retrospect of some period of Jeremiah's ministry (ch. vi. 27–30):

27 An assayer I have set thee among My people
    To know and test their ways;
28 They are wholly intractable stuff,
    Traders in slander—
    Brass and iron all—
    Corrupt in life.

29 The bellows snorts from the fire:
    The lead is consumed!
    In vain does one smelt and smelt;
    Their vileness will not out.
30 'Rejected Silver' men call them,
    For Yahwe rejects them.

The text of these verses is so confused, the metre so uncertain, and the presence of glosses so suspected, that it is impossible to make out the exact sense of the image employed. We have the general idea of the assayer labouring to extract precious metal (whether

gold or silver does not clearly appear) from a mass of
refractory ore, and defeated in his aim. Whether the
particular point be that the whole is oxidised into dross,
or that the mass refuses to melt so that its worthless
elements might be expelled, we have perhaps too little
knowledge of metallurgical processes among the Hebrews to decide. In the application, therefore, only the
main thoughts can be recognised; and they are such
as these: that the 'remnant of Israel' (vi. 9), the Judah
of Jeremiah's time, is a crude compound of better and
worse materials, whose value was to be determined by
the amount of sound morals and true religion which it
might contain; that it was the aim of Jeremiah's
ministry to discover this value; that it had been an
arduous and protracted process; and that the final
result proved the nation to be utterly reprobate and
rightly rejected by Yahwe.

Dr W. Erbt, in his original and suggestive work on
Jeremiah and His Time, was perhaps the first to emphasise the biographical significance of this passage.
He finds in it the evidence of a change of method which
was adopted by the prophet and determined the form
of his ministry during the middle period of his history.
Jeremiah had started life as a 'prophet to the nations'
(i. 5), announcing Yahwe's imminent intervention in a
universal catastrophe, heralded by the Scythian irrup-
tion. This phase of his ministry was brought to a close
by the promulgation of the Deuteronomic law, of
which he was at first a zealous partisan. But his observation of the effect of that transaction on the moral
condition of the people gradually convinced him that
the reform movement was being manipulated in the
interest of sacerdotalism in a way that deprived it of all
religious value. He accordingly laid aside the *rôle* of a
preacher of national doom, and set himself to the
diplomatic task of breaking up the alliance between the

two parties which had amalgamated in support of
Deuteronomy,—the hierarchical nationalistic party,
which regarded the merely formal institution of the
Covenant as a sufficient guarantee of Yahwe's favour,
and the prophetic party which was concerned for the
fulfilment of its ethical requirements in the life of the
community. He thus became 'Yahwe's gold-assayer,'
striving to win individuals to the cause of truth and
righteousness for which he stood. This task was accomplished in the early part of the reign of Jehoiakim, when
the hierarchical section of the priesthood was installed
in control of the Temple worship, and the prophetically
minded party was driven into opposition, with Jeremiah
as its natural leader. Just then it became apparent once
more that the fate of Judah hung on a great world-
movement among the nations; and Jeremiah resumed
the form of his early ministry, appearing on the stage
of politics with a message of judgment more inexorable
by reason of the conclusions he had reached regarding
the hopeless impenitence and irreligion of all classes of
his countrymen[1].

Now, with regard to this ingenious construction of
Jeremiah's history, it is enough for our immediate
purpose to remark that it not only goes beyond any
evidence that can be adduced in its support, but as an
explanation of the passage before us it fails at the
crucial point. What is here described is an abortive
attempt to discover any good element in the mass of
Judean society, whereas on the theory Jeremiah achieved
a considerable success. That Jeremiah gathered round

[1] This statement of Erbt's theory, which I hope is correct, is condensed from observations scattered through the pages of his book,
Jeremia und seine Zeit; see pp. 92, 136, 141, 145, 148, 184, 190 f.
The point which is not quite clear is whether he regards Jeremiah's
efforts after a political separation of the two parties as successful or the
reverse.

him adherents and disciples in the course of his work is likely enough; but that it was his special aim to seek them out there is no proof whatsoever. And it is very improbable that he ever set himself the political task of creating an opposition party within the ranks of the priesthood. Nor is there the least suggestion of a change of method at any particular period of the prophet's life. The testing principle is just the word of the Lord, declared by him from beginning to end of his career,— that word which is 'as fire, and as a hammer that shatters the rock' (xxiii. 29)[1].

But while there is nothing to suggest a change of *method*, there is clearly indicated a changed *attitude* of the prophet to his work, and a new conception of the divine purpose which is fulfilled by his mission. Contemplating the effect of his preaching on his generation, he could not fail to see that those who rejected it were hardened in unbelief, so that their last state was worse than their first. The question thrust itself upon him:

---

[1] In this connexion it is instructive to compare the different ways in which the idea of the smelting pot is used by Isaiah and Ezekiel. To Isaiah it is an emblem of a purifying judgment, the result of which would be the removal of injustice and the restoration of the ancient civic virtues in the State: 'I will bring down My hand upon thee, smelting out thy dross in the furnace, and taking away all thine alloy. And I will restore thy judges as at the first, and thy counsellors as at the beginning: thereafter thou shalt be called the city of righteousness, the faithful citadel' (Isa. i. 25 f.). By Ezekiel the image is used of the actual destruction of the Hebrew State by the Chaldean armies: the crucible is the city of Jerusalem, in which all the refuse of Israel's national life is to undergo its final trial by fire; and the object of the smelting is the demonstration of the utter worthlessness of the people for the ends of God's kingdom (Ezek. xxii. 17–22). Jeremiah has the same view as Ezekiel of the result of the operation; but he differs both from Isaiah and Ezekiel in treating the fire as a symbol, not of the providential action of Yahwe in His crowning judicial intervention, but of the prophetic word, whose rejection by the people showed them to be a mass of perdition, and sealed their fate.

Why this compulsion to speak in the name of Yahwe, when it not merely brought scorn and persecution on himself, but failed to exercise any saving influence on those who heard? And the answer that comes to him is the conviction that he is Yahwe's instrument to test the spiritual condition of his nation, to expose the shallowness and unreality of its pretensions to religion, and to unfold the moral principles which make its destruction inevitable.

It would clear up some problems if we knew at what stage of his life this revelation came to Jeremiah. On the assumption that the prophecies are in the main chronologically arranged the passage has naturally been taken as a summary of his pre-Deuteronomic ministry, the period of the Scythian oracles and the polemic against the popular religion. The thought, however, seems to imply a longer experience of conflict with unbelief; and to date it so early certainly excludes the possibility that Jeremiah ever cherished good hope of Josiah's reformation. Erbt is probably right in assigning the oracle to a later time, and in regarding it as a retrospective reflexion on his whole activity during the reign of Josiah. Its significance is hardly overestimated if we think of it as marking the point when his absolute prediction of the doom of Judah was finally ratified by the verdict of his own conscience on the sin of his people, and his mind was brought to acquiesce in the divine sentence of rejection.

I have dwelt on this point at what may seem undue length, because it bears on an idea which is deeply grounded in the prophetic theology, if not in the nature of religion itself. Jeremiah was not the first prophet who saw that the revelation of spiritual truth is a double-edged weapon,—that its indirect effect may be, and in certain conditions will be, the opposite of its primary intention: that instead of producing insight

and conviction it may, or must, result in a deadening of
the moral and religious sensibilities. It is a conviction
which flashed on the lofty mind of Isaiah at the moment
of his call. 'Go and say to this people, "Hear continually
without perceiving; and see continually without understanding." Make the heart of this people fat and its
ears dull, and smear its eyes; *lest* it should see with its
eyes and hear with its ears and understand with its
heart, and repent and be healed' (Isa. vi. 9 f.). In the
case of Jeremiah it is more natural to suppose that the
truth was slowly apprehended as the lesson of experience; but to him also it became clear that the word of
God is a savour of death unto death even more than of
life unto life. There is something perplexing to us in
this attitude of the prophets towards the effect of their
message. It is partly to be explained, no doubt, by the
tendency of the religious mind of the Old Testament
to refer all things directly to the will of God. It may be
that with their profound faith in divine sovereignty the
prophets could not distinguish in the result between
what was the essential purpose of God and what was
due to the reaction of human freedom against that
purpose. That which was the inevitable effect of their
preaching was identified with the intention of Yahwe
in sending them to preach; and there were times when
this judicial aspect of their mission filled the whole
horizon of their thought. If we criticise their position
from the standpoint of the Christian idea of God, we
are only thrown back on a mysterious law of the spiritual
world which is frequently appealed to in the New Testament. In the light of a fuller revelation of the character
of God it is, indeed, impossible to think of His purpose
except as a purpose of grace and mercy which, while
respecting the independence of created personalities,
and working patiently to evoke the free response of
their will, genuinely seeks the salvation of all through

the revelation of the truth. Yet on the other hand the
moral universe is so constituted by its Maker that the
sinful abuse of freedom brings its own punishment in
hardening of the conscience, and a growing incapacity
for fellowship with God. Thus it is true that God sent
not His Son into the world to condemn the world, and
yet by his coming the world is condemned. 'And this
is the judgment, that light is come into the world, and
men loved darkness rather than light, because their
works were evil' (John iii. 19). This is the permanent
religious fact which underlies the stern predestinarian
doctrine of the prophets, and is the basis of their
assurance that the purpose of Yahwe will finally prevail
in spite of the sin and unbelief of men.

Is this, however, Jeremiah's final word on Yahwe's
purpose with Israel? The question is relevant, because
it happens that the classical illustration of the divine
sovereignty—the image of the potter and the clay[1]—
seems to have originated with Jeremiah; and we
naturally inquire what truth it conveyed to his mind.
He tells us at the beginning of ch. xviii how it first
came to him. He found himself one day in a potter's
workshop in the lower quarter of Jerusalem, intently
watching the process by which he deftly fashioned on
the wheel out of one clay different vessels just as he
chose. He saw that the potter was not always immediately successful. Something would go wrong, and then
he would squeeze the clay into a shapeless lump and
start afresh, till he attained the result he sought. The
prophet's thoughts were at this time occupied with the
problem of his people's fate; and a sudden inspiration
revealed to him the analogy between the work of the
potter and Yahwe's dealings with Israel. He realised
that it was no chance impulse that had moved him to

[1] See Isa. xxix. 16, xlv. 9, lxiv. 8; Wisd. Sol. xv. 7; Sirach xxxiii. 14;
Rom. ix. 21.

go down to the potter's house that day; he had been
led thither by the hand of God that he might receive
the message enunciated in *v.* 6: 'Can I not like this
potter do with you, house of Israel? Behold, like potter's
clay are ye in My hand.'

There is no reason to question the reality of the
incident, or the authenticity of the oracle so far as I
have quoted it. The following verses (7–10) interpret
the analogy in a sense so remote from its plain implications that they must be set down as the well-meant
homily of an over-zealous commentator. Jeremiah's own
interpretation as given in *v.* 6 stops short with an
assertion of the barren doctrine that Yahwe can do
with His people whatsoever He chooses. But is that
the whole of the lesson he learned in the potter's house?
We cannot say that that is impossible; and yet the
image suggests so much more to us that we can scarcely
think the prophet himself did not find in it a more
consoling idea than he has put into words. For surely
the interest of his observation lies in the potter's treatment of the *spoiled* vessel. He is not content with
crushing it; he does not throw it away, but begins anew
and fashions out of it another vessel 'as seemed good
in his eyes.' All that is meaningless if Yahwe's power
over Israel is to be manifested only by its destruction.
'As seemed good in His eyes!' The phrase in itself
may not carry us very far. It may mean nothing more
than 'according to His arbitrary pleasure[1].' But even
so, if it was Yahwe's pleasure to make of the same clay
'another vessel,' must He not have in His heart some
grand design which had been thwarted once but could
not be defeated finally? So the lesson of the potter's
wheel spells itself out to us; and while we cannot be
certain that Jeremiah read all this into it, we have no
reason to say he did not. We may believe that the truth

[1] Deut. xii. 8; Jud. xvii. 6; Prov. xii. 15, xxi. 2, etc.

which dawned on him is that Israel is in the hands of an omnipotent and gracious God, whose inflexible justice compels Him to crush to the dust the pride of the old Israel—the 'worthless vessel' (Hos. viii. 8)— but who will out of its ruin create a new people of God, formed for Himself to set forth His praise[1].

Whether consciously or unconsciously, Jeremiah has thus found the fitting emblem for the highest conception man can form of the divine sovereignty in relation to human freedom. God wills the perfection of His creatures; and though there is that in human nature which resists and retards the accomplishment of His purpose, and may seem to frustrate a long course of patient discipline, the Almighty worker does not forsake the work of His hands, but labours persistently, unceasingly, and in the end effectually, for the reconciliation of all things to Himself. To Jeremiah as to the Apostle, the last word on the mystery of predestination is a doxology: 'O the depth of the riches both of the wisdom and the knowledge of God! How unsearchable are His judgments, and His ways past finding out!... For of Him, and through Him, and unto Him, are all things. To Him be the glory for ever. Amen' (Rom. xi. 33, 36).

[1] Comp. Buttenwieser, *op. cit.* p. 210.

CHAPTER IX

UNREAL WORSHIP—TEMPLE AND SACRIFICE

WE have seen in a previous chapter[1] that the Deuteronomic reformation culminated in the centralisation of the national worship in the Temple at Jerusalem. That, indeed, so far as appears, was the one tangible and enduring result of the spiritual movement which finds expression in the book of Deuteronomy. The ethical demands of the Covenant failed to touch the conscience of the nation, and in spite of the good example of the king (Jer. xxii. 15 f.) there is no evidence of any sustained or successful effort to purify public life from the abuses which had called forth the denunciations of the prophets. As has often happened in the history of religion, that which was begun in the spirit was perfected in the flesh. The high ideal cherished by the best minds of the prophetic party, of a holy and righteous community living in moral fellowship with Yahwe and assured of His protection, degenerated into an empty formalism which substituted a superstitious reverence for the Temple for love to God and obedience to His will. The Temple became, even more than the Law-book, the talisman of the spurious piety that sprang up in the latter half of Josiah's reign; and although this was not wholly due to the influence of Deuteronomy, there can be no doubt that the enforcement of the law of the One Sanctuary was a powerful incentive to the popular delusion of its inherent sanctity.

It is an instructive fact in the history of prophecy that this Temple-superstition was in part a heritage

[1] pp. 94 f.

from the ministry of Isaiah. Isaiah's doctrine of the
inviolability of Yahwe's earthly sanctuary on mount
Zion is a somewhat elusive part of his theology. It
seems to rest on a mystic interpretation of the local
presence of Yahwe in His Temple as a symbol of the
unseen divine order about to be revealed through His
intervention in the history of the world. As the 'waters
of Shiloah that go softly' (viii. 6) are a type of God's
continuous but secret working in the present, so the
foundation laid in Zion (xxviii. 16) is a pledge to faith
of the indestructibility of the true Israel in the impending crisis of judgment. These are fundamental convictions with Isaiah, and in so far as mount Zion is the
material image of such ideas we can understand the
place which it occupies in the prophet's thought. But
it is clear that the representation is not merely ideal or
figurative. In the later prophecies of Isaiah it assumes
a concrete form, becoming the ground of his assurance
that the sacred mount will prove impregnable to the
assault of the Assyrian world-power. The signal verification of this presentiment in the destruction of
Sennacherib's army made a profound impression on the
popular imagination; but it was an impression which
allowed the spiritual presuppositions of Isaiah's faith
to evaporate. To him the deliverance of Jerusalem had
meant 'something far greater than the raising of a siege
and the annihilation of an army. He had expected that
the arm of the Lord would be recognised in this
deliverance, and that the chastened spirit which had
been evoked by those days of anxiety and fear would
ripen into a genuine national conversion. He had
looked, in short, for the emergence at last of the
Remnant of penitent and believing Israelites who after
the great catastrophe would form the nucleus of the
future kingdom of God[1].' These hopes were frustrated

[1] *Cambridge Bible*; Isaiah (1915), i, p. xliv.

by the impenitence and blindness of the people, the
only practical fruit of the crisis being an abortive
attempt to root out the heathenism of the provincial
sanctuaries on the lines afterwards followed by the
Deuteronomic reformers. On the nation as a whole the
vindication of Isaiah's faith had no other effect than to
foster a belief in the inviolability of the Temple, which
ultimately hardened into a dogma of the popular religion.
How far the reforming prophetic party was ready to
compromise with this tendency we are in no position
to judge. Since they looked back to Isaiah as their
founder it is natural to suppose that their view of the
Temple as Yahwe's dwelling-place was based on his
teaching, although it is more than probable that the
notion of empirical inviolability tended to dissociate
itself in their view from the spiritual intuitions which
gave religious worth to the conception. At the same time
it must be insisted, in opposition to a common critical
opinion, that the book of Deuteronomy itself lays no
stress whatever on the peculiar claim of Jerusalem to
be the one place of worship, and is entirely free from
any suggestion of a magical connexion between Yahwe
and the Temple. The materialistic idea of the sacredness
of the Temple was but a crude popular perversion of
the essential principle of the Deuteronomic legislation.

That Jeremiah had watched the growth of this
superstition with a clear perception of its deadening
effect on the religious life of the people, appears first
of all from a poetic fragment, of unknown date, preserved in ch. xi. 15 f. The superior text of the LXX
enables us to recover the general idea, although the
rendering given is very uncertain in details. Yahwe is
the speaker:

15 What has My darling to do in My house?
　　Vile are her doings!

Can scraps of fat and sacred flesh
　　Turn calamity from thee?
　　Then might'st thou rejoice!

16 An olive-tree, green, resplendent in beauty!—
　　So wert thou called.
　　With noise of furious stormwind (?)
　　Its foliage is blasted,
　　Its branches destroyed[1]!

Here we have an utterance of Jeremiah's private
reflexions on the new attitude of the people to the
Temple and its worship. As he stands in the crowded
court beholding the multitude at its devotions, his
spirit is stirred, and the question rises to his lips, What
do they mean by it?—What can God think of it? Are
these men so oblivious of the character of the Being
whom they ignorantly worship as to imagine that the
performance of sacrificial rites in a sacred place will
answer His demands, or avert His wrath? In a striking
image, derived perhaps (as Duhm suggests) from some
allusion in a Temple-hymn, the prophet sees Israel,
once like an evergreen olive-tree in the house of its
God (Psa. lii. 10 [8]), blasted and withered by a sudden
and irremediable stroke of divine judgment. Now these,
as Cornill has already pointed out, are precisely the
thoughts which were to find public expression in the
famous Temple-oration of the time of Jehoiakim, to
which we now turn.

It may well be that the pressure of a grave national
crisis was needed to reveal even to Jeremiah the full
extent of the hold which this obsession had obtained
on the minds of his contemporaries. Such a crisis was
brought about by the disastrous battle of Megiddo, in
which Josiah was slain; and that event must have been

---

[1] I make no attempt to justify the conjectural translation of 16 b.
The passage is hopelessly corrupt in all versions.

still fresh in public memory when the prophet felt himself called by God to warn the people of their delusion. He found his opportunity at a great convocation in the Temple court in the beginning of the reign of Jehoiakim (xxvi. 1 ff.). If we could accept an attractive conjecture of Wellhausen, we might find a suitable occasion for this concourse in the tidings of Josiah's defeat and death, which caused a spontaneous rush of the populace to the Temple, as the sole surviving stay of their faith in Yahwe. This reading of the situation derives some support from the fact that in the very circumstantial narrative of ch. xxvi a king is never mentioned. But the exclamation 'We are delivered[1]' in vii. 10 seems to show that the dominant mood was one of relief rather than of panic and dismay. It would seem, therefore, that a somewhat later occasion is indicated—Duhm suggests the coronation of Jehoiakim —when a more cheerful spirit prevailed, and the belief in the inviolability of the sanctuary drew fresh encouragement from the fact that the State had been preserved, and a native monarch still sat on the throne of David. Be that as it may, the defeat of Josiah had dealt a shattering blow to the illusory hopes that had grown up under the shadow of the Covenant. Men had 'looked for peace, but good came not: for a time of healing, and lo! sudden terror!' (viii. 15, xiv. 19). And it is significant that just at this time the Temple superstition emerges in unabated strength and vitality. It goes far to prove that reliance on the Covenant as a formal compact between Yahwe and the nation, and a spurious reverence for the Temple, were distinct and separable factors in the religion of the time, so that when the former collapsed under a stroke of adverse fortune the latter

---

[1] נִצַּלְנוּ: for which, however, Cornill would read נַצְּלֵנוּ: 'Deliver us.'

survived as a fanatical conviction in the popular mind. Incidentally, it warns us against the error of so confusing the two things that a protest against the cruder superstition is mistaken for an indirect polemic against Deuteronomy itself. Deuteronomy had doubtless done much to enhance the prestige of the central sanctuary, but it had been far from the intention of its authors to make the Temple a fetish; and there is nothing in Jeremiah's attitude at this juncture which can fairly be construed as antagonism to the religious aims which had animated the party of reform.

Let us look, then, at the words spoken by Jeremiah on this occasion. They are recorded in two forms, substantially identical, but with significant variations. There is a condensed report from a biographer in xxvi. 4–6, and a fuller account, presumably based on Jeremiah's own memoirs, in vii. 3–15[1]. The latter, however, consists of two dissimilar parts. The first half (*vv.* 3–7) is a *conditional* promise of continued possession of the *land*, if the people will amend their sinful lives; it is largely made up of stereotyped editorial formulae; and, apart from the words of the people quoted in *v.* 4, has nothing to do with the Temple. The second half (*vv.* 8–15) is an *absolute* prediction of the devastation of the *sanctuary* and the rejection of the nation, slightly amplified by a later hand, but distinguished by a force and originality of expression which vouch for its substantial authenticity. These represent irreconcileable points of view; and we must assume either that two different addresses of Jeremiah, delivered on different occasions, have been amalgamated, or (what is much more probable) that *vv.* 3–7 are a supplementary composition by a Deuteronomic commentator, such as we frequently find in the book. Fortunately, a very

[1] It is no longer questioned by critics that vii. 1–15 and xxvi refer to the same incident.

slight change suffices to make *vv.* 8–15 an independent
whole: we have only to supply in *v.* 8 the 'lying words'
cited in *v.* 4 from the mouth of the people. With this
insertion, and the omission of redundant relative
clauses, the actual speech delivered by Jeremiah will
read somewhat as follows:

Thus saith Yahwe:

Trust not in these misleading words, 'The palace of
Yahwe, the palace of Yahwe, the palace of Yahwe, is all this!'
What? Steal and murder! and commit adultery! and swear
falsely! and sacrifice to Baal! and then come and stand before
Me in this house and say 'We are delivered':—in order to
perpetrate all these abominations! Is it a robbers' den that you
take My house for? Verily as such do I also regard it, saith
Yahwe. But go now to My sanctuary which was in Shilo, where
I placed My name at first, and see what I did to it because of
the wickedness of My people Israel. And now because you do
all these deeds, I will do to this house in which you trust as I
did to Shiloh; I will cast you out from My presence as I cast out
your brethren, the whole seed of Ephraim.

The summary in ch. xxvi gives a slightly different
turn to the discourse by introducing the element of
contingency which is excluded by the terms of vii. 8–15:
'*if* ye will not listen to Me...*then* I will make this house
like Shiloh.' But it is doubtful if this be the actual form
of the address. Certainly, the priests at least took it up
as an unqualified threat (*v.* 9); although Jeremiah
allows that if the people will mend their ways Yahwe
will alter His purpose, yet throughout the proceedings
he is accused and defended and ultimately acquitted
as one who has uttered a categorical prediction. We may
therefore conclude that the prophecy was absolute in
its terms, and that vii. 8–15 reproduce most nearly its
ipsissima verba.

Jeremiah must have known that he took his life in his

hand when he went up to deliver this tremendous message. It must have been the first time that he publicly and explicitly announced the destruction of the Temple and the holy city; and he knew that to do so was to defy both the interests of the priesthood and the fanaticism of the mob. The effect of his words was comparable to that of Amos's first announcement of the downfall of Israel in the royal sanctuary at Bethel in the time of Jeroboam II (Amos vii. 10 ff.). But the old respect for the office of a prophet, which had shielded Amos from personal violence, had been undermined by the persecuting *régime* of Manasseh, and the priests had no difficulty in inciting the populace to an assault on Jeremiah's life. Happily, the freedom of prophesying still found its champions in that tumultuous assembly; and through the intervention of the lay aristocracy and certain 'elders of the land' Jeremiah was set free. The circumstances of his escape are dealt with in the note below, and need not divert our attention from the matters which more immediately interest us: viz. the meaning of this prophetic repudiation of the Temple and its worship, and in particular the contrast which it reveals between the prophetic and the Deuteronomic ideals of religion[1].

---

[1] With regard to the manner of Jeremiah's escape, Professor Butten-wieser (*Prophets of Israel*, pp. 24 ff.) propounds a novel and ingenious theory which raises a very important question concerning the attitude of the Deuteronomists to the prophets. On the usual reading of ch. xxvi the bench of nobles at once acquitted Jeremiah on the ground that his prophetic inspiration secured for him the right of free speech in public: 'No capital charge lies against this man, for in the name of Yahwe our God he has spoken to us' (*v.* 16). The argument is then clinched by the precedent of Micah the Morasthite cited by some of the provincial elders who were present (*vv.* 17–19). The part assigned to Ahikam the son of Shaphan in *v.* 24 is left utterly obscure. Now, Buttenwieser, by changing a single word in *v.* 16 (אֵין to אַיִן: 1 Sam. xxi. 9), turns the negative sentence into an affirmative, and explains the situation as follows:

We may take it for granted that no honest Deuteronomist would have regarded Jeremiah's words as a

The judges after hearing Jeremiah's defence pronounce sentence of
death: 'Verily this man has incurred the death penalty, for *in the name
of Yahwe our God* he has spoken to us.' Against this decision some of the
country elders protest, appealing to the case of Micah. But their protest
is overruled; and in the end Jeremiah owes his deliverance to an
individual, Ahikam, who contrives to 'spirit him away' in some manner
not described.—It must be recognised that this theory, if it could be
substantiated, would offer a perfectly intelligible view of the proceedings,
and would even improve the consecutiveness of the narrative. But it
seems to me to be cumbered with insuperable difficulties, of which the
grammatical change proposed for *v.* 16 is the least. The crucial question
is, How could prophesying in the name of Yahwe be in itself a ground
of condemnation? Buttenwieser's answer is based on the law of prophecy
in Deut. xviii. 20–22, a passage which, he believes, has been misunderstood by all expositors. The point of that enactment he takes to be that
the prophet who presumes *in the name of Yahwe* to speak contrary to
the law (of Deuteronomy) shall be put to death. To speak against the
law is itself an offence, whether punishable by death or not, but to do
so in the name of Yahwe constitutes a capital crime. This Jeremiah, by
his own confession (*vv.* 12–15) had done; hence his case comes under
the statute, and sentence is pronounced accordingly.—But Deut. xviii.
20 ff. cannot possibly have the sense which is thus put upon it. It is a
baseless suggestion that the passage is intended to safeguard the authority
of the law against the teaching of such prophets as Amos, Isaiah, Micah
and Jeremiah. There is not a word to suggest legal restriction of the
freedom of true prophecy, but on the contrary an explicit affirmation
of its right to declare whatsoever Yahwe has commanded (*vv.* 13 f.).
Nor is anything said about speaking contrary to the law. To translate
the words ולא יהיה הדבר ולא יבא in *v.* 22 by 'that which shall not
be nor occur'—meaning that which is opposed to the principles of
Deuteronomy—is a sheer travesty of Hebrew syntax. *V.* 22 is the answer
to the question of *v.* 21: How shall we know the word which Yahwe
has *not* spoken? To express Buttenwieser's idea in Deuteronomic
phraseology the answer must have been: 'When a prophet speaks not
in accordance with the statutes and judgments which I am commanding
you this day, he speaks presumptuously in the name of Yahwe.' But the
real answer is: 'When a prophet speaks in the name of Yahwe, *and the
word does not occur nor come to pass,* that is the word which Yahwe has not
spoken; the prophet has spoken it presumptuously' (בְּזָדוֹן).—Applying

direct polemic against the law-book; for Cornill is surely wrong in thinking that the expression '*the* words of falsehood' in *vv.* 4 and 8 can be understood as referring to that book. The false words are the words quoted from the mouth of the people—possibly taught to the people by the priests, but certainly not found in Deuteronomy nor expressing an idea there inculcated. It is another question whether a strict Deuteronomist would have been whole-heartedly in sympathy with Jeremiah's protest. He would have agreed that reverence for the house of God was no substitute for moral obedience, and that the Covenant had no validity unless its ethical requirements were put in practice. But might he not have felt that the prophet was too peremptory and *exigeant*, a little too severe in his judgment on the defective morals of the community, too unmindful of the value of even a formal recognition of God, and much too hasty in his conclusion that the reformation

this to the case of Jeremiah, we see (*a*) that from beginning to end there is no hint that he had spoken against the law. (*b*) That he had spoken in the name of Yahwe cannot be the *gravamen* of the charge brought against him. His real offence was to have spoken against the Temple and the city (*vv.* 9, 11; cf. *v.* 12): that he had falsely presumed to do so in the name of Yahwe could only be at most an aggravating circumstance. Now this real offence is not referred to at all in the verdict of the nobles, nor is there any suggestion that his pretension to inspiration was false. If the last clause of *v.* 16 were a reason for condemnation in accordance with Deut. xviii. 22, it would at least have required the Deuteronomic word בְּזָדוֹן (presumptuously) to be added. (*c*) The theory makes Jeremiah and his judges to play at cross purposes. To the accusation that he has prophesied against the city, he replies that he has spoken in the name of Yahwe. It is unnatural to suppose that what was a plea of 'not guilty' on the lips of the prophet should turn into a verdict of 'guilty' on the part of the judges, without any indication that his claim was denied.—We are therefore obliged, at whatever cost to the orderliness of the narrative, to fall back on the commonly accepted view that the judges decided in favour of Jeremiah, that they were supported by the elders of the land, and that after all Ahikam the son of Shaphan had to interpose to prevent him from being lynched.

had finally failed? To suppose that such thoughts were in the minds of many good men in Judah is no more than to do justice to the sincerity of those whose religious aspirations were satisfied by the Deuteronomic ideal. To understand Jeremiah, we must realise the difference between his position and theirs; and the difference comes openly to light in the Temple address.

In the first place, Jeremiah declares that the public religion, the religion of which the Temple is the centre and symbol, is an organised hypocrisy. In it religion was divorced from morality as completely as in the earlier days when worship was accompanied by flagrant immoralities. Men whose daily lives were a violation of every law of God presented themselves in the Temple, in the fond belief that its inherent sanctity ensured the stability of the social order within which they could practise their 'abominations' with impunity. It may be difficult to tell how much of pure superstition mingled with their worship, and how far it was down-right hypocrisy; the line between worship of an unethical power and unethical worship of a spiritual Being is hard to draw; and Jeremiah's condemnation applies to both alike. The Temple, he says in effect, is not what men call it or imagine it to be, but what by their actions they make it. It might have been the place where Yahwe's gracious presence was experienced if they had hallowed His name by lives lived in piety and righteous-ness; but used as they use it it has become even in Yahwe's eyes a cave for robbers to shelter themselves in.

Now the Deuteronomists must certainly be acquitted of any intention to bring about this state of things. They set out to organise *religion*, and in that they had achieved a considerable outward success. They did not see, however, that true religion is not a thing that can be organised. It must spring spontaneously from the contact of the human spirit with the living God; and the attempt to manipulate it from without can only result in its counterfeit, *hypocrisy*. The prophet may utterly fail to evoke the spirit of religion in his hearers; but at least he knows the real thing when he sees it, and stedfastly refuses to be put off with a sham. The mere reformer, on the other hand, is apt to compromise with appearances, and to think that when he has established a formal observance of religious ordinances he has gained much, though less than he could have wished. These two types of mind confront each other in Jeremiah and the better representatives of the Deuteronomic point of view. To the latter it would seem a hopeful sign that the Temple court was thronged day by day by reverent worshippers, even if their lives fell short of their profession. To Jeremiah it was simply a profanation of the holiness of God, and the most hopeless spectacle that the mind could contemplate. It was nothing to him that the reformers had meant well; he is concerned with the realities of the situation, and judging the movement by its fruits he pronounces it a sowing among thorns.

Accordingly, in the second place, Jeremiah announces that since the Temple has become the symbol of a false religion God is about to make an end of it, and with it of the nation which trusted in it. He does this, as we have seen, categorically, not as a conditional threat or warning, but as a fixed purpose of Yahwe. Here again he places himself in direct opposition to the Deuteronomic policy even in its most creditable aim. The leading principle of that policy was to save the State by putting its religious institutions on a footing worthy of the character, and deserving of the favour, of the nation's God. The book of Deuteronomy abounds in conditional threats, alternating with promises, meant to keep the people loyal to the national Covenant on which its preservation depended: if its authors could

have believed that an irrevocable doom hung over the
State they would never have put their hands to the
work. It is neither surprising nor blameworthy that
they failed to recognise the absolute character of the
prophetic announcements on this subject. We have
referred in a previous connexion[1] to the difficulty of
distinguishing the absolute element in prediction from
the element of contingency which is involved in a call
to repentance; and indeed it would seem that the
prophets themselves were not always clear whether
their utterances partook more of the one character or of
the other. Still there were predictions whose absolute
import was for the moment unmistakable, and this
Temple address of Jeremiah is one of them. The
priests who heard it had no doubt on that point, and
the elders who opposed them could only defend the
prophet by citing the equally absolute prediction of
Micah which had nevertheless not been fulfilled. That,
no doubt, implies a belief that no prediction is really
absolute in the final sense that its fulfilment is inevitable;
but it does not alter the fact that Jeremiah had pronounced the doom of the Temple to be as certain as the
fate that had overtaken the old sanctuary of Shiloh. And
this was a position which could in no way be reconciled
with the fundamental conceptions of the Deuteronomic
party.

In the Temple address, therefore, the prophet parts
company with the reformers, or those of them who
still clung to the hope that by the accomplished reformation the State had been saved. The difference
between them was at last exposed, and it concerned the
essence of religion. To Jeremiah religion was reality—
real fellowship with a real moral deity, and whatever
obscured that relationship was a hindrance to religion
and must be swept away. To the men who had taken

[1] pp. 74 ff.

control of the Deuteronomic movement, and were now
the spiritual leaders of the people, religion was a form
—a mere profession of homage expressed in ceremonial
functions; and to such religion the Temple and its
ritual were the necessary channels of communication
between God and His people. A God who could
destroy the Temple was a God whom they did not
understand and could not worship. Yet He was the
God of the prophets, and events speedily proved that
He was the God of history. The lesson of history was
too hard for that age to learn, and was to remain
unlearned for centuries. To the Jews of Christ's day
the second Temple was what the first had been to
priest and people in the time of Jeremiah: a pledge of
God's presence, and a rallying-point for the fanaticism
which a superstitious faith always engenders. Jeremiah's
polemic against the sanctity of the Temple was but the
prelude to the final emancipation of the spirit of religion
from the forms of a local and material worship; and the
first Christian martyr completed what was lacking in
the sufferings of Jeremiah by testifying that Jesus of
Nazareth would 'destroy this holy place.' The victory
of the new faith was not secure until the Master's
words were fulfilled: 'Seest thou these great buildings?
There shall not be left here one stone upon another
which shall not be thrown down[1].'

A condemnation of the Temple worship necessarily
implied a judgment on the value of the sacrificial system
as a whole. This is the theme of another Temple address
by Jeremiah, which has been preserved in the sequel
of the great discourse which we have just considered
(ch. vii. 21–23). The denunciation of public worship
as practised in the sanctuaries of their time had always
been a prominent feature in the preaching of the pre-

[1] Acts vi. 14; Mark xiii. 2, etc.

exilic prophets. This note is struck with passionate emphasis in the first proclamation of the prophetic gospel by Amos. 'I hate, I despise your processions, And have no relish for your festivals: Your sacrificial gifts I abhor, And I will not look on your offerings of fatlings. Take away from Me the noise of your songs: Your harp-playing I will not hear. But let justice flow like water, And righteousness like a perennial stream. Did you bring sacrifices and offerings to Me In the wilderness forty years long, House of Israel? saith Yahwe...' (Amos v. 21–25; cf. iv. 4 ff., v. 4 ff.). With equal vehemence Isaiah declaims against the ritual of the Temple at Jerusalem, and asserts its incompatibility with the character of Yahwe. 'What to Me are your many sacrifices? saith Yahwe; I am sated with holocausts of rams, And fat of fed beasts. In blood of bullocks and he-goats I delight not. When you come to see my face, Who has required this at your hand? Trample My courts no more: Bringing of gifts is vain, Sacrificial smoke is abomination to Me. New moon and sabbath I cannot endure; Fasting and sacred seasons My soul hateth, They are a burden to Me: I am weary of bearing it. Yea, when you spread out your hands I will hide My face from you; Yea, when you make many prayers I will not hear. Your hands are full of blood...' (Isa. i. 11–15)[1]. Hosea teaches the same doctrine in a very compact, if less absolute form: 'I delight in goodness and not sacrifice; And in knowledge of God apart from burnt-offerings' (Hos. vi. 6); he speaks scornfully of the Israelites going with their flocks and herds to seek Yahwe, and not finding Him (v. 6; cf. iv. 19). In the undisputed prophecies of Micah (chs. i–iii) there is no express mention of cultus; but in a later chapter of the book, commonly assigned

[1] For slight changes and omissions in the text, see Dr Gray's commentary.

to the reign of Manasseh, the prophetic point of view comes to its clearest and most eloquent expression. 'Wherewith shall I come before Yahwe, And bow before God on high? Does Yahwe take pleasure in thousands of rams, In myriads of rivers of oil? Shall I give my firstborn for my transgression? The fruit of my body for the sin of my soul? It is told thee, O man, what is good; and what Yahwe requires of thee: To do justice, and love mercy. And to walk humbly with thy God' (Micah vi. 6–8).

In these utterances of Jeremiah's precursors we have a measure of the opposition between the prophetic and the popular conceptions of religion. Ancient worship culminated in animal sacrifice, and apart from sacrificial worship religion could not exist. Sacrifice was the chief and indispensable means of maintaining intercourse between God and man. The bond uniting the deity and his worshippers was conceived as a physical one, and nothing was needed to keep it intact save the due observance of the stated ritual. Morality might be important, and transgressions of the divinely appointed order might be punished by judgments more or less severe; but the threatened breach could always be healed, and the anger of the god appeased, by enhanced zeal in the performance of sacrificial rites. How the slaughter of animals had come to occupy this supreme position in ancient ritual is not a question that greatly concerns us here; it is enough that the act was universally regarded as the necessary condition of approach to the deity, and of securing his favour. And that these ideas permeated the popular religion of Israel in the time of the prophets we see clearly from the passages quoted above. To the people sacrifice was the vital part of religion not only on the human side, but also on the divine. Yahwe was as dependent on their service as they were on His succour; if sacrifice were abolished the relation between them and their God would indeed be dissolved, but as an unworshipped deity Yahwe would no longer have a *raison d'être*. Hence they concluded that though Yahwe had a regard for morality, he must have a still greater regard for His own honour, and would never press His demand for righteousness so far as to abandon the nation which did formal homage to His divinity. And this, which to the popular view was incredible, is precisely what the prophets maintained that Yahwe was about to do.

Now it is commonly held that the prophets' repudiation of sacrifice was not absolute, but relative to the prevalent delusion that cultus apart from morality has an inherent value in the sight of God. That is to say, they did not reject sacrifice as such, but only as offered by a people that had lost the true knowledge of God. It seems clear, however, that the prophetic principle goes further than that. Not only is sacrifice of no avail as a substitute for righteous conduct, but a perfect religious relationship is possible without sacrifice at all. This is plainly taught by Amos when he points to the forty years in the wilderness as a time when sacrifice was unknown. There is no doubt that Amos shared the view of Hosea that the desert sojourn was the ideal period in Israel's history; and the obvious inference is that if Yahwe could be properly served without sacrifice then, He could be so still. Sacrifice, therefore, is no necessary term of communion between Yahwe and Israel: it does not belong to the essence of religion. And that the principle extends to the cultus in general, and was held by other prophets, is strongly suggested by the fact that they never demand a purified ritual, but always and exclusively the fulfilment of the ethical commands of Yahwe[1].

[1] In opposition to the view here expressed, Smend reminds us (*Alttest. Religionsgeschichte*, p. 197 *n*.) that the cultus which the prophets.

This at all events is the obvious meaning of Jeremiah's remarkable utterance in ch. vii. 21 ff. 'Add your holocausts to your (private) sacrifices[1] and eat flesh! For I did not speak with your fathers nor give them commandment, in the day when I brought them out of the land of Egypt, concerning holocaust and sacrifice. But this thing I commanded them, Obey my voice, etc.' The error here rebuked is not simply the practical abuse of sacrificial ritual by men who sought thus to compound for their moral delinquencies; it is the notion that Yahwe had ever instituted sacrifice at all. The whole system, and all laws prescribing or regulating it, are declared to lie outside the revelation on which the national religion of Israel was based. It must have been hard for the prophet's hearers, and it is not easy for us, to understand such a position in face of the tradition which traced the origin of the most ancient ritual codes to the authority of Moses. Jeremiah makes no attempt to show how sacrifice had come to be so deeply lodged in the ceremonial praxis of his people, or to set himself right with the prevalent belief that it was divinely ordained. His conviction of its non-essential character is the outcome of his prophetic knowledge of God, and is so strong that he is prepared to defy all

denounce is the cultus of a people with whom Yahwe is about to break off relations, and that they had not before them the problem of how in all respects the intercourse between God and people was to be realised and expressed. That is true so far as it goes. But the prophets had the problem in view at least so far as to hold up to their contemporaries the ideal of a religion wholly based on moral fellowship between God and man, and in which sacrificial worship was at best an irrelevance, and at worst an offence.

[1] עוֹלוֹת and זבחים: the point being of course that the former were wholly consumed on the altar as an offering to Yahwe, whereas the latter partly furnished the material of a feast to the worshippers. For all Yahwe cares, says the prophet, you may eat the one along with the other!

traditional opinion, and affirm that it could never have been commanded by the God who had revealed Himself through Moses to Israel. And in this he makes explicit the latent opposition between the prophetic conception of religion and that which found in sacrifice an indispensable means of communion with Yahwe.

But how, we must ask, does this declaration bear on the prophet's estimate of the law of Deuteronomy? The sacrificial element is not prominent in Deuteronomy, nor is it greatly emphasised, but it is there; and moreover we cannot doubt that the acceptance of the code had fostered the tendency to set undue value on ritual as compared with moral duties. It would appear, therefore, that the principle enunciated by Jeremiah involves rejection of the claim of Deuteronomy to be a divine law imposed on Israel. That is, in fact, the only interpretation consistent with seriousness of purpose on the part of the prophet. We cannot suppose him capable of the ineptitude of solemnly denying that God had instituted sacrifice at the Exodus while admitting that He had done so forty years later in the land of Moab. Nor is it fair to say that he is using the language of rhetorical exaggeration, or that he means only to deny that sacrifice was the *primary* interest of the Mosaic legislation. His words strike at the root of the common illusion which regarded sacrifice as an essential constituent of the worship of Yahwe; and when he asserts that God had given no law about it at the beginning he must mean that such laws, whether found in Deuteronomy or anywhere else, were unauthorised additions to the covenant made with the fathers. It does not follow of necessity that Jeremiah had been an opponent of the reformation of which Deuteronomy was the legal instrument, or that he could have taken no part in promoting it. We cannot even say that he saw reason to change his mind about the Code itself.

He had never imagined that sacrifice was of the essence of religion; but then it is by no means clear that the Deuteronomists regard it as such. Their purpose was not to insist on the necessity of sacrifice, but so to regulate it as to purge it of heathenish abominations. Jeremiah might well sympathise with this aim, looking on the purification of the cult as a thing desirable in itself, and fraught with no dangerous consequences to religion. It was only when the people were being taught that Temple and ritual were a *sine quâ non* of religion, and when the 'lying pen of the scribes' was busy fabricating rules in this sense, that he took up the strong position of branding these things as a hindrance to true fellowship with God, and a perversion of the historic religion of Israel from its native ethical genius.

CHAPTER X

PROPHETIC INSPIRATION

FROM an early period of his ministry Jeremiah had recognised the disastrous influence of the two professional religious orders in Jerusalem—the Prophets and the Priests. The alliance of these two classes for selfish and venal ends is referred to as the most disquieting symptom of the moral degeneracy of the people. 'A monstrous and horrible thing has come to pass in the land: the prophets prophesy falsely, and the priests give *Tôrā* at their side; and my people love it so; and what will ye do at the end thereof?' (v. 30 f.). 'For low and high they are all out for gain; from prophet to priest they all deal in falsehood. And they heal the hurt of my people superficially, saying, "Peace! Peace!" when there is no peace' (vi. 13 f. = viii. 10 f.). The distress which filled the prophet's mind at the sight of this profanation of the most sacred institutions of the national religion is powerfully expressed in an oracle which probably belongs to his earlier years (xxiii. 9–11):

> 9 Broken is my heart within me,
>   All my bones quiver!
> I am like a drunken man,
>   Like one overcome by wine.
> Before Yahwe and His glorious majesty.

> 10 For with adulterers the land is filled;
>   Their course is bad, their power not right.
> 11 Yea, both prophet and priest are profane:
>   'Even in My house I have found their wickedness':
>   Is Yahwe's oracle.

Of the priests as a separate body Jeremiah has not much more to say; but the prophets of the type referred to in these passages occupied much of his thought, and called forth his severest censure. They were in large measure responsible for the blind optimism and indifference to moral issues which prevailed after the promulgation of Deuteronomy. 'Then I said: "Ah, Lord Yahwe! Behold the prophets are saying to them, Ye shall not see the sword, and famine shall not come to you; but assured peace I will give you in this place"' (xiv. 13). They are for the most part a shadowy group in the background of the picture; although one vigorous personality of this stamp appears on the stage in Hananiah of Gibeon, whose memorable encounter with our prophet in the fourth year of Zedekiah throws an instructive light on the opposition between the true prophet and the false.

I

There is no mystery about the position or the antecedents of this order of men in the Israelitish commonwealth. They were the degenerate survivors of a phase of prophecy which had once played an influential and honourable part in the history of the national religion. In its origin Hebrew prophecy had been the highest expression of the national spirit, at a time when patriotic and religious enthusiasm were one thing, and the cause of Yahwe was identical with the cause of Israel. Its inspiration was sustained by an indomitable confidence in the future of Israel, founded on a lofty conception of the power of Yahwe, and a firm belief in His will to advance the interests of His people. This was its characteristic down to the appearing of Elijah, in whom for the first time religion is divorced from patriotism, and the claims of Yahwe are seen to be so absolute that they must be vindicated even at the cost of Israel's destruction. And it is noteworthy that just at this time we have the first indication of a schism in the ranks of the prophets, in the dramatic scene where Micaiah ben-Imlah stands alone before Ahab and Jehoshaphat as a prophet of woe against 400 prophets of Yahwe who assure the king of success in his enterprise against the Syrians (1 Kings xxii). The incident is typical of the whole subsequent development of prophecy. The canonical prophets were a minority of chosen individuals who read the signs of the times with a clearer insight into the character of Yahwe and the principles of His government than their contemporaries, and who perceived that it was His purpose to bring Israel's national existence to an end. The threatening aspect of events, in which these prophets discerned the signs of coming judgment, only stirred in their opponents a fanatical enthusiasm for the national cause, which broke out in the ecstatic manifestations which had always been regarded as the mark of possession by the spirit of Yahwe. False prophecy, in short, so far as it had any root of sincerity, was fundamentally an unprogressive survival of the ancient prophecy of Israel, under conditions to which it was no longer adequate, and under which it was apt to deteriorate into mere flattery of the popular opinion, or even into a means of livelihood (Mic. iii. 5–8).

The problem how to distinguish the true prophet from the false was thus an old one in Israel, and was beset by peculiar difficulties on the level of religious knowledge on which the mass of the people stood. In early times it had little or no ethical significance. A prophecy was true if it was verified by the event; and a true prophet was simply one whose vaticinations uniformly proved to be correct: his moral character was not in question. Samuel had the reputation of being a true prophet because 'whatsoever he speaks unfailingly

comes to pass' (1 Sam. ix. 6). The question first became of religious importance when the destinies of
the State were concerned; and especially when a succession of men appeared who consistently prophesied
national disaster, while the bulk of the order flattered
the hope of a brilliant future. In externals there was
nothing to distinguish the one kind of prophet from
the other. Both spoke in the name of Yahwe; both spoke
with the accent of personal conviction; and both could
appeal to ecstatic experiences as the seal of the genuineness of their oracles. Yet they could not both be true
interpreters of the one thing which it was important
to know—the actual purpose of Yahwe, which would
be fulfilled in history. Accordingly in the contest of
Micaiah with the 400, the question is expressly raised,
and answered in an unexpected fashion: 'Which way
went the spirit of Yahwe from me to speak by thee?'
Micaiah throws no doubt on the reality of his opponents'
inspiration: they were inspired, he says, to prophesy
falsely—inspired by a lying spirit sent forth from Yahwe
to lure Ahab to his doom. For the rest he is content to
leave the issue to the arbitrament of events: 'Thou
shalt see in that day when thou goest into an inner
chamber to hide thyself'; 'If thou return at all in peace,
Yahwe has not spoken by me' (vv. 25, 28).

Now this question has a unique place in the thinking
of Jeremiah. The canonical prophets before him had,
so far as we know, met opposition in the strength of
an immediate personal conviction of the truth of their
own message, and an inward certainty of the fulfilment
of their word, without attempting to explain the
phenomenon of spurious inspiration. But to Jeremiah's
introspective bent of mind a negative attitude was
perhaps impossible. He thoroughly understood the
influence which these false prophets had with the
people, and contrasted it sadly with the failure of his

own mission. He knew that he himself was classed as
one of the raving fanatics who appeared from time to
time in the Temple, exciting the populace by frenzied
oracles uttered with all the manifestations of inspired
possession (xxix. 26 f., xx. 1 f.). Nay, it would almost
appear as if he himself was liable to be impressed by
the extraordinary manner in which these men could
sometimes deliver their message. In his encounter with
Hananiah he seems to have quailed for a moment
before the vehemence of his opponent's enthusiasm,
and to have felt a misgiving as to whether he might not
be right. It required an interval of self-recollection to
regain the confidence to confront Hananiah with an
energy of conviction greater than his own (xxviii. 6 ff.).
It was imperative that he should inquire what criterion
of inspiration he possessed which justified him in believing that his own revelations were true and those of
his rivals false, that his own visions were real and theirs
delusions.

Moreover, the question was in the air in his time.
The contemporary book of Deuteronomy has two
passages dealing with false prophecy, though in a way
that shows little if any advance on the twofold position
of Micaiah. In ch. xiii the rule is laid down that
no prophet who seeks to seduce the people from their
allegiance to Yahwe is to be listened to under any
circumstances. Such a prophet, if he seems to be
authenticated by the fulfilment of some sign which he
has given, is sent by Yahwe, not indeed to mislead the
people, but to test its fidelity to His covenant. In ch.
xviii the seemingly inconsistent principle is enunciated,
that the false prophet is to be detected by the non-
verification of his predictions. The contradiction is
perhaps only apparent. In the first case the reference is
to a mere arbitrary sign attached to the alleged revelation, which might or might not come to pass without

affecting the truth of the prophet's teaching; in the second the thing predicted is the very substance of the message itself. In each case, however, an objective norm is set up by which the validity of a prophetic announcement can be tested: in the one case, conformity to the national religion; in the other, the course of events. The authors of the Deuteronomic legislation were thus aware of the dangers involved in the unrestrained exercise of freedom of prophesying; and in their attempt to regulate and control it, we have the first intimation of the radical opposition between the written code and the living voice of prophecy which ultimately led to the extinction of the latter.

For all these reasons Jeremiah was held up by the problem of inspiration as none of his predecessors had been. In his treatment of it we find, not a theoretical solution of the difficulties of the subject, but rather a movement towards a clarification of the prophetic consciousness which points forward to a higher level of religion, at which the devout wish of the great founder of Hebrew prophecy could be realised: 'Would that all the Lord's people were prophets!' (Num. xi. 29).

II

Jeremiah's polemic against the popular prophets of the time is mostly contained in a series of oracles delivered at various dates, and collected in ch. xxiii. 9 ff., under the heading *LANNĔBÍ'ÎM* ('Concerning the prophets'), and commencing with the striking lines already quoted on p. 185. The passage has been considerably amplified by commentators, especially towards the end of the chapter; and it is difficult to tell precisely how much of it was really written by Jeremiah. But the main lines of his criticism are clearly discernible. He declaims against the current prophecy of the day on three grounds: *first*, the character of its representatives;

secondly, the substance of their message; and *thirdly*, the forms in which they gave it out as the word of Yahwe.

(1) Jeremiah repeatedly denounces the prophets as men of immoral life.

13 In Samaria's prophets I saw unseemliness;
    They prophesied by Baal and misled My people.
14 In Jerusalem's prophets I have seen a horror:
    Adultery, walking in lies, and strengthening the hand of
      ill-doers.
  They are all to Me like Sodom,
    As the inhabitants of Gomorrah (xxiii. 13, 14).

Similarly the false prophets who appeared among the exiles in Babylon are accused of committing adultery with their neighbours' wives (xxix. 23). And not only do these prophets share in the prevalent vices of the upper class (v. 7 ff.), not only do they place no check on rampant wickedness (xxiii. 17); but the contagion of their evil example is a chief source of the general corruption of morals: 'From the prophets of Jerusalem pollution has gone out through the whole land' (xxiii. 15). It is, of course, not necessary to suppose that a sweeping class-judgment like this held true of every member of the class. There were doubtless honest and respectable individuals among them. But the scandal must have been sufficiently notorious to throw discredit on the whole style of teaching which emanated from that class, and to destroy its pretensions to be the word of God. And we can readily believe that men of the temperament favourable to a spurious religious excitement were peculiarly open to sensual temptation; while their absence of moral courage led them first to flatter and then to imitate the vices they failed to condemn. It is above all this indifference to moral good or evil in the social life of the people that stamps them as impostors when they speak in the name of Him who is of eyes too pure to behold iniquity. The mark of the true prophet is that he strives to 'turn back My people from their evil way' (xxiii. 22). His words and actions approve themselves as in accord with the holy will of God, and he gives his life to promote the extension of true godliness in the nation to which he is sent.

(2) The teaching of these prophets corresponded to their character. It was a message of peace to all and sundry, without regard to their moral condition. 'They keep on speaking to the scorners of Yahwe's word, "Peace shall be yours" and to every one who walks in the obduracy of his heart they say "No evil shall come near you"' (xxiii. 17). In the true prophets the anticipation of the doom of the nation went hand in hand with their judgment on its sinful condition; and in face of their preaching it argued great shallowness of moral perception to assure the people under all circumstances of the favour and help of Yahwe. But these men, being themselves destitute of high or strict principles of morality, could see nothing in the state of the nation calling for the righteous judgment of God. Their whole effort was to produce a sense of security by proclaiming 'Peace, Peace,' when there was no peace.

In opposition to this tendency Jeremiah takes up a position which might seem to us one-sided and extreme. He appears to assert that only the prophet of disaster is truly sent by Yahwe, that only the destructive, annihilating prophetic word is the genuine word of God. 'Is not my word like a fire, like a hammer that shatters the rock?' (xxiii. 29). And in his challenge to Hananiah he goes so far as to make it a mark of the true prophet that he prophesies of war and famine and pestilence; although he adds in qualification that a prophet of peace *may* be recognised as truly inspired provided his word comes to pass (xxviii. 8, 9). Obviously some qualification is needed; for just about the same time Jeremiah himself addressed a prophecy of hope to the exiles in Babylon, and one that could not be tested by fulfilment till after seventy years. But with regard to the principle itself, it may have two implications. In the first place, the chronic condition of the nation was such that a prediction of judgment had a strong presumption in its favour. In the second place, any prophecy which fell in with the natural disposition to look at the bright side of things could be explained as of human origin, and therefore needed attestation by the course of providence before it could be accepted as divine. More than this Jeremiah can hardly have meant. Laxity of moral conviction and a readiness to prophesy smooth things went naturally together.

(3) Lastly, Jeremiah holds that these prophets were either deluded or dishonest in their use of the traditional forms of prophetic revelation. 'Lying vision, and idle divination, and deceit of the mind, is what they prophesy to you' (xiv. 14). He sees the evidence of falsehood *first* in the want of originality and independence: 'they steal My words from one another' (xxiii. 30); *next* in their mimicry of the prophetic mode of utterance: 'they take their tongue and bring forth an oracular utterance[1]'; and *last* in their palming off of lying dreams as real prophetic visions (xxiii. 32).

Now, it is at this point that we might look for some attempt to differentiate between the experience of the true prophet and that of the false. If there is a possibility of deception in this matter there must, we are apt to think, be some valid criterion by which the revealing activity of the divine spirit can be distinguished from the ordinary operations of the mind. But it is doubtful if any such criterion can be found in Jeremiah's treatment of the problem. He uses three expressions to

---

[1] וינאמו נאם: that is, I take it, they simulate the peculiar intonation which was supposed to be due to supernatural inspiration; and which was no doubt characteristic of ecstatic speech.

describe the qualifications of the true prophet in contrast to the false. (a) He is one who has 'stood in the council of Yahwe' (xxiii. 18, 22); (b) he has 'heard the word of Yahwe' (xxiii. 18, 21, 28, xiv. 14); (c) he is 'sent' by Yahwe (xxiii. 21, 32, xiv. 14). If we knew the right interpretation of these metaphors we might learn what Jeremiah's view of genuine inspiration was. But they are ambiguous, and leave us in uncertainty on the crucial question of the significance he attached to the ecstatic side of prophetic experience. Does this standing in the council of Yahwe denote a visionary experience, like the sublime scene described by Micaiah in 1 Kings xxii. 19–22, or a spiritual condition removed from every trace of ecstasy? Is hearing the word of Yahwe to be understood as an audition which seems to proceed from an external voice, or merely as an intuitive perception of what the mind of Yahwe is? And similar questions might be asked with regard to the consciousness of being 'sent' or commissioned by Yahwe. Direct answers to these questions cannot be given. But looking to Jeremiah's teaching on this subject as a whole, and comparing his utterances one with another, certain fundamental positions may be laid down.

1. He has no *psychological* test by which true prophecy can be distinguished from false. It might be thought from some expressions that he assigns a superiority to the audition over the vision, and again to the vision over the dream. But even if there be some ground for these distinctions, they are only relative, and do not reach to the bottom of the problem. He knows that there is a lying vision which originates in the human mind; but there is also a true vision 'from the mouth of Yahwe' (xxiii. 16); and such visions he undoubtedly claims to have seen. But he does not pretend that there is anything in the vision itself which will stamp it as springing from the one source or the other. And all

investigation of the subjective phenomena of religion confirms the conclusion that it is impossible to discriminate between true inspiration and false by the *form* of the experience through which ideas present themselves to the mind.

2. The real test which Jeremiah applies to his opponents is the test of *morality*. It is not so much in the form of their prophetic experience as in the substance of their prophetic teaching that he discovers the proof that they are no true spokesmen of Yahwe. In their indifference to the sin of the people, in their positive encouragement of evil-doers, and in their own immoral lives, they proclaim their entire ignorance of Yahwe's truth. It is the men themselves who are false; and to a false heart no true revelation is vouchsafed. Hence he knows that they are no accredited messengers of the God whose essence is righteousness, that the visions by which they seek to authenticate their message cannot come from Him, and must therefore be in some way the product of their own minds.

3. Jeremiah is conscious of standing in a personal relation to God, which we may call confidential, and of which the false prophets can have no experience. It is expressed by the phrases already mentioned as descriptive of the true prophet: he has stood in the council of Yahwe, has heard his word, has been sent by Him. His whole conscious life is pervaded by this conviction, which had come to him at the moment of his call— that before his birth he had been predestined and consecrated to the mission of a prophet. It is this which gives him the assurance that the truth which he perceives, whether it come to him through a vision, or an audition, or by direct spiritual intuition is a revelation of the mind and will of Yahwe. This immediate consciousness of having the mind of God is the ultimate secret of true prophetic inspiration, which, being in-

communicable, can neither be analysed nor applied as an objective criterion of an alleged revelation. It is strictly analogous to the experience of religious certainty in general—the *testimonium internum Spiritus Sancti,* 'bearing witness with our spirits that we are children of God.' He who has it knows that he has it, though he who lacks it may be deceived in thinking he has it; just as a man who is awake may be sure he is not dreaming, whereas a man in a dream may readily fancy himself awake.

There is a striking passage in the book of Numbers, in which the manner of Yahwe's intercourse with Moses, the incomparable prophet, is contrasted with His methods of revealing His will to the ordinary prophet (Num. xii. 6–8):

> If there be a prophet among you,
> In the vision I make myself known to him,
> In the dream I speak with him.
> Not so My servant Moses:
> In all My house he is found trustworthy.
> Mouth to mouth I speak with him,
> Plainly and not in riddles;
> And the form of Yahwe he beholds.

Here we have presented, dimly but unmistakably, the conception of a mode of revelation which transcends the ordinary range of prophetic experience. The latter sees δι' ἐσόπτρου ἐν αἰνίγματι, and hears indistinctly; God communicates with the prophet through the refractory medium of visions and dreams, and consequently his knowledge of the divine mind and purpose is obscure, fragmentary, and defective. The pre-eminence of Moses is expressed by figures to which we cannot, indeed, attach a precise or certain signification, but which convey the general impression of a spiritual state in which the will of God is apprehended directly and consciously, and with clear insight into its scope and reasons. The position of Moses in the theocracy is compared to that of the confidential servant in the household, whom his Lord has found trustworthy, who shares his master's thought, is initiated into the principles of his administration, and stands on terms of personal intimacy with him. To Moses Yahwe reveals Himself as He is; He communes with him in articulate rational language, face to face, as when 'a man speaketh with his friend.' Now it may be a question whether this form of communion with God is conceived as the highest reach of the prophetic consciousness, or as something which lies beyond prophecy and ought to be called by another name; and in the next chapter we shall look at that question in the light of Jeremiah's religious experience. It is plain, of course, that the point of view of the writer in Numbers is not exactly that of Jeremiah. Jeremiah does not admit that Yahwe has anything at all to do with the visions, real or pretended, of the false prophets: they are the product of their own thought and imagination. Nevertheless it seems to me that the conception of Moses' relation to Yahwe contained in that passage does correspond somewhat with Jeremiah's consciousness of his own intercourse with God, and is perhaps the nearest expression of it in language which he himself would have understood. It is impossible to suppose that any earlier Old Testament writer had a higher idea of inspiration than he had; and we may reasonably hold that in that face-to-face converse with Yahwe, that comprehensive insight into His purpose, which are there attributed to Moses, we have a typical representation of what Jeremiah regarded as the essence of true prophecy. The basis of all genuine inspiration is a mind 'in tune with the Infinite,' a moral sympathy with the principles on which the universe is governed, and a consciousness,

none the less real because incommunicable, of personal
fellowship with the God who reigns over all, and who
reveals His secret purpose to His servants the prophets.

Amid the confusions of the spurious prophetic
manifestations of his time Jeremiah finds a refuge in
the thought of the unescapable omniscience and omnipresence of God. This idea is expressed in a sentence
which Cornill has justly described as one of the most
enigmatic and surprising in the whole prophetic
literature (xxiii. 23 f.):

> 23 Am I a God of the Near,
>   And not a God of the Far?
> 24 Can any hide himself in secret places
>   Where I shall not see him?
> The heavens and the earth—
>   Do I not fill them?
>   Is Yahwe's oracle.

It is difficult to perceive the precise bearing of these
words on the problem of prophetic inspiration as dealt
with in the context. What, in such a connexion, is
meant by asserting that God is far off and not near?
And how is this statement related to the further statement that none can hide himself from the all-seeing
eye of Yahwe? An interesting and highly original
interpretation put forward by Cornill answers these
questions somewhat as follows. The two verses express
a contrast: *v.* 23 refers to the mistaken notion of God
which the false prophets entertain, *v.* 24 to the experience of a true prophet. Yahwe is not a next-door
neighbour, at the beck and call of every one who chooses
to assume familiarity with Him: He is the high and
lofty One who inhabiteth eternity, inaccessible to the
impertinent intrusion of human audacity and presumption. But just as little as God can be found by the
irreverent and irreligious mind, so little can the man

truly called by Him to be a prophet find a retreat in which the imperious summons will not reach him—a truth which Jeremiah had learned for himself by his own experience. The exegesis is too subtle to be convincing; although the ideas are profoundly true and in every way worthy of Jeremiah. On the other hand the ordinary interpretation—that Yahwe is not a nearsighted being, who only sees what is before his eyes, but One who from a remote height surveys all and penetrates every secret place where the false heart seeks to hide itself—is a little flat and trivial and unsatisfying. Perhaps the best commentary on the passage is the 139th Psalm. 'O Lord, thou hast searched me and known me; Thou knowest my downsitting and mine uprising, Thou understandest my thought afar off. Thou searchest out my path and my lying down, And art acquainted with all my ways. For there is not a word in my tongue, But lo, O Lord, thou knowest it altogether. Thou hast beset me behind and before, And laid thine hand upon me: A knowledge too wonderful for me; So high, I cannot attain to it! Whither shall I go from thy spirit? Or whither shall I flee from thy presence? If I ascend up into heaven thou art there: If I make my bed in Sheol, behold, thou art there. If I take the wings of the morning, And dwell in the uttermost parts of the sea; Even there shall thy hand lead me, And thy right hand hold me.' To the prophet as to the Psalmist omnipresence and omniscience are one thing. Jeremiah is not here denying the nearness of God; he is merely asserting that He is *also* far: that He is both immanent and transcendent, filling heaven and earth as a living conscious mind, setting every event and every secret thought in the light of His countenance. And the application of this truth to the facts of prophecy may be that real prophecy has, as we might say, a cosmic significance. It is not a series of

casual, spasmodic, abnormal illuminations, having no
relation to ultimate reality; but a reflexion in human
thought of the infinite Wisdom which reigns throughout
the universe and through all the ages: a revelation of
one overruling purpose by which 'the whole round
world is every way bound with gold chains about the
feet of God.' To Jeremiah the word of Yahwe is the
eternal truth of things, the immutable truth which will
shatter the existing order, and destroy the whole world
of lies on which men were building their confidence.
As the spokesman of this imperishable word he looks
with scornful amazement on the pretensions of the
false prophets who bring the rushlights of their puny
fabricated oracles into the bright sunshine of his own
sure knowledge of God and of the destiny in store for
his nation (xxiii. 28 f.):

> 28 The prophet that has a dream,
>   Let him relate a dream;
> And he that has My word,
>   Let him declare My word in truth.
> What has the chaff to do with the wheat?
>   Is Yahwe's oracle.
> 29 Is not My word like fire,
>   Like a hammer that shatters the rock?

CHAPTER XI

INDIVIDUAL RELIGION—THE INNER LIFE OF JEREMIAH

AMONG the extant writings of Jeremiah there is a striking series of poetic utterances which, through a tacit agreement of recent scholars, have come to be known as the 'Confessions of Jeremiah.' The passages are interspersed here and there in the middle part of the book, from the end of ch. xi to ch. xx, in an order imposed not by the prophet himself but by the editors of his literary remains[1]. Although few in number they have a peculiar interest, both from a biographical and from a religious point of view. They supply material for a chapter on the inner life of Jeremiah, such as could be written in the memoir of no other prophet. They form no part of his public message to his contemporaries, and were probably never published in his lifetime; but, as Wellhausen has finely observed[2], it would seem that some consciousness of the permanent value of his meditations moved the prophet to commit them to writing, for the guidance and edification of future generations of seekers after God. And we cannot be too grateful for their preservation. It is not too much to say that if these precious fragments had perished, not only would the most vital element in Jeremiah's individuality and influence have remained unknown, but the devotion of the Jewish Church would have been immeasurably poorer in that strain of personal piety

[1] Chs. xi. 18–23, xii. 1–6, xv. 10–21, xvii. 9 f., 14–18, xviii. 18–23, xx. 7–12 (xx. 14–18).

[2] *Israelitische und jüdische Geschichte* (5th Ed.), p. 149.

which saved its religion from degenerating into a soul-
less legalism.

The characteristic of the Confessions is that in the
form, sometimes of monologue, but more frequently
of strangely ingenuous and arresting colloquy with
God, they lay bare the inmost secrets of the prophet's
life, his fightings without and fears within, his mental
conflict with adversity and doubt and temptation, and
the reaction of his whole nature on a world that
threatened to crush him and a task whose difficulty
overwhelmed him. There is nothing quite like them in
the range of devotional literature. Communings of the
soul with God as tender and intimate, meditations as
profound, prayers as fervent and sincere, may be found
in the Psalms and the great classics of the spiritual life;
but Jeremiah's experience is unique in this respect, that
it springs out of a prior official relation to God which he
had in virtue of his prophetic vocation. It is true that
the call to be a prophet was itself a religious experience,
involving direct and continuous intercourse of the
prophet with God; but from the nature of prophecy
this intercourse was limited to Yahwe's dealings with
the nation of Israel, and left unsolved, or even intensi-
fied, the problem of personal religion as it presented
itself in the prophet's own life. No man felt this more
acutely than Jeremiah. There were times when he could
rejoice in the knowledge that the Lord had spoken to
him and called him to a service which was perfect
freedom. At other times he felt his work a burden too
heavy to be borne; his exclusion from the common
joys and satisfactions of human existence filled him
with a wistful regret, and he would fain have been
released from the constraint of the divine word. At
such moments there burst from him those cries *de pro-
fundis* which are the ground note of the Confessions.
In his distress he spreads his complaint before God,

praying for the vindication of his message and the victory of his cause, and seeking a sure foundation for his life in the eternal purpose. Such in outline is the trend of Jeremiah's experience as unfolded in the passages before us. We shall find here a certain expansion or sublimation of the prophetic consciousness into the larger relationship which is properly called religion —a relation of which one term is God, and the other is the human soul, in its desolation and weakness and need, and its irrepressible craving for assurance of its worth to the God who made it. That transformation, for all we can tell, may have taken place more than once in the history of prophecy, but the solitary record of it is the Confessions of Jeremiah, which we will now proceed to consider.

I

As a guide to the following exposition I give here a translation of the entire series of confessional utterances, with the exception of the first two (xi. 18 ff. and xii. 1 ff.) which will be found on pages 110 f. Although it contains some disputable renderings, and disguises numerous difficulties of text and interpretation which baffle the translator, it will I hope convey to the reader some adequate idea of the range of thought, emotion and experience which he is invited to explore in the rest of this chapter.

A General Complaint and Prayer (xv. 10–18)

10 Woe is me, my mother, that thou hast borne me
A man at strife with all the world!
Nor borrower nor lender am I;
And all men curse me!
11 Say, Lord, if I have not persisted
With Thee for the enemy's good[1]:

---

[1] In this insoluble *crux interpretum* I have partly adopted a suggestion of Prof. C. R. Brown, reading אִם לֹא שָׁרִיתִי אִתְּךָ לְטוֹבָה

And pleaded with Thee in the evil day,
    In the day of distress!

*   *   *   *   *   *   *

15 Thou knowest it, Yahwe!
    Remember, and visit me graciously.
    Avenge Thyself on my persecutors,·
    And not in Thy long-suffering!
    Know that for Thee I have borne reproach
16   From all who despise Thy word[1].

But to me is Thy word a delight,—
    The joy of my heart;
For Thy name has been named upon me,
    O Yahwe of hosts.

17 With the merry crew I sat not rejoicing;
    Lonely I sat because of Thy hand:
    For with spleen Thou hast filled me.
18 Why is my grief perpetual?—
    My wound mortal,
    That will not be healed?
Wilt Thou be to me like a winter brook,
    As waters that fail?

The Divine Answer (xv. 19–21)

19 Therefore thus saith Yahwe:

    If thou return, I will restore thee;
    Thou shalt stand before Me:
    If pure thoughts thou utter, unmixed with base,
    Thou shalt be as My mouth.
    These men shall come round to thee,
    But not thou to them.

שְׁרִיתִיךָ (אֶל־הָאֹיֵב. with suff. of indirect object, would probably be too bold.) The general sense is fortunately clear from the following line; and שׂרה, the verb used of Jacob's wrestling at Peniel (Gen. xxxii. 29 [28]; Hos. xii. 4, 5 [3, 4]), suits the context admirably. The last three words are from the LXX, only transposed from the second distich to the first. *V.* 12 is untranslatable; and *vv.* 13, 14 are alien to the connexion (cf. xvii. 3, 4).

[1] Reading, with the consonants of the LXX: מֹנֲאֲצֵי דְּבָרְךָ כֻּלָם.

20 I will make thee to this people
　　A wall strong as brass:
They will fight, but shall not o'ercome thee;
　　For I am with thee to save thee,
To deliver thee 21 from the hand of the wicked[1],
　　From the grip of the terrible.

Yahwe the Searcher of Hearts (xvii. 9, 10)
　9 Deep[2] beyond sounding is the heart.
　　　And sick beyond cure:
　　　Who can know it?

　10 I, Yahwe, search the heart,
　　　And try the reins;
　　　To give to a man as his ways,
　　　The fruit of his doings.

A Prayer for Healing and Succour (xvii. 14–18)
　14 Heal me, Yahwe, that I may be healed;
　　　Save me that I may be saved;
　　　For Thou art my praise!

　15 Lo! They are saying to me,
　　　'Where, then, is Yahwe's word?
　　　Let it but come!'

　16 But I have not pressed for the evil day[3],
　　　Nor desired the day of woe:
　　　Thou knowest.
　　What has come forth from my lips
　　　Lies plain before Thee.

　17 Be not a terror to me,
　　　Thou, my trust in the evil day!

[1] Some superfluous clauses omitted in 20 b, 21.
[2] Reading עָמוֹק with the LXX, instead of עָקֹב (cf. Ps. lxiv. 7 [6]).
The Heb. text, however, may be right.
[3] לֹא־אַצְתִּי יֹם רָעָה, instead of לֹ' אֵ' מֵרֹעֶה, omitting the following אַחֲרִיךְ. For other renderings, see the comm.

¹⁸ May my foes be put to shame, and not I:
 May they be dismayed, and not I!
 Bring on them the day of evil;
  Destroy them with double destruction.

A Conspiracy against the Prophet's Life (xviii. 18–23)

¹⁸ 'Come,' they have said, 'Let us hatch
 Against him a plot!
(For never shall Torah fail the priest,
 Nor counsel the sage, nor word the prophet!)
Come, with the tongue we will smite him,
 And carefully watch his words ¹.'

¹⁹ Watch Thou *them*, O Yahwe!
 And hear what my enemies say.
²⁰ Should evil be rendered for good ²?
 Think how I stood before Thee
To speak for their good,
 To turn Thy wrath from them.
^{22b} While they digged a pit to entrap me,
 And snares did lay for my feet.

²³ But Thou, O Yahwe, well knowest
 All their designs for my death.
Let not their guilt be atoned for,
 Nor their sin blotted out from Thy sight.
May they stumble and fall before Thee!
 In the time of Thy wrath deal with them.

---

¹ The Heb. 'and not heed all his words,' in the mouth of Jeremiah's enemies, has no meaning. Omit 'not' with LXX, and take the verb in a bad sense = 'watch for something to be used against him' (Cornill). In *v.* 19 I follow Schmidt in reading 'to them' for 'to me.'

² In *v.* 20 the clause 'they have digged a pit for my soul' is obviously a variant from *v.* 22 *b*. This suggests, as Erbt points out, that 22 *b* followed close on *v.* 20, and that consequently *vv.* 21, 22 *a*, which break the connexion, are an addition to the original oracle. Duhm and Cornill would reject the whole of 21–23 as unworthy of Jeremiah; but see pp. 211, 223 f. below.

The Word of the Lord a Reproach and a Burden (xx. 7–12)

7 Thou hast deceived me, Yahwe; and I was deceived:
  Wast stronger than I, and prevailedst.
 I am a laughingstock all the day;
  All men deride me.

8 Whene'er I speak I am mocked[1];
  Of violence and wrong is my cry;
 For Yahwe's word is to me a reproach
  And derision all day long.

9 If I said, 'I will seek to forget Him,
  And speak no more in His name,'
 'Twas like glowing fire in my breast,
  Shut up in my bones.
 I was weary with keeping it under;
  I could not hold out.

10 I hear the whisper of many[2]:
  'Denounce! Ay, we'll denounce him!
 All you who are friends of his bosom,
  Watch him askance.
 He may haply be fooled, and give us the power
  To wreak our revenge.'

11 But Yahwe is on my side,
  A Hero of might.
 Therefore my foes shall stumble,
  And shall not prevail.
 Shamed shall they be that they acted amiss,
  With eternal, never-forgotten disgrace.

----

[1] Reading with LXX אֶשָּׁחֵק for אֶזְעָק.

[2] מָגוֹר מִשָּׁבִיב is omitted as a gloss from xx. 3, yielding a wrong sense in this context. The rest of the verse is difficult, and the rendering given precarious. I read with LXX שְׁלֹמוֹ שָׁמְרוּ צַלְעוֹ for the Heb. שלמי שמרי צלעי.

¹² But, Yahwe of hosts, Thou righteous Searcher!
   Who seest the reins and the heart:
   Let me see Thy vengeance upon them;
   For on Thee I roll my complaint.

Jeremiah curses his Birth (xx. 14–18)

Curs'd be the day I was born,
   The day when my mother bore me—
      Be it unblessed!
Curs'd be the man who brought to my father
   The good news: 'A man-child is born'—
      Making him glad!

May that day[1] be like the cities
   That God overthrew,
      And pitied them not!
May its morning hear the cry of distress,
   Its noon the shout of battle!
Because it slew me not in the womb,
   That my mother had been my grave,
      And her womb pregnant for ever.

Why came I forth from the womb
   To see trouble and sorrow,
      To consume my days in shame?

II

The first question that arises with regard to these passages is whether they form a connected series, recording the stages of a definite, though more or less protracted, spiritual crisis in Jeremiah's life, or whether they reflect passing moods to which he was subject at all periods of his career. And if the former view be adopted we have further to inquire to what part of his life this crisis belongs. I have already mentioned the probability that the first two passages (in chs. xi and xii) were written at the time of his flight from

------

[1] The text reads 'that man.'

Anathoth in the fifth or sixth year of his ministry (see pp. 109 ff.). But the later ones presuppose a longer experience of opposition and failure than Jeremiah could look back upon at that time. The usual opinion of scholars is that these date mostly from the last years of his activity, so that the inward conflict which they record was carried on amidst the external trials and dangers of which we have a full report in the narrative of Baruch. It is pretty generally surmised, for instance, that the passages in ch. xx have a biographical connexion with the night spent in the stocks described in the immediately preceding verses. There is little evidence for or against this presumption. On the whole I incline to the view that the entire series falls within the middle period of his work, before he had become a prominent actor on the stage of politics. The kind of persecution alluded to in chs. xviii and xx, with its crafty and furtive devices to entangle him in his talk, and find a ground of accusation against him, is not exactly what we should expect when he was at open war with the hierarchy and the court; it even suggests that his audience was confined to a narrow circle of friends and adherents, so that it was difficult for his enemies to ascertain the precise tenor of his teaching. And it is not at all improbable that this was really the character of Jeremiah's ministry during the last twelve years of Josiah. It seems to me that we can understand Jeremiah better if we think of the spiritual agony of the 'Confessions' as the Gethsemane, rather than the Calvary, of his life. When we behold the calm courage and self-possession with which he faces death and outrage and imprisonment under Jehoiakim and Zedekiah, we get the impression of a man whose inward struggles are over, who has emerged with the victory over himself, and braced for his closing part. And the marvellous lucidity and composure of his outlook on the future

destiny of God's kingdom seems based on the knowledge of his own indissoluble relation to God, and the
clear insight into the essentially religious constitution
of human nature, which he gained largely through the
experience which is enshrined in his 'Confessions.' I
think we are entitled at least to proceed on the assumption that there is a psychological continuity in the
passages we are about to consider—that they exhibit in
its different aspects one great spiritual conflict which is
the key to Jeremiah's inner life.

III

The central interest of the 'Confessions' is the
struggle in Jeremiah's mind between fidelity to his
prophetic commission and the natural feelings and
impulses of his heart. This resolves itself into several
elements, which may be partly isolated and looked at
separately.

The first and most obvious feature is the extraordinary effect on the mind of the prophet of *persecution
and obloquy*. He had been prepared for opposition by
his call to office, and had received the promise of
strength to endure it (i. 8, 17 ff.); but in the strange
and unexpected forms in which it was actually encountered by him, it almost unmanned him. He had
all the oriental's shrinking from ridicule, and sensitiveness to calumny; and both were his portion in full
measure. He is a laughing-stock all day long, an object
of derision to all; as often as he speaks he is mocked
(xx. 7, 8); his enemies assail him with the tongue (xviii.
18); every one curses him (xv. 10). His sympathetic
nature was wounded by the hatred and contempt to
which he was exposed, by the alienation of his fellows
and their misconstruction of his motives. He felt
keenly his isolation from the joys and common interests
of social life: 'I have not sat in the assembly of merry-

makers, rejoicing; because of thy hand I sat solitary'
(xv. 17; cf. xvi. 1 ff.). But besides all this he knew that
he had enemies who cherished designs on his life. It is
from the first of the Confessions that we learn of the
plot to assassinate him in Anathoth (xi. 18 ff.) and the
allusions of xviii. 18, 22, xx. 10 show that in Jerusalem
more subtle methods were employed to compass his
destruction. The knowledge of this produced in him a
feeling of resentment, which breaks out in imprecations
on his foes, startling in their concentrated force of
passion (see xi. 20, 22 f., xii. 3, xv. 15, xvii. 18, xviii.
23, xx. 11). There is a tendency among commentators
to clear Jeremiah of responsibility for such utterances
and assign their composition to later scribes who knew
not what spirit he was of. But they are too constant a
feature of the Confessions to be got rid of by the
hypothesis of interpolation, either on the subjective
ground that they are unworthy of Jeremiah, or because
they violate some doubtful metrical canon. That they
have been amplified here and there by later hands is
easily conceivable, and where there are signs of dis-
location of text (as in xviii. 20 ff.) we may reasonably
surmise that this has taken place; still, enough remains
to show that the prayer for vengeance was a real element
in Jeremiah's attitude towards his personal foes. The
business of the expositor is to understand and explain
the fact, not to deny its possibility (see pp. 223 f. below).

Jeremiah's distress, however, had a deeper cause in
the *failure and rejection of his prophetic message*. 'Behold
they say to me, Where is the word of Yahwe? Let it
come!' (xvii. 15). And this has two sides. On the one
hand it is a comfort and delight to him that 'for Yahwe's
sake he suffers reproach' (xv. 15); that it is the word of
the Lord which is to him 'a reproach and a derision all
day long' (xx. 8). There were times when his fellowship
with God was a source of deep spiritual joy (xv. 16),

when he was content to sit solitary because of His hand
(xv. 17), sustained by the consciousness that Yahwe
had spoken to him, and that 'His name was named
upon him' (xv. 16). But at other times, the seeming
futility of his work, the absence of any confirmation of
his word, filled him with despondency and exposed
him to temptation. Why was he left so long to be
mocked at as a discredited prophet of evil? Why
should Yahwe be to him as a deceitful brook, as waters
that fail? (xv. 18). He even dallied with the thought of
casting off the burden of prophetic responsibility, and
living the common natural life of men. But that was
only to aggravate his suffering. The word of the Lord
which had been an outward reproach now became an
inward torture: 'If I say, I will not think of Him nor
speak any more in His name, it is in my heart as a
burning fire shut up in my bones' (xx. 9). Yahwe has
brought him into a strait from which he can find
neither exit nor retreat. 'Thou hast deceived me, O
Yahwe,' he cries, 'and I have been deceived; Thou
hast been too strong for me and hast prevailed' (xx. 7).

Reading between the lines of the Confessions, we
can trace, in the next place, a process of *self-examination*
on the part of the prophet—a scrutiny of his motives
lest he has been in any way unworthy of his calling.
It is instructive to observe the point to which his
introspection is directed. We note the vehemence with
which he repels the insinuation that he has had a secret
delight in anticipating the doom which he announced
as Yahwe's inevitable sentence. He repeatedly calls
God to witness that he has not gone beyond the message
he was entrusted with: that he 'has not been urgent
for evil, nor desired the day of woe' (xvii. 16): that on
the contrary he has striven to act as a mediator with
Yahwe on behalf of the people, and of those very men
who were his sworn foes (xviii. 20, xv. 11). Yet the

very earnestness of his protestation suggests that he
was conscious of a moral danger at this point, into
which he had possibly fallen. 'The heart,' he says, 'is
more inscrutable than anything, and mortally sick:
who can know it?' (xvii. 9). Had he perhaps crossed the
invisible line between a holy zeal for the manifestation
of the divine righteousness and a selfish desire for his
own vindication? or between an awed submission to
Yahwe's purpose of judgment and a gloomy satisfaction
in being its instrument and herald? He has so far
within him the answer of a good conscience that he
can bring the obscure workings of his mind into the
light of God's omniscience, that he may know if there
be any wicked way in him. 'I, Yahwe, search the heart,
and try the reins, to give to each man according to his
ways, according to the fruit of his doings' (xvii. 10;
cf. xi. 20, xii. 3, xx. 12). But whether in that holy
presence he feels himself entirely clear in this matter is
a question which he does not answer, or answers only
indirectly in the divine admonition which recalls him
to a sense of his responsibility (xv. 19 ff.; see below).

Lastly, these poems reveal to us Jeremiah's experience of *prayer*. They are the outpouring of his heart to
One who seeth in secret and can reward openly. And
there is no doubt that the open reward is the object of
the prophet's most intense desire. He prays for healing
(xvii. 14)—which may mean either spiritual healing of
his sick heart[1] (xvii. 9), or removal of the troubles
which oppressed him and perhaps had undermined his
physical health—he prays for help against his adver-
saries (xvii. 18), for vindication of the cause he represents, and also (as we have seen) for vengeance on his
persecutors. But to Jeremiah prayer is more than
petition. It is intimate converse with God, in which his
whole inner life is laid bare, with its perplexities and

[1] So Duhm, Cornill, etc., connecting directly with *v*. 9.

struggles and temptations; and he unburdens himself of the distress which weighs down his spirit, in the sure confidence that he is heard and understood by the God to whom all things are naked and open. Now such prayer contains in itself the assurance of its answer; and in one striking passage, which we must regard as the climax of the 'Confessions,' Jeremiah comes to clear consciousness of the answer which solves the problem of his personal relation to God. 'Thus saith Yahwe, "If thou return, and I restore thee, thou shalt stand before Me; and if thou bring forth what is precious, unmixed with what is base, then thou shalt be as My mouth. These (enemies of thine) shall come round to thee, and not thou to them. And I will make thee to this people as an impregnable wall of brass...for I am with thee to help thee and to deliver thee..."' (xv. 19 ff.).

We can scarcely be wrong in thinking that this illumination, which comes to Jeremiah in answer to prayer, marks a turning-point in his life. It seems to point to a certain obscuration of his prophetic consciousness, as if the impulse of his youthful consecration had been exhausted by the continued strain and labour of his work. He appears to realise that he had come near to forfeiting his office by losing its spirit, and that he needed a renewal of his vocation, a reinstatement in his mission, if he was to continue to act as a prophet of Yahwe. He learns, further, that the condition of victory over the world is victory over himself. He who had sat as a gold-refiner, testing the lives of the men around him and finding them to be refuse silver (vi. 27 ff.), now discovers that all is not pure gold within himself. He sees that he must separate between the noble and the base in his own mind. In the presence of God he recognises that there is something unworthy and ignoble in those human feelings to which he has given such free and fearless expression—his querulous complaints against providence, his impatience for the verification of his predictions, and especially his vindictive spirit towards his enemies. Thoughts like those he has uttered mar his communion with the pure and holy Being whose name has been named upon him, and unfit him for His service. Only as he cleanses himself from these lower impulses of his nature, and brings forth things noble and right, can he stand before Yahwe and speak as His mouthpiece to his fellow men. Only so can he recover the joyous sense of God's favour which he 'had loved long since, and lost awhile,' or be clothed with the strength that overcomes the world. He is made to feel that the word of God is sharper than any two-edged sword, and pierces to the dividing asunder of soul and spirit, and is a discerner of the thoughts and intents of the heart. He gains a glimpse of the truth that the pure in heart alone can see God, and that only through what is Godlike in man are God's mind and purpose discerned.

IV

In the experience which I have thus attempted to analyse there is involved, as I have already remarked, a modification of the prophetic consciousness which gives to Jeremiah his peculiar importance in the history of the religion of Israel. It is necessary to devote a few paragraphs to the elucidation of this point; and in order to do so, it is worth while to glance briefly at the previous development of Hebrew prophecy along two lines: first as a theocratic institution, and next as a mode of divine revelation.

(a) When we speak of prophecy as a theocratic institution we mean that the prophet had a recognised position and function in the unwritten religious constitution of the Hebrew state. He was the medium of communication between Yahwe, the divine King of Israel, and His people. Prophecy was the power which in the hands of Samuel had welded the nation into a political unity by the establishment of the monarchy; and throughout its history it had never abdicated its mission to criticise the acts and policy of the secular rulers of the state. It claimed this right not, as is sometimes imagined, as the organ of democratic opinion, but (in idea at least) as the representative of Yahwe's prerogative, the organ through which He exercised His regal authority over Israel. Its place in the national life was, therefore, as constitutional as the kingship, of which in a sense it had been the creator. Both were religious institutions: the king was Yahwe's executive agent or vicegerent; the prophet was His mouthpiece; and in the inevitable conflicts which arose between the secular interests of the monarchy and the ethical demands of the true religion the prophet spoke with a moral authority which appealed to a deeply-rooted sentiment in the mind of the community.

It might indeed be objected that this function of prophecy was annulled in the case of the great prophets who, from Amos downwards, had announced the dissolution of the bond between Yahwe and Israel; and in principle that is true. These men were conscious of a personal vocation and an individual mission, which owed nothing to the public recognition of their office. But if the theocratic conception was virtually transcended, the consequences had not been drawn. The whole ministry of Isaiah is a proof that the thought of Yahwe's kingship was a living truth to his mind and a sustaining motive of his activity; and it was applied by him to political matters in the full conviction of Yahwe's claim to a controlling voice in the ordering of affairs of state. The essential fact is—and this is as true of Amos and Hosea and Micah as of Isaiah—that the prophet was still a vehicle of Yahwe's message *to the nation*. The correlate of the prophet, if I may so express it,—the recipient of his revelation—is Israel as a corporate entity; the response to the divine word, the only response that matters, has to be given by the nation as a whole; what the prophet himself feels about it is a question strictly irrelevant to his mission. He stands wholly on the side of God as the medium through whom He has chosen to reveal His mind to His people. He is of course a self-conscious medium; his reason, his conscience, his perceptions of spiritual and religious truth, are all actively employed in the discharge of his duty. But there is no internal schism, no reaction of any part of his being against the word of the Lord; or if there be a conflict (as in the case of Hosea), it is transferred from the human mind to the divine, and becomes part of the one indivisible message which the prophet has to utter. Such is the conception we are led to form from the recorded experience of these prophets; and even if they had their moments of hesitancy and inward revolt, still the fact that they do not disclose them shows that they did not regard them as having positive religious value either for themselves or for others.

Now the public ministry of Jeremiah was entirely modelled on this theocratic idea of the function of the prophet in the state, and differed in no material respect from that of his predecessors. Like them he stood over against the people as the organ of Yahwe's revelation, appealing to the national conscience, and labouring to bring about a national conversion. He knew that he preached to deaf ears, and that his labour would be in vain—that Judah would not, and (as he ever more clearly saw) *could not*, repent; and that therefore the word of Yahwe must be verified in its destruction[1].

[1] There seems to be nothing to support the theory of Erbt, that he ever turned aside from this main task, hopeless though it was, to work for the conversion of individuals, or even (like Isaiah) to form a new spiritual fellowship composed of men in whom his word found a believing response.

In all this Jeremiah is 'as one of the prophets.' But it is evident that the theocratic conception of the prophetic office could not survive the downfall of the Jewish state, which alone had supplied the requisite conditions for the normal exercise of the prophet's calling. We cannot doubt that the presentiment of that impending catastrophe overshadowed Jeremiah's mind, and impelled him to seek a deeper foundation for his prophetic relation to God than in the things that were shaken and ready to pass away. And in his Confessions we see something of the inward process through which a larger vision came to him.

We see that the controversy between Yahwe and Israel was reflected in his own consciousness, in a heart-rending conflict between his natural love for his nation and his sense of what Yahwe's righteousness demanded. As a true and loyal Israelite, he was slow to abandon the hope that the alienation might be removed; and in this hope he had sought to bridge the gulf between Israel and its God by his personal intercession. Once and again the impulse to intercessory prayer had welled up from the depth of his affection for his brethren (xviii. 20, xv. 11), but only to be checked by the stern mandate of the inner voice that spoke to him through his conscience. 'Pray not thou for this people, neither lift up cry or prayer on their behalf, and do not intercede with Me; for I will not hear thee' (vii. 16; cf. xiv. 11 f., xi. 14). At such moments the inexorableness of the divine justice came home to him with overwhelming power, and compelled him to acquiesce in the sentence of rejection on the nation. At the same time we see that the effect of his preaching in the prevailing temper of indifference and impenitence had been to set the opinion of the people strongly against him, and isolate him completely from their fellowship. Thus on both sides 'his efforts to heal the breach between Yahwe and the nation had only resulted in a sharp antagonism between himself and his compatriots' (Wellhausen, *Isr. u. jüd. Gesch.* p. 149). He was forced to realise that he stood alone on the side of God, the bearer of a revelation which found no response anywhere except in his own heart. With greater truth than Elijah he could have said 'I, even I only, am left, and they seek my life to take it away' (1 Kings xix. 10, 14). It was as if the believing remnant which to Isaiah had represented the spiritual kernel of Israel and the hope of its future had shrunk in Jeremiah's view to the limits of his own individual life[1].

In such a situation we may say that one of two things must happen. Either the prophet will despair of religion, the word of God on which it depends having proved to be seed which can find no soil in human nature wherein it could germinate, or a purely destructive force without power to build and plant and renew. Or else he will find in himself, in his own assent to its truth and his sense of its imperishable worth, the germ and pledge of a new religious relationship, and a proof that there is that in the human heart which will not let the truth of God perish. The second is what happened with Jeremiah. Disowned by men and driven in upon himself, he found in the truth of his rejected prophecy an indissoluble link of communion between his own soul and God. Amid all his tribulations and the defeat of his lifework, it was a blessedness of which nothing could rob him that Yahwe, the God of Israel, had spoken to him, and received him into His fellowship. And in this individual response to the voice of God he discovered an earnest of that instinctive and universal sense of the divine in which he recognised the permanent essence of religion (viii. 7; see pp. 120 ff. above).

[1] See Wellhausen, *op. cit.*; 1st Ed., p. 77; a passage omitted in later editions.

(*b*) When we look at prophecy, in the second place, as a human medium of revelation, we can trace a progressive emancipation of its spiritual essence from the ecstatic or visionary forms in which its earlier manifestations consist. At the lowest stage of prophecy of which we need here to take any account, inspiration and ecstasy are identified. Revelation was an occasional thing; the prophet or seer was a man endowed with a peculiar psychopathic susceptibility to divine suggestion or influence, who delivered his oracles piecemeal as they came to him. His message consists either of words uttered unconsciously in a state of trance, or of an announcement of what he has seen and heard in vision; his conscious mental powers playing no essential part in the process. We have an example of this type of prophecy in the Old Testament in the heathen sooth-sayer Balaam—'the man whose eye is closed, who seeth the vision of the Almighty, fallen down and having his eyes uncovered' (Num. xxiv. 3, 4, 15, 16)—and perhaps another in Micaiah ben-Imlah in the time of Elijah and Ahab (1 Kings xxii. 15 ff.). On the higher level repre-sented by the great prophets of Israel this crude and fragmentary conception of inspiration is left far behind. Visions and auditions, mysterious inward promptings to speech and action, are still a part of the prophet's experience; but the field of revelation is no longer confined to them alone. The *meaning* of the vision passes into the prophet's thinking, and becomes the nucleus of a comprehensive view of God and the world, from which spring ever fresh intuitions of truth and calls to duty. That these again may clothe themselves involun-tarily in symbolic imagery is a fact which does not in the least detract from the essentially spiritual character of the prophet's discernment of the mind of God. He reflects upon what he has seen and heard, and interprets its significance to himself and his hearers; and the substance of his revelation is not the mere vision or audition itself but the truth which it has evoked or symbolised in his mind. Thus his reasoning and moral faculties are actively engaged in the discovery and delivery of his message; and all that comes home to him with immediate certainty as the result of his initiation into the divine purpose is as truly the word of God to him as the content of the vision itself. The clearest illustration of this phase of prophecy is seen in Isaiah, whose inaugural vision gave the first impulse to his life's thought and activity, and yet was not published till several years after his work began. But Amos and Hosea and Micah all stand on the same high plane of prophetic inspiration.

The difference between Jeremiah and these earlier prophets is merely that the ecstatic and the intuitive or reflective elements of his experience are more sharply distinguished in his mind than appears to have been the case with them, and that he relies more explicitly than they on the intuition. We saw in our last chapter[1] that his controversy with the false prophets of his day led him to deny all revelational value to the vision as a mere psychological fact. He does not doubt the reality of his own visions, nor does he deny that his opponents have visions of a sort; but he finds the ultimate criterion of inspiration in a personal knowledge of Yahwe which he has and they have not. So in the Confessions he apprehends the word of God in two forms: an impersonal form, which is a survival of the ecstatic mode of revelation; and a personal form, which appeals directly to his conscience and reason. The former appears in the internal pressure which compels him to speak in the name of Yahwe, and against which he struggles in vain (xx. 9); and the latter in the divine answer to his perplexities and prayers which commands the assent of his

[1] pp. 194 f.

moral and religious sense by its inherent self-evidencing
power (xv. 19 ff.). Now this second form of inspiration
may be said to be the vanishing-point of the prophetic
consciousness, where it shakes off the last remnant of
subconscious thought, which had served its purpose in
the providential education of the people of religion, and
gives place to what had always been the spiritual
essence of true prophecy—the intuitive certainty of
divine truth, and the illumination of the whole conscious mind by the Spirit of God.

The peculiar importance of Jeremiah's position in
the religious history of Israel might be tersely expressed
by saying that he embodies the transition from the
prophet to the Psalmist. In the same sense in which he
is called the last of the prophets, he may be regarded
as the first of the psalmists. No doubt there were
psalmists before Jeremiah, as there were prophets after
him; but just as the one movement culminates and comes
to its purest expression in his person, so the other owes
much of what is vital and precious in its spirit to his
influence. Prophecy's last effort, Dr Davidson has said,
was to reveal itself in a life; and we can add that that
life, in which prophecy effloresced, contained the germ
of the devotional poetry of the Psalter.

The secret of the transmutation lies before us in the
'Confessions,' and has been partly elucidated in the
foregoing exposition. We have seen how the prophetic
vocation became to Jeremiah the centre of a new and
more intimately human relation to God, which expanded into a life of prayer and communion, in which
all that concerned him, his temptations, his perplexities,
and the burden of his work, formed the subject of an
intimate introspective dialogue between himself and the
divine voice that echoed mysteriously through the

secret chambers of his soul. It was this reaction of his human subjectivity on the fact of his prophetic call which unsealed within him the perennial fountain of true piety—the religious receptivity of the individual. Out of the Hebrew prophet, there is created in Jeremiah a new spiritual type—the Old Testament saint: the man who, when flesh and heart fail, finds in God the strength of his heart and his portion for ever (Ps. lxxiii. 26). It remains for us to sketch briefly the outstanding features of this type of piety, as exhibited in Jeremiah.

1. Its first and most obvious characteristic is its strongly marked *individualism*. In the case of Jeremiah this is naturally accounted for by the peculiar circumstances of his life; and it may be that only an altogether exceptional experience like his could have found a path from the national and prophetic religion of ancient Israel to the personal religion of the later Jewish Church and Christianity. At all events it is with his experience that we are here concerned; and the significant fact is that in writing the 'Confessions' he felt himself absolutely cut off from religious fellowship with men. The bond between him and his nation was broken, or ceased to be a religious bond, from the time when he realised that he stood alone for Yahwe against a people whom he still loved, but for whom he might not pray. Individual men are present to his thoughts only as foes, persecutors, and despisers of God's word. He seemed to himself the one religious person in his generation, the only man who knew Yahwe and stood in immediate relation to Him. In this consciousness of spiritual isolation, it seemed further to Jeremiah that the whole cause of Yahwe in the world hung on his individual life—upon his inward fidelity to the truth revealed to him, and also on his outward vindication in the sight of men. This is the explanation, even if it be not a justification, of his passionate desire for the discomfiture

of his enemies. Either they must go under or he; either they or he must be put to everlasting shame and confusion. And forasmuch as he was persuaded that the truth of God stood or fell with him, he felt assured of final victory over his foes, and prayed with a good conscience that he might see Yahwe's vengeance upon them. If we judge this attitude of mind from the standpoint of the Christian ideal, we must recognise the truth of Smend's remark that 'Jeremiah was no martyr in the New Testament sense[1].' He could not himself hold on to the truth if Yahwe should leave him naked to his enemies' scorn. He had not learned the secret of victory through defeat and death.

Such was the cradle of individual religion, as it came to birth in the person of Jeremiah. Now individualism is not the last word in religion, nor was it Jeremiah's last word. The time came, as we shall see in a future connexion, when his private relation to God, combined with other elements in his thinking, broadened out into the conception of a new community of the people of God, based on direct personal knowledge of God such as he alone at this time possessed. Nevertheless, both in his experience and in the history of revelation, individualism was a necessary stage towards the formation of the new humanity whose Head is Christ. It is also perhaps a stage which is repeated in every life that attains to saintly excellence. There are in every deeply religious life moments when earthly relationships fall away, when the life of active service is suspended, and the soul is left alone with God, having nothing in heaven or earth to desire besides Him. The deepening of religion on its subjective side, begun in Jeremiah and continued in a succession of like-minded psalmists, is the best part of the legacy which Judaism has bequeathed to the Christian Church. It explored and brought to

[1] *Alttestamentliche Religionsgeschichte* (2nd Ed.), p. 261.

light the capacity of the human spirit for fellowship with the Divine, which was the preparation for the gathering together into one through Jesus Christ of the children of God who are scattered abroad (John xi. 52).

2. The basis of Jeremiah's personal religion is his trust in the unerring righteousness of God. He was the first to carry that great prophetic idea into the sphere of the individual life. Yahwe was to him the Righteous Judge, the all-seeing Searcher of hearts, who gives to every man according to his deeds (xvii. 9, xii. 3, xx. 12). This conception of God is a reflexion of the process by which he experienced the divine working within him. He was too sincere not to be conscious of his fundamental integrity, but too sensitive morally not to be aware of the possibilities of evil that lurked in the inscrutable depths of his nature. We have seen how he shudders at the discovery of the deceitfulness of his heart, with what jealousy he examines into the purity of his motives, how earnestly he strives to rid himself of all illusion and unreality and self deception. This we call the operation of conscience; but to Jeremiah it is the eye of Yahwe searching the thoughts and intents of the heart, and bringing to light things hidden from himself. And once more the process starts from the close personal relation to God imposed on him by his prophetic mission. If Yahwe has called him to be a prophet, He must see in him something which fits him for His service and friendship; and Jeremiah recognises it to be his supreme moral task to be this something, to eliminate the baser elements of his character and live wholly and resolutely in the good and true, that he may stand approved and without offence in God's holy sight. He is of those who walk in the light, and have fellowship with the God who is light, and in whom is no darkness at all.

Now this note of *moral sincerity*, springing from a

vivid realisation of the omniscience and righteousness of God, is one that is repeatedly struck in the meditations and prayers of the Psalter. The deeply exercised writer of the 51st Psalm knows that 'truth in the inward parts'· is the indispensable condition of restoration to Yahwe's favour and the joy of his salvation; the writer of the 139th revels in the thought of God's exhaustive and unescapable knowledge of him, and closes his meditation with the remarkable prayer, conceived in the very spirit of Jeremiah: 'Search me, O God, and know my heart: Try me and know my thoughts: And see if there be any way of wickedness in me, and lead me in the way everlasting'; and other illustrations might be cited. At times such utterances may strike us as deficient in evangelical humility. There is often an insistent protestation of integrity which savours of self-righteousness; we miss the utter abnegation of merit, the emptying of self, the absolute dependence on a goodness and a love outside of ourselves which regards not our desert but our need, such as are expressed in many favourite Christian hymns[1].

But on the other hand the strong ethical sense of the Psalmists and Jeremiah supplies a needful corrective to the opposite error to which evangelical piety is itself

[1] For example, in Christina Rossetti's:

None other Lamb, none other name,
    None other hope in heaven or earth or sea.
None other hiding-place from guilt and shame
    None beside Thee!

My faith burns low, my hope burns low;
    Only my heart's desire cries out in me
By the deep thunder of its want and woe,
    Cries out to Thee.

Lord, Thou art life, though I be dead;
    Love's fire art Thou, however cold I be:
Nor heaven have I, nor place to lay my head,
    Nor home, but Thee.

exposed. For if the too obtrusive consciousness of moral sincerity as a claim on the divine mercy involves the danger of spiritual pride, the absence of the thing itself would be fatal to all true godliness; and there is a hypocrisy of self-depreciation into which a spurious and sentimental spirituality is apt to fall. In any case it was a great step in the history of religion to turn from the formalism of an external worship, and the legalism of a national covenant, and to find God in the heart of the individual, as One whose holy and searching presence strengthens every good purpose and pure aspiration that dwells there, and who sets secret sins in the light of His countenance. By the grace of God Jeremiah took that step, and opened up a way of access to God which many devout souls, following in his footprints, found to be the way everlasting.

3. Jeremiah is original above all in the exercise of *prayer*. Prayer is the universal form in which communion with God finds expression, and is rightly described as the 'vital breath,' the 'native air' of individual religion. How far the older prophets were men of prayer is a question which we have slight means of answering. The theory of Oehler, Riehm, Giesebrecht and others, that the prophetic revelation always came in answer to prayer, is mainly a generalisation from the case of Jeremiah, which may or may not be legitimate. We may suspect that in this respect, as in so many others, Jeremiah's experience was *sui generis*. Now it is an interesting fact in his spiritual history that his first efforts in prayer were intercessory or mediatorial prayers for the nation whose doom he was compelled to pronounce. He had felt that such intercession was unavailing. It was not in accordance with the will of Yahwe as revealed to him; it was but the protest of his natural feeling against the conviction that the judgment was inevitable. And it was partly through the rejection

of his prayer for others that he learned to pray for himself. He has been named by Wellhausen 'the father of true prayer,' as being the first in whom the higher spiritual qualities of prayer come to light. Devotional writers speak of a 'ladder of prayer'; by which they mean the successive stages through which the individual enters into the full possession of the grace and privilege of prayer. But there is a similar ladder in the historical evolution of religion; and among the innumerable steps in that ladder there are three which may be distinguished. The lowest is that of petition for the fulfilment of some particular desire, or the removal of some external evil, solely in the interest of the individual himself. Such prayer is common to every known form and phase of religion. The second stage is that on which Jeremiah enters. Here prayer is the effort of the soul to bring every thought and feeling into harmony with the will of God, and to find its true good in being right with Him. Although it is neither selfish nor self-centred, it contains a certain residuum of self-will—an unresolved difference of the two wills, arising from the man's inability to conceive that what he deems to be necessary for his good can possibly be other than what God wills that he should have: in Jeremiah's case the overthrow of his enemies. There is a third stage, to which perhaps he hardly attains, where the thought of self is entirely lost, and the mind surrenders itself wholly to the divine will as that which alone is truly good. 'Father, not my will but Thine be done.'

4. And this leads me to some concluding observations on the *limitations* of Jeremiah's religious experience, judged of course by comparison with the Christian ideal. Nearly fifty years ago, Bernhard Duhm, since known as one of the most gifted interpreters of the mind of Jeremiah, wrote these words: 'If it had been possible for him to find the indispensable idea of the

religious community, so necessary for the existence of
the religious individual, he would have *anticipated
Christianity*; and as his person so often reminds us of
Christ, so his theology would remind us of the Christian
conception of the kingdom of God[1].' If this statement
implies, as it appears to do, that but for that one *lacuna*
in his thinking, Jeremiah could have been the founder
of the Christian religion, it is a rash and empty speculation, which the distinguished author would probably
not defend to-day. Jesus Christ would have said that
though among men born of women there had not
arisen a greater than Jeremiah, yet he that is least in
the kingdom of heaven is greater than he. Putting that
aside, however, I think that the defects of his piety are
mainly traceable to a single root: viz. an incomplete
possession by the spirit of love, which is the medium
of perfect communion with God. It is strange at first
sight that one who had such a profound conviction of
the love of Yahwe for Israel drew so little upon it for
himself. God is to him the all-seeing, all-righteous
Judge, rather than a loving Father. It is true that in
the recognition of his personal worth by Yahwe he does
experience the divine love in a measure; but we can
scarcely speak of him as one in whom the love of God
was perfected. He did not enter into the truth that God
is love, and he that dwelleth in love dwelleth in God,
and God in him. His was not the perfect love that
casteth out fear; for great as his faith in Yahwe is it
does not deliver him from fear that His cause may
suffer shipwreck through the triumph of his foes.
Again, does he not come under the sweep of the great
Johannine maxim that 'he that loveth not his brother
whom he hath seen, how can he love God whom he
hath not seen'? His feeling towards his persecutors is
natural and excusable, and in a sense just, but it is not

[1] *Theol. d. Proph.* p. 251.

the spirit of love which inspires a prayer for their
destruction. Jeremiah had not learned the lesson of the
Cross, or the mind which in the agony of death could
pray, 'Father, forgive them, for they know not what
they do'; 'Lord, lay not this sin to their charge.' A later
generation read something of that lesson in the long
drawn out tragedy of his career, but Jeremiah went
down to the grave, stedfast to the end in his loyalty to
the truth, but without the consolation of seeing that
the pleasure of the Lord had prospered in his hands.

CHAPTER XII

THE NEW FOE FROM THE NORTH

THE battle of Megiddo (608 B.C.), and the stirring events which rapidly followed, mark the opening of a new chapter in Jeremiah's life. What we may call the Deuteronomic period, with its comparative prosperity, its political optimism, and its religious insincerity, had come to an end, and soon the ship of state was labouring in a heavy sea which called for more skilful steersmanship than its rulers could bring to their task. The crisis found Jeremiah still in the prime of life—probably not more than forty years of age—and he faced it with the serene courage and wisdom of one who stood in the council of the Lord and knew His purpose. While the religious and prophetic convictions which underlay all his work remain unchanged, his energies are directed into a new channel. Hitherto he seems to have held aloof from political action, confining himself to the hortatory side of his mission, while maturing in secret those conceptions of the essential nature of religion which were to be his guiding light in the stormy years that lay before him. But from about 608 onwards he appears to have exercised a political ministry hardly less influential than that of Isaiah in a previous generation. He certainly becomes one of the outstanding public figures of the time, and plays an active part as an adviser in public and national affairs.

We must note in passing that it is about this time that we begin to see Jeremiah through the eyes of a sympathetic and well-informed contemporary, Baruch, the son of Neraiah, to whose *memorabilia* we are probably indebted for most of our knowledge of the prophet's public appearances. It is just possible, therefore, that if Baruch had become acquainted with Jeremiah sooner, or if his narrative had commenced at an earlier period, we might have a different impression of the prophet's previous activity from that which we form from his own extant oracles, detached as they mostly are from any definite situation. But on the other hand it is equally probable that it was the new publicity on which Jeremiah had entered that drew Baruch to his side, and established the close and fruitful intimacy which obtained between the prophet and his biographer. However that may be, we have now to study Jeremiah as an actor on the stage of politics, and to see how his fundamental principles were worked out in their application to a rapidly developing political situation.

Now it is a significant feature of the ministry of Jeremiah that its latest phase returns to its earliest in the renewed expectation of danger from the north. He had commenced as a prophet by announcing that 'Evil looms from the North and great destruction' (vi. 1; cf. iv. 6). In the Scythian terror of his youth he had heard the muttering of the storm that was to break on his people and hurl them to destruction; and doubtless he had looked for a speedy realisation of his vision of woe. But the danger had passed away: the northern sky cleared up, and it seemed as if assured peace had come to Judah through the mercy of its God. For twenty years Jeremiah had borne the reproach of a false and discredited prophet. Again and again the mocking taunt had assailed his ears: 'Where is the word of Yahwe? Let it come, pray!' (xvii. 15). Yet he remained unshaken in the confidence that his message had been true, and he preserved the oracles in which it had been expressed as words of Yahwe whose verification was certain. And now at last the Foe from the North appears again in a more formidable guise; he is not the Scythians, but a new power raised up by God to be the instrument of His people's overthrow. Yahwe, who had seemed to be asleep, proves Himself to be 'wakeful over His word to fulfil it' (ch. i. 12). And the prophet's youthful foreboding, clarified by larger knowledge of the world and of the forces that make history, returns upon him with redoubled conviction as he sees more and more clearly the unfolding of the providential purpose of judgment on the impenitent people of Israel. This new power is the Chaldean empire of Nebuchadnezzar. Let us first trace the series of events which brought this power within the prophet's horizon.

We start from the battle of Megiddo. That battle, we are told by the writer of the book of Chronicles (2 Chron. xxxv. 21 ff.; cf. 1 Esdras i. 26 ff.) was fought by the Egyptian monarch against his wish, being forced on him by the fatal obstinacy of Josiah. What motive induced the king of Judah to provoke the unequal conflict we are not told: most probably it was a resolve, fortified by reliance on the Covenant with Yahwe, to maintain the independence of the sacred territory which, though not immediately threatened, would undoubtedly have been lost in the event of an Egyptian success. The real objective of Pharaoh Necho's expedition was the Euphrates, where he hoped to establish himself in possession of all Syria as it fell from the enfeebled grasp of the Assyrian empire. And in fact the fall of Nineveh in 606 found him still in command of the coveted province. He was able to veto the popular election of Shallum, or Jehoahaz, to the vacant throne of Judah, and installed as his viceroy the eldest son of Josiah, Eliakim, bestowing on him his better known name of Jehoiakim. There was, however, a rival claimant to the lordship of western Asia with whom Necho had still to reckon. Nabopolassar, the Chaldean king of

Babylon, dispatched an army under his son Nebuchadnezzar to the upper Euphrates, where the Egyptians
suffered a crushing defeat in the decisive battle of
Carchemish (605 B.C.). Necho was compelled to
evacuate all his Asiatic conquests, and leave Nebuchadnezzar, who had just succeeded to his father's throne,
undisputed master of Syria and Palestine. 'The king
of Egypt came no more out of his land' (2 Kings
xxiv. 7).

Jeremiah could not have been a passive spectator of
these critical events. It is certainly surprising that no
extant prophecy of his can be plausibly read as a warning against the infatuated policy which led to the disaster
of Megiddo[1]. We can imagine what Isaiah's action
would have been in such an emergency. How he would
have thundered out his denunciations of the recklessness
and short-sightedness of the militarists: how he would
have unmasked their secret intrigues, and used every
means in his power to awaken public opinion to the
danger of their project! Jeremiah showed himself
capable of equally vigorous action on a later occasion
(chs. xxvii, xxviii), and if he was silent at this time
the most probable reason is that he had not yet taken
up the *rôle* of political adviser which was soon to be
thrust upon him.

The first certain indication of his absorbing interest
in current political events is his lament over the fate in
store for the young prince Jehoahaz when he was
summoned before Pharaoh Necho at his headquarters
at Riblah (2 Kings xxiii. 33). It would seem that the

---

[1] In 1 Esdras iii. 28 it is assumed that Jeremiah must have warned
Josiah against this step. Schmidt (*op. cit.* p. 278) surmises that the
incident of the broken bottle in ch. xix. 1–xx. 6 may have reference to
this ill-fated enterprise; and Erbt (p. 148) suggests a similar origin for the
short oracle of xiii. 12 f.; but there is little to support either of these
interpretations.

protracted obsequies of the dead king Josiah were being
performed[1], when Jeremiah appeared before the wailing
multitude and recited this dirge (ch. xxii. 10):

> Weep ye not for him that is dead,
>> Neither bemoan him.
> But weep, yea weep, for him who goes away;
>> For he shall return no more,
>> Nor see his native land.

It is a mistake, however, to suppose that this plaintive
elegy reveals a political bias on the part of the prophet[2].
Political faction was no doubt actively at work in regard
to the succession to the crown. Jehoahaz had been
elected by popular acclamation in opposition to the
heir-apparent Jehoiakim. Since Necho deposed and
imprisoned him and put his elder brother on the throne,
we may reasonably infer that Jehoiakim had made
interest with the Pharaoh, and became the centre of a
pro-Egyptian party in Jerusalem. His adherents were a
section of the aristocracy and the priesthood. Jehoahaz
may therefore have stood for the policy of his father
Josiah, the policy of national independence in reliance
on Yahwe; and his election would show that democratic
opinion was on that side. But Jeremiah's oracle is no
more an expression of sympathy with that view than of
antagonism to the policy of Josiah, which so far as we
can see must have been identical with that represented
by Jehoahaz. It is simply an outpouring of personal
emotion, inspired by the prophetic insight which
assured him that the unhappy prince who was to return
no more had 'left behind' no 'powers that would work
for him,' but that fresh misfortunes and causes of mourning lay before the people as it stumbled blindly forward
toward the dark mountains.

---

[1] It may be supposed that the reign of Jehoahaz was even shorter
than the arbitrary three months assigned to him in the Chronology
(2 Kings xxiii. 31).   [2] Erbt, *op. cit.* p. 269.

To this period belongs the great Temple oration of chs. vii, xxvi, which we have already examined in a former connexion[1]. Since its contents are not political we need not dwell further on it here, except to note that Jeremiah at this time found support in the higher ranks of society. It is significant that Ahikam, a son of one of the original promoters of Deuteronomy, was on his side, in opposition to the priests and prophets, who were partisans of the perverted interpretation of the Code against which Jeremiah protested. But apart from that, there is evidence of a marked difference of temper between the priesthood and the secular nobility. The priests were Jeremiah's natural and inveterate enemies, and their behaviour on this occasion excites no surprise. The lay aristocrats may not have been his friends; they may not have been members of the prophetic party, or deeply concerned for the interests of religion; but at least they were a body of open-minded and unprejudiced men, who were prepared to resist the encroachments of priestly bigotry, and maintain the right of prophecy to a free voice in the forum of public opinion. The fact is interesting in view of the change which passed over the spirit of the governing class, first under the influence of Jehoiakim's despotic rule, and later through the rise to power of a lower social stratum after the first deportation to Babylon.

Our next glimpse of Jewish politics is in the fourth and fifth years of Jehoiakim: the time when the battle of Carchemish put an end to the Egyptian suzerainty in Palestine. It was either the news of this event or a prophetic anticipation of it that moved Jeremiah to take the most momentous step in his public career. He resolved to make a last effort to reach the conscience of his countrymen by a solemn recital of all the words of warning which Yahwe had imparted to him since the

[1] pp. 168–174.

beginning of his ministry. With the assistance of
Baruch, a professional writer, he prepared a roll of his
prophecies ready for public reading when a suitable
occasion should present itself. He had to wait several
months[1]; but at last, in December of the year 604, the
proclamation of a national fast afforded the fitting
opportunity. Jeremiah was at this time for some reason
'hindered[2]' from appearing in the Temple, and dele-
gated the hazardous task to Baruch (ch. xxxvi). It is clear
that by this time tidings of what had happened on the
Euphrates had reached Jerusalem, and both in the court
and among the people the gloomiest apprehensions prevailed. The prospect of another invasion like that of
Sennacherib in 701 was enough to fill the boldest with
alarm; and the king, shivering over his winter fire
(v. 22), must have shivered inwardly as he contemplated
the miscarriage of the mistaken policy which for four
short years had kept him on the throne. Now, if ever,
Jeremiah may have thought, the nation was in a mood
to listen to his message.

[1] From a comparison of xxxvi. 1 with xxxvi. 9 it would seem to follow
that at least nine months elapsed between the writing and the reading
of the roll. But this improbably long interval is reduced to a *minimum*
of three months if we assume that the *years* are reckoned according to the
old Hebrew calendar from harvest to harvest, while the numbering of
the *months* follows (as always) the Babylonian calendar, whose year
began in the spring. The fifth year of Jehoiakim would then be from
Oct. 604 to Sept. 603, and the ninth month of that year would be Dec.
604; and if the roll was written in the end of the fourth year of the reign
it could have been read within little more than three months from that
time. So Steuernagel, *Einleitung*, p. 539.

[2] עָצוּר, v. 5. The word is used in some obscure technical sense in
1 Sam. xxi. 8, Neh. vi. 10, but neither of these passages throws any
light on the cause of Jeremiah's exclusion. It is clear from the narrative
that imprisonment (as in xxxiii. 1, xxxix. 15) is not indicated; and we
seem reduced to the alternative between some Levitical defilement con-
tracted by the prophet, and an interdict imposed on him by the Temple
authorities in consequence of the incidents recorded in ch. xxvi.

The sequel showed that he had not altogether mis-
judged the effect of this novel appeal to the chastened
disposition of the people. The multitude listened to
Baruch without murmur or tumult. Even the priests
and prophets were awed into silence and inaction. It is
a little more difficult to divine the attitude of the nobles.
It appears that we have to distinguish two groups of
the aristocracy. The first is the *sārîm*, the ministers of
State and royal councillors, who during the public
reading of the roll were in conclave in the palace in the
chamber of Elishama the secretary: five of these are
named. The other group consists of the 'servants of the
king'—the courtiers proper, and the royal princes, who
were in attendance on their master in an inner chamber
of the winter palace; and of these, three happen to be
mentioned. When we observe this distinction the situation becomes a little more clear. It is evident that the
ministers were deeply impressed. When the proceedings
in the Temple court are announced to them, they send
for Baruch, and make him sit down and read the
volume in their hearing. When he had finished they
took counsel together (LXX), or sat with awe-struck
faces (MT), and decided that they must report the
matter to the king. But first they urge Baruch to go
with Jeremiah into hiding, obviously in order to screen
them from the vengeance of Jehoiakim. Of the courtiers,
on the other hand, it is recorded in *v.* 24 that they, like
the king, 'trembled not nor rent their clothes': i.e.
they felt or affected a supercilious contempt for the
words of the prophet. We thus see that there was a
cleavage between the king with his immediate *entourage*
and the high officials who conducted the business of
state: whence we may conclude that Jehoiakim had not
yet succeeded in forming a government after his own
mind. It is noteworthy that among the well-disposed
aristocrats the family of Shaphan, so stedfast in its

loyalty to Jeremiah, is again represented (*vv.* 10 f.), and a son of Shaphan was one of the three (in LXX two) ministers who tried to prevent the king from burning the roll[1] (*v.* 25)[2].

The important point for us is that this was a reproduction of old prophecies of doom extending back to the beginning of Jeremiah's ministry. The significance of this fact is unmistakable. It means that to Jeremiah the end is now in sight, and the way of its coming in the main apparent. The new power of Babylon is the instrument fashioned by Yahwe for the execution of His purpose to destroy the remnant of His people Israel. In the contest being waged on the banks of the Euphrates the prophet recognises one of the great turning points of history, which change the face of human affairs and direct the stream of national destiny into new channels[3]. Henceforth the sceptre of empire

---

[1] The LXX, however, reads the opposite.

[2] A critic would give a good deal to know the contents of the roll read by Baruch on this occasion. It cannot have been very long, for it was read through three times within a few hours. Neither can it have been very short, if it contained all the words spoken by Yahwe to Jeremiah 'against Jerusalem and Judah' up to that time. Everything goes to show that it is all comprised within the first 25 chapters of the present book, excluding of course prophecies of later date than 604, and the numerous editorial expansions of those which remain, and probably excluding also the private confessions and prayers of Jeremiah, and possibly the promises of restoration in ch. iii, and other pieces irrelevant to the prophet's immediate purpose. All this is more or less uncertain; and it is very doubtful if the common opinion be correct, that the recovery of the original roll would give us the key to the structure of the present book of Jeremiah.

[3] If we could believe, as some good scholars do, that ch. xlvi contains genuine oracles of Jeremiah, we should have evidence that he watched the struggle with a gloating satisfaction over the impending overthrow of Egypt. But the whole of that chapter is so unlike anything else from the pen of Jeremiah that I must regard it as the work of an anonymous, perhaps contemporary, poet, with a genius akin to that of Nahum. The mixed authorship of the foreign prophecies in chs.

has been transferred in God's providence to Nebuchadnezzar, and he is irresistible until his mandate is exhausted. The political implications of this conviction
are not yet drawn out: that is reserved for later instruction. The immediate purpose of the prophet is to drive
home the truth that the judgment is near, and the
manner of it determined.

The publication of these early prophecies, long after
the Scythians had ceased to be the troublers of Asia,
and when the Babylonian empire was the rising power
in the east, would be enough of itself to prove that
Jeremiah identified the Chaldeans with the Foe from
the North of his youthful visions. A more direct proof,
however, may be found in the first thirteen verses of
ch. xxv, when read in their original text and connexion. It is a bold but very plausible conjecture that
in these verses we have the conclusion[1] of the volume
of prophecies dictated by Jeremiah to Baruch in the
year 604. Following the simpler text of the LXX, and
omitting superfluous clauses, we obtain the following
peroration:

[1 The word that came to Jeremiah concerning the whole
people of Judah, in the fourth year of Jehoiakim son of Josiah,
king of Judah.]

3 Since the thirteenth year of Josiah, son of Amon, king of
Judah, to this day, three and twenty years long, I have spoken
to you early and late, 5 saying 'Turn you every one from his
evil way and from the wickedness of your actions; thus shall you
dwell in the land which Yahwe has given to you and your
fathers for ever and ever.' 7 But you have not listened to me.
8 Therefore Yahwe has spoken thus: 'Forasmuch as you have
not listened to My words, 9 I send and bring *a people from the
North*, and bring it against this land and its inhabitants, and all

xlvi–li is generally recognised; and the effort to disentangle a Jeremianic
nucleus in the various oracles hardly repays the labour spent upon it.

[1] Rather than the *Introduction*, as Rothstein and others have thought.

the peoples round about it. I will lay them waste, and make them a perpetual desolation and hissing and derision; [10] I will banish from them the sound of joy and mirth, the voice of the bridegroom and of the bride, the sound of the mill stones and the light of the lamp. [11] And they shall serve among the nations seventy years. [13] Thus will I bring upon this land all My words which I have spoken against it, even all that is written in this book[1].'

It will be seen that the date is the same as that of ch. xxxvi, and that the passage closes with a reference to a 'book' clearly assumed to be known to the hearers or readers. We are naturally led to the conclusion that this book is none other than the roll which Jehoiakim cut up and burned, but which was afterwards

[1] This restoration of the text is arrived at by a somewhat intricate but quite convincing train of critical reasoning, for the details of which the reader must be referred to the larger commentaries (such as Cornill or Rothstein), or to Buttenwieser's lucid summary (*op. cit.* pp. 46 f.). The chief source of confusion lies in the fact that the oracles against foreign nations (now found in chs. xlvi–li of the Hebrew) stood at one time in the MT (as they still do in the LXX) immediately after *v.* 13, as read above. This is proved by certain modifications of the text in Hebrew which obviously presuppose the immediate sequence of heathen prophecies, of which modifications the LXX has curiously enough kept clear. Thus in *v.* 11 the words 'they (i.e. the people of Judah) shall be servants among the nations' (LXX) were changed so as to read 'these (the foreign) peoples shall serve the king of Babylon'; and some smaller alterations reveal the same assumption. The threat against Babylon in *v.* 12, although found both in the LXX and the MT, must be a later insertion; its repetition in *v.* 14 is peculiar to the Hebrew. In the LXX the collection of foreign prophecies has as its heading: 'That which Jeremiah prophesied against the nations.' When these prophecies were removed by the editors of the Hebrew text to the end of the book, this heading was inadvertently left; and now forms the last clause of *v.* 13: '(this book) which Jeremiah has prophesied against all the nations.' The result is that a passage originally written as the conclusion of a book against Judah (as is expressly stated in *v.* 1 and understood in *vv.* 3 ff.) was transformed into the introduction to a series of oracles against the heathen nations. The explicit references to Nebuchadnezzar and the Babylonians are all absent from the LXX, and must have been added in the course of the Hebrew redaction.

rewritten by Baruch, and that *vv*. 3–13 are the original peroration of that book, to which an editor has prefixed a title giving the correct date of its composition. And it is to be noted that throughout the passage (as the LXX shows) the Babylonians are never once named, but only vaguely described as a 'people from the North[1].' Such a designation would have little appropriateness as applied to the Chaldeans apart from the association of ideas established by previous anticipations of danger from that quarter.

Among Jeremiah's later poems there is one which breathes something of the spirit of the early Scythian poems, and in which the Babylonians are again spoken of as coming from the North. It is addressed to Jerusalem as the ideal shepherdess of the nation, whose fair flock is scattered by a desert wind in the day of Yahwe's anger (xiii. 20–27).

> 20 Lift up thine eyes, and see[2]
>   How they come from the North!
>   Where is the flock that was given thee—
>   Thy beautiful flock?
>
> 21 What wilt thou say when thou findest
>   Set o'er thee as heads
>   Them whom thyself mad'st familiar
>   With thee as friends[3]?
>   Will not agonies seize thee
>   Like a woman in travail?
> 22 Or if thou say in thy heart
>   'Why has this come upon me?'—

[1] It is true that in xxxvi. 29 Jehoiakim is represented as saying that the king of Babylon was mentioned in the roll. That only means, however, that in the opinion of the narrator Jehoiakim knew perfectly well what was in Jeremiah's mind.

[2] The sing. address is to be maintained throughout, as in LXX.

[3] In *v*. 21, read יִפְקְדוּ; and transfer לְרֹאשׁ from the end of the fourth line to the second.

> For thy many transgressions thy skirts are upturned,
> 　Rudely exposed thy limbs!

23 If the negro can change his skin,
> 　Or the panther his stripes,
> Then may you, accustomed to evil,
> 　Learn to do good!

24 So I chased them away like chaff
> 　Blown by the desert wind.

25 This is thy lot, the portion assigned thee
> 　By Me, saith Yahwe—
> Since Me thou hast wholly forgotten,
> 　Trusting in lies.

*　　*　　*　　*　　*　　*　　*

27 On all the hills of the landscape
> 　I have seen thy horrors[1].

> Woe to thee, Jerusalem! Thou wilt not be clean-
> 　For how long yet?

The northern foes are here described as those whom Jerusalem has known of old as 'lovers'; i.e. has had illicit religious and political relations with them (cf. 2 Kings xx. 12 ff.; Ezek. xxiii. 12 ff.). How will she feel when they become her tyrants, and treat her with the indignities used to a rejected concubine slave? For this is the fate appointed her by Yahwe, on account of her sins. Yet the poem closes with a sigh of poignant regret, which calls to mind two earlier apostrophes to Jerusalem, and forms a climax to them. In iv. 14 we read:

> O Jerusalem, cleanse thee from sin,
> 　If thou wouldst be saved.
> How long shall lodge in thy breast
> 　Thy dissolute thoughts?

[1] The poem has suffered some disturbance of its original structure. I agree with Erbt that *v.* 23 (addressed to *individuals* of the nation) is, though undoubtedly Jeremiah's, out of place here; and it is plausible, with the same scholar, to place *v.* 24 immediately after 20. His reasons for rejecting 22 are less convincing. *V.* 26 is untranslatable for more reasons than one.

In vi. 8:

> Be warned, O Jerusalem, lest my soul
> Be estranged from thee.

And here:

> Woe to thee, Jerusalem! Thou wilt not be clean
> For how long yet?

The same fond clinging to Jerusalem, the same reluctance to abandon hope of her future, appears in each of these ejaculations, and reveals an aspect of Jeremiah's mind which is apt to be overlooked: viz. his underlying faith in some permanent principle of good enshrined in the history of Israel. And, strange to say, this hope is not extinguished even at the last. For, as Duhm points out, the purification of the sacred city is a long and weary process, but not impossible. The prophet's thoughts already stretch beyond the judgment to a time of restoration and blessedness—a hope which was to blossom forth in the ideal visions of a new Israel which brightened the evening of his life (see below, Chap. xvi).

If the poem last quoted belongs, as it may, to the period of the Chaldean victory at Carchemish, we may with less hesitation assign to the same situation the more sombre utterance of ch. xiii. 15–17, which gives an impressive picture of the doomed nation walking in self-willed pride to destruction under the waning light of the day of grace:

> 15 Hear and give ear, and be not proud!
> For Yahwe has spoken.
> 16 Give Yahwe your God the glory,
> Ere it grow dark:
> Before your feet stumble
> On darkening mountains,
> And you wait for light, but darkness is there,
> And he turns it to gloom.

17 But if you will not hear it:

> In secret my soul shall weep
> Because of your pride;
> And my eye run down with tears,
> For Yahwe's flock is led captive.

The captivity of Yahwe's flock is here spoken of in the accent of prophetic certainty, as if it were an accomplished fact; although many years were to elapse and many new situations to be faced before the end actually came. For the time being Jehoiakim saved his throne by tendering a prompt submission to Nebuchadnezzar. But after three years of half-hearted allegiance his restless ambition and political rashness led him to tempt his fate by renouncing his fealty. Nebuchadnezzar, who must have had weightier cares on his hands at the moment, retaliated by letting loose guerilla bands of Chaldeans, Arameans, Moabites, etc., to keep him in play till he himself should be in a position to deal with him effectually (2 Kings xxiv. 2) [1]. In the midst of these troubles Jehoiakim died, leaving his widow and eighteen-year-old son, and his unhappy country, to reap the consequences of his perfidy and folly.

A difficult and obscure prophecy of Jeremiah is perhaps to be explained by the circumstances of this revolt. It stands in ch. xxii. 20–22, in the collection of oracles on the kings of Judah, between those on Jehoiakim and on Jehoiachin; and that is probably its true chronological setting—at the end of Jehoiakim's reign.

> 20 Go up to Lebanon and cry!
> In Bashan lift up thy voice!
> Cry from the mount of Abarim,
> For broken are all thy lovers [2].

[1] This is probably the background of the prophecy of ch. xii. 7–12.

[2] See the following Note.

21 I spoke to thee in thy time of ease;
Thou saidst, 'I will not hear!'
Such was thy way from thy youth till now,
Thou wouldst not hear My voice.

22 All thy friends the wind sweeps off,
Thy lovers are captive gone;
Ashamed and confounded shalt thou be
For all thy evil ways.

Here the personified people is called on to ascend the heights of Lebanon, Bashan and Abarim, the three mountainous regions north and east of the land, and see that all its defences[1] are broken down. It is not unlikely that, as Erbt has suggested, this signifies the break-up of a coalition of West-Asiatic states against Babylon, in which Judah was involved. That such a coalition existed at the time of Jehoiakim's rebellion we are nowhere informed; but it is very credible, and indeed in the circumstances of the case almost a matter of course. Moab and Ammon are excluded by 2 Kings xxiv. 2; but there remain Tyre and other northerly states; and Tyre is known to have been hostile to Babylon at this time[2]. These would be the 'lovers' and 'friends[3],' who are as good as led into captivity, leaving Judah naked to her enemy. In a single sentence Jeremiah drives home the lesson of the coming catastrophe: disobedience, indifference to Yahwe's warnings, especially in the time of respite and fancied security that followed the inauguration of the Covenant—this is the moral cause of the ruin that is impending, the shame and confusion that will fall upon the nation.

[1] One is tempted to read מבטחיך for מאהביך in v. 20. שבר is seldom used of human beings.

[2] See Kittel, *Geschichte*, ii, p. 549 *n.* 1; Erbt, *Jeremia u. s. Zeit.*, p. 277.

[3] In v. 22, we may point רְעַיִךְ instead of רֹעַיִךְ ('shepherds').

Before leaving the reign of Jehoiakim we may quote two impassioned philippics of Jeremiah, which reveal the embittered relations that existed between that monarch and the prophet. The first and more illuminating of the two was called forth by the erection of a sumptuous palace on Mount Zion in which Jehoiakim evidently took a peculiar pride. Built by forced labour, with callous disregard of the rights of the wage-earners, and lavishly decorated after approved foreign models, it symbolised a conception of royalty which Jeremiah repudiated with his whole heart (ch. xxii. 13–17):

13 Woe to him who builds his house with injustice
　　His storeys with wrong!
　Who makes his fellow-man serve for nought,
　　And keeps back his wage.
14 Who says 'I will build me a spacious house,
　　With roomy chambers;
　Well-lighted with windows, panelled with cedar,
　　And bright with red paint!'

15 Is it thus thou wouldst play the king—
　　By outvieing in cedar?
　Did not thy father eat and drink,
　　And do himself well[1]?
　Yet he practised justice and right,
16 　Judged the cause of the needy and poor:
　Was not this to know Me in truth?
　　Saith Yahwe (of hosts).

17 But *thou* hast nor eyes nor thought
　　For aught save thy gain:
　For the innocent blood thou canst shed[2],
　　The murder thou canst do!

If we suppose this oracle to have been delivered in

---

[1] So we may render the Heb. phrase with Duhm and Cornill, inserting here (with LXX) וְטוֹב לוֹ instead of the double [לו] אז טוב of the Heb. (15 *b* and 16 *a*).　[2] Omitting וְעַל הָעֹשֶׁק.

public, perhaps in front of the unfinished palace, we can understand the implacable resentment which was roused in the mind of the king against Jeremiah! The most interesting feature of the passage, however, is the by no means overdrawn eulogy of Josiah's regal virtues, which are held up as a rebuke to his unworthy son. An earnest, God-fearing man, enjoying in measure the pleasures of the table (in this resembling Charlemagne, and William the Silent, and other distinguished personages), but resolute in administering justice and upholding the rights of the poor; such is Jeremiah's portrait of the king who had made Deuteronomy not only the law of the realm, but also the rule of his own life 'Was not this to know Me?' saith Yahwe.

The second oracle on Jehoiakim (xxii. 18, 19) probably gives the exact form of the curse pronounced by Jeremiah on the king after his burning of the roll, summarised by Baruch in xxxvi. 30.

> [18] Woe upon this man,
>   Upon Jehoiakim[1]!
> None shall lament for him: 'Alas, my brother!'
>   Or: 'Alas, O sister!'
> None shall bewail him: 'Alas, O lord!'
>   Or: 'Alas for his majesty!'
> [19] With the burial of an ass shall he be buried,
>   Dragged along and flung forth
>   Without the gates of Jerusalem.

It is by no means certain that this prediction was not fulfilled. Although 2 Kings xxiv. 6 gives the impression that Jehoiakim died a peaceful death, it is noteworthy that nothing is said of his burial[2]; and the statement in

---

[1] In the Heb. text the opening lines of the poem have been lost in the superscription. The first line above stands in the LXX; the second is supplied by a felicitous conjecture of Cornill.

[2] The only other king of Judah whose burying place is not recorded is Hezekiah (2 Kings xx. 21): the omission here is certainly accidental, but it does not follow that it is accidental in the case of Jehoiakim.

the LXX of 2 Chron. xxxvi. 8 that he was buried in the garden of Uzza may have been borrowed from the similar notices about Manasseh and Amon (2 Kings xxi. 18, 26). Two possibilities remain open: the death of this unpopular monarch may have been followed by a tumult in which his dead body was dishonoured by the mob. Or the Chaldeans, when they entered the city, may have disinterred the corpse and exposed it to the indignities here described (cf. ch. viii. 1 ff.). Some kind of fulfilment the prophecy must have had, or its substance would hardly have been preserved in two separate forms.

To the brief reign of Jehoiachin we may confidently assign the following poem, addressed to the young king and his mother. It probably describes the success of the guerilla bands of Chaldeans, etc., in cutting off the southernmost cities from contact with Jerusalem (xiii. 18, 19):

> [18] Say to the king and queen-mother,
>   'Sit low in the dust!
> For down from your heads is fallen
>   The crown of your pride!
> [19] The towns of the Southland are closed,
>   With none to open!
> All Judah is gone into exile—
>   Clean swept away!'

Jeremiah's political attitude at this time is revealed in two oracles on Jehoiachin, which surprise us by the uncompromising severity of their judgment on the fate of the king. Their tone is probably due to certain popular aspirations which gathered round his person rather than to anything in the character of Jehoiachin himself. The first of the two (ch. xxii. 24 ff.) must have been spoken at the beginning of the reign, and gives the impression that the young prince was a favourite of the people, and that his accession was welcomed as a release from the self-willed tyranny and disastrous policy of his father. All such hopes Jeremiah was compelled to shatter. Though Coniah (Jehoiachin) were really—as the people thought—the signet ring on Yahwe's right hand, yet Yahwe would pluck him off and hurl him into a foreign land where he would die. The second (xxii. 28–30) was published after Jehoiachin had surrendered and thrown himself on the clemency of Nebuchadnezzar, and been carried a prisoner to Babylon. It is obviously intended to counter-act a prevalent expectation that he would speedily return triumphant over all opposition, and reign as the legitimate heir to the kingdom of his fathers.

<blockquote>
28 Is he an image despised and broken—
This man Coniah?
Or a vessel misliked?
Why was he hurled and cast forth[1]
To a land that he knew not?
29 O land, land, land! Hear the word of Yahwe:
30 'Write this man down as childless,
A man unprosperous all his days;
For none of his seed shall prosper
Sitting on David's throne,
And ruling in Judah again!'
</blockquote>

It was therefore, we may surmise, for no fault of his own, but simply to cut off the delusive hopes that attached themselves to his person, that Jeremiah issued this unsparing denunciation of one whose misfortunes were fitted to awaken sympathy. The point of the pre-diction is not that Jehoiachin shall die childless (which as a matter of fact he did not), but that he may be written down as childless so far as any prospect of his descendants occupying the throne was concerned. Through this passage we obtain a glimpse of an aspect of the new political situation which, as we shall see in the next chapter, was to determine Jeremiah's attitude profoundly for several years to come.

---

[1] Omitting הוא וזרעו and changing the verbs to sing.

CHAPTER XIII

THE WAY OF LIFE AND THE WAY OF DEATH

THE first deportation of Jews to Babylon took place about the year 597 B.C. With Jehoiachin there went into exile, though not like him into imprisonment, the *élite* of the Judean population: the priests, the nobles, the soldiers, and the skilled artisans; and of these elements the first colony of exiles was formed on the banks of the Euphrates. Most of the liberal-minded and experienced statesmen who had shielded Jeremiah from the fury of the mob and from the vindictive enmity of Jehoiakim had been taken away, and their places were filled by a lower class of men whose interests were opposed to theirs, and among whom the prophet must have found very few friends. During the next eleven years the current of Jewish life ran in two parallel channels, one in Jerusalem and the other in Babylonia; and there was intense animosity among the exiled aristocracy against the *parvenus* in the homeland who had usurped their privileges and appropriated their possessions.

At first Jeremiah's sympathies were with the exiles. They are the 'good figs' of the vision recorded in ch. xxiv, as contrasted with the 'rotten figs,' which symbolised the worthless remnant left in Jerusalem. But soon there arose in Babylonia a seditious agitation against the Chaldean government which called forth the sternest condemnation on the part of the prophet. It was, as we have seen, to counteract this movement that he uttered the second of his oracles against Jehoiachin, whose liberation was hoped for, and under whom the exiles expected the restoration of an independent Jewish kingdom with themselves in the seats of power. This was the occasion of the remarkable letter to the exiles contained in ch. xxix, in which Jeremiah carries the counsel to political quietism further than any other prophet had done. It not merely inculcates submission to the irresistible power of the Chaldean empire, or merely making the best of an unhappy situation, but it urges the cultivation of a friendly spirit towards the foreign state of which these men were involuntary members (v. 7). And it closes with a warning against the influence of the prophets who were fanning the agitation, and whose appearance in Babylon was hailed by the exiles as a sign that though banished from the Temple and the holy land they were not cast off by Yahwe (vv. 8, 15 ff.).

There is no doubt that this message was precisely the kind of advice which the new king Zedekiah would have wished the exiles to lay to heart; and indeed, if (as some think) the mention of seventy years as the limit of the Chaldean domination (v. 10) be a later insertion, it would have been acceptable to the imperial government. It is quite conceivable, therefore, that it was sent with the knowledge of the king and the Babylonian Resident in Jerusalem; for Jeremiah must have had access to court circles when he was able to use royal plenipotentiaries as bearers of his letter (v. 3). In any case we can see that the letter is informed by sound political judgment no less than by religious conviction; and it may even be based on some knowledge of the liberal spirit which animated the policy of Nebuchadnezzar. But to make this the main purpose of the document—to regard it as a mere political manifesto with no higher object than to further the interest of Babylon—is to miss its profound religious significance.

To that aspect of it we shall return when we come to consider Jeremiah's teaching on the future of religion.

The sequel to the reception of the letter throws some light on the state of parties in Jerusalem. It is very intelligible that the anti-Babylonian faction among the exiles resented Jeremiah's interference, and took measures to have him silenced. But it is perhaps significant that the remonstrance they addressed to Jerusalem for this purpose was sent not to the king but to Zephaniah the priest, who as responsible for order in the Temple is reproached for allowing a dangerous lunatic like Jeremiah to go at large (xxix. 24 ff.). But the priest contented himself with reading this missive to Jeremiah. From the assumption that this was a friendly act, it has been concluded that the higher offices in the Temple were now filled by men of a different stamp from those who had persecuted the prophet in the past. It is more likely, however, that Shemaiah, the writer of the letter, and Zephaniah were working together, and that the priest's purpose was to frighten Jeremiah, although he did not dare to imitate the cruelties perpetrated by Pashhur under the rule of Jehoiakim (ch. xx. 1 ff.).

Soon afterwards we find that the revolutionary spirit had broken out in Judea. About the middle of Zedekiah's reign emissaries from several neighbouring states assembled in Jerusalem to concert measures of revolt from Babylon (ch. xxvii. 1–4). Jeremiah put forth all his energies to prevent the nation being plunged into a second disastrous war with Nebuchadnezzar. The fact that he alone appears as opposing the conspiracy has led some critics[1] to suppose that the party favourable to Babylon had been driven from power by a pro-Egyptian ministry which sought to force the king into an anti-Chaldean alliance. That theory does not seem

[1] Schmidt, *op. cit.* pp. 313 f., 325.

to be necessary or even probable. It was obviously
contrary to the interest of Zedekiah to fall in with a
movement which must have aimed at his own deposition
in favour of his nephew Jehoiachin. The inflammable
patriotism of the populace was easily played upon by
fanatical prophets of the type of Hananiah of Gibeon
(ch. xxviii), who were doubtless in touch with the
parallel movement among the exiles; and when their
influence was reinforced by the prospect of help from
Egypt and a coalition of adjacent countries, it might
readily have become too formidable to be controlled
by the court. There is no positive evidence that Zedekiah and his advisers had yielded to the popular
clamour; and it is permissible to suppose that they
breathed a deep sigh of relief when the agitation died
down as suddenly as it arose. Into the details of the
narrative and discourses of chs. xxvii and xxviii, and
the difficult literary question of the relation of these
chapters one to the other, we cannot enter here. It must
suffice to say that, whether through Jeremiah's influence
or for some other cause, the conspiracy collapsed. It
may have been to clear himself from the suspicion of
disloyalty that Zedekiah sent to Babylon an embassy
headed by two friends of Jeremiah, sons of two prominent
promoters of the Deuteronomic reformation: Eleasa
the son of Shaphan, and Gemariah the son of Hilkiah
(ch. xxix. 3)[1].

From this time to the outbreak of the final rebellion
—a period of about five years—we have no information
about the course of events in Jerusalem, or of the
personal fortunes of Jeremiah. When the curtain is

  [1] If ch. li. 59–64 were genuine, and Zedekiah in person had to go
to Babylon to explain matters, we might have reason to conclude that
he had been more deeply compromised than is suggested above. But
there are some grounds for suspecting that the notice there is only a
legendary duplicate of xxix. 3.

again raised the city is invested by a Chaldean army (ch. xxxiv. 1 ff.), and the doubtful issue of the siege is weighing heavily on the mind of the king (xxi. 1 f.). This means that the anti-Babylonian influence had gained the upper hand in the royal council. Zedekiah is surrounded by a body of hot-headed and reckless political gamblers who, relying on Egyptian support, have staked everything on the chance of a successful resistance to Nebuchadnezzar. The king is a mere puppet in their hands (ch. xxxviii. 5), a weak, irresolute, characterless individual, extremely anxious to know what was right, but utterly incapable of doing it. Jeremiah seems to have understood the difficulty of his position, and treats him with a deference and sympathy such as he never showed to the proud and masterful Jehoiakim. At an early period of the siege he even assured Zedekiah of a peaceful end and an honourable burial (ch. xxxiv. 4 f.), a prophecy dismally falsified by the event (2 Kings xxv. 6 f.; Jer. lii. 10 f.). And the king on his part secretly revered the prophet, and would gladly have leaned on his advice. Four times according to the received text[1] he consulted him regarding the issue of the war; and twice (or once) he saved him from a cruel death at the hands of his enemies.

This part of Jeremiah's life is crowded with incidents of the highest biographical interest, but we can only touch upon them slightly here. For the first part of the siege he was at liberty (ch. xxxvii. 4), and so far as we read unmolested. The change came when the Chaldean generals were compelled temporarily to suspend the blockade on account of the approach of an Egyptian relieving force, and the people of Jerusalem, in spite of Jeremiah's continued warnings, believed they were to see their foes no more. The wealthy citizens now com-

[1] In reality perhaps only twice. On the probability of duplicate narratives in the biography of Jeremiah see below, pp. 258 n., 274 n.

mitted a public wrong which called forth a vehement protest from the prophet. At the beginning of the siege they had made a solemn covenant before Yahwe to release all Hebrews whom they illegally kept as slaves, but no sooner did the danger appear to be over than they violated their oath, and forced their Hebrew brethren and sisters back into servitude (ch. xxxiv. 8 ff.). It has been suggested that Jeremiah's denunciation of this flagrant breach of faith was the cause of the malignity with which he was henceforth pursued by the ruling class in the city. The explanation seems somewhat superfluous. There was enough, as we shall see presently, in Jeremiah's general attitude to the war-party to account for the determined attempt on his life which was soon to be made.

Of Jeremiah's arrest and imprisonment two conflicting accounts appear to have been current. According to the first, which we read in ch. xxxvii. 11–21, he purposed to take advantage of the withdrawal of the besieging army to pay a visit to his native village[1]. When he reached the gate, however, he was arrested by the officer on duty on a charge of deserting to the Chaldeans; and in spite of his protestations of innocence he was seized, beaten, and thrown into the cistern-chamber in the house of Jonathan the secretary, which had been turned into a state-prison for the nonce. There he would have been left to perish of cold and hunger but for the king's anxiety to get from him some re-assuring word of God regarding the great issue that

[1] The object of the visit is very obscurely expressed by the phrase לחלק משם בתוך העם (v. 12). The LXX renders 'to purchase (food) from thence'—a very natural object for the visit, but one difficult to find in the Heb. verb, however vocalised. It is usually supposed that the proposed visit had something to do with the sale of family property which was the occasion of the later interview with his cousin Hanamal (xxxii. 6 ff.).

hung in the balance. At a secret interview in the palace Zedekiah puts to him the timid question, 'Is there any word from Yahwe?' Jeremiah answers curtly, 'There is! You shall fall into the hands of the king of Babylon.' Then he makes a petition for his own personal safety, praying that he may not be sent back to the house of Jonathan to die. The king accordingly gives orders that he should be kept under *surveillance* in the court of the guard; and there he remained, receiving a daily ration of bread until all the food in the city was consumed.

The other account is given in ch. xxxviii. Jeremiah is denounced to the king by a group of nobles, on the ground that his constant assertion of the futility of resistance, coupled with persistent incitements to desertion, were undermining the courage of the soldiers and citizens. Having extorted Zedekiah's reluctant permission to work their will on the prophet, these men thrust him into a miry cistern, belonging to one of the royal princes, in the court of the guard. Thence he is rescued by an Ethiopian eunuch named Ebed-melech, who impresses on the king the evil he had done[1] in handing Jeremiah over to the will of his enemies, and procures an order to extricate the prophet from the cistern, a task which was accomplished with much difficulty. Zedekiah then, with elaborate precautions against discovery, arranged a private interview at some place between the palace and the Temple. Having first obtained a solemn promise that he would not be given over to the men who sought his life, Jeremiah urged the king in the name of Yahwe to surrender to the Chaldeans. The king made the strange excuse that he dreaded being made the victim of insult or outrage by the Jews who had already found refuge in the Chaldean camp. Jeremiah assures him that *that* fear is groundless,

[1] So LXX.

but that he would deservedly be exposed to a far more bitter taunt unless he broke away from the counsel of the men who were leading him to ruin. He describes a vision which Yahwe had showed him of the women of the palace being led out in procession to the officers of the Babylonian army; and as they pass before their king they chant this mocking song:

> They goaded thee on and coerced thee—
> The men of thy trust;
> When thy feet were plunged in the mire,
> They turned thee their backs.

(Ch. xxxviii. 22.)

Here Zedekiah, irresolute as ever, cut short the interview, adjuring the prophet not to divulge to any one what had passed, but to pretend that he had merely petitioned the king against being again consigned to the house of Jonathan. By this prevarication the suspicious curiosity of the *sārîm* was allayed, and Jeremiah henceforth was left in peace in the court of the guard until the fall of the city[1].

---

[1] The two accounts are commonly considered to refer to two separate and consecutive incidents in the history of Jeremiah's persecutions, the second recording a fresh attack on his life after the first had been frustrated by the intervention of the king. It is no doubt possible to connect them in that way, if we can suppose that the offence with which he is charged in xxxviii. 1 ff. could have been committed while he was a prisoner in the court of the guard. That appears to me hardly credible; and since the hypothesis that he had regained his freedom after his first imprisonment is excluded by xxxvii. 21, we seem shut up to the conclusion that the opening of ch. xxxviii takes us back to the time when Jeremiah was still at liberty (xxxvii. 4), and gives an independent report of the circumstances of his arrest and committal to a dungeon. It may be necessary to suppose that ch. xxxviii was originally preceded by a *résumé* of the prophecies quoted by his accusers in *vv.* 2, 3, such as we find almost *verbatim* in xxi. 8, 9, xxxiv. 2 (cf. xxxii. 2–5), all of which were obviously spoken while he was still free to come and go in the city. The indications of overlapping come out most clearly in the verses dealing with the interview between Jeremiah and Zedekiah (xxxvii.

It is difficult, for reasons stated in the note below, to overcome the impression that these are two independent and irreconcilable narratives of Jeremiah's persecution by the nobles and his secret meetings with the king. Which of them represents most faithfully the actual circumstances it is impossible to decide. Although the second raises more difficulties than the first, we should

17–21 = xxxviii. 14–27). Apart from the general improbability that two such interviews should have taken place in similar circumstances within so short a time, the close parallelism of the narratives strongly suggests that they are but different versions of the same event. In both the king seeks an oracle regarding the fate in store for himself and the city; in both Jeremiah announces the issue, in the first absolutely, in the second with an exhortation (which he knows to be useless) to avoid the uttermost calamity by surrender; in both he asks and obtains protection from the men who were bent on his destruction. This last point is specially significant, inasmuch as xxxviii. 26 brings us back to the same situation as xxxvii. 20. The petition that he might not be sent back to die in the house of *Jonathan*, recorded in the first narrative, has a meaning when he had just been brought from that place to meet the king which it could not have in the second, where in fact no such request is actually mentioned. Finally, in both accounts Jeremiah is left in the court of the guard till the end of the siege. Steuernagel (*Einl.* pp. 557 f.) and Buttenwieser (*Prophets*, pp. 53 ff.) recognise a doublet in the account of the interview, while holding that the narrative is continuous up to that point. It seems to me that the duplication extends to the whole of ch. xxxviii.

If the case before us were an isolated one, it might be reasonable to treat the narrative as a unity, and overlook the indications of dual authorship which have been pointed out. But there are several other cases of a similar kind which taken together make it probable that the story of Jeremiah's life existed in at least two versions, of which it is impossible to say that one is more authoritative than the other. The clearest example is the undoubted parallel between xxxix. 1–14 and xl. 1–6: the account of Jeremiah's liberation after the capture of Jerusalem. Again, several scholars have felt that xxi. 1–10 and xxxvii. 3–10 cannot refer to two different deputations from the king to Jeremiah, but must be variant accounts of the same incident. And there are some obvious doublets in the speeches of chs. xlii–xliv. Hence the theory of a twofold narrative of this episode in Jeremiah's career affords the most plausible solution of the discrepancies between xxxvii. 11 ff. and xxxviii.

not be justified in dismissing it as legendary and re-taining the other as historical. It is more probable that each rests on incomplete knowledge of details, the divergences being such as might naturally arise from the reports of different eye-witnesses. We must there-fore be content to accept as historical the main facts, in which they agree: that Jeremiah was suspected of treasonable sentiments and utterances by the leaders of the war party, and narrowly escaped death at their hands; that the king consulted him secretly and would gladly have followed his advice if he had dared. We have now to inquire how far Jeremiah's conduct laid him open to such suspicions.

We have seen already that for twenty years preceding the fall of Jerusalem, Jeremiah's political attitude had been governed by the conviction that the power of Babylon was established in the purpose of the Almighty, and was irresistible till its mission was fulfilled. From the time of the victory of Carchemish he had looked on the Chaldeans as the destined instruments of Israel's humiliation, through whom all his prophecies of woe were to be realised. At a later period—the time of the projected coalition against Babylon (chs. xxvii, xxviii) —he speaks of Nebuchadnezzar as the servant of Yahwe, His earthly vicegerent for the time being, to whom He had committed the dominion over the world within Judah's horizon; so that to refuse submission to his authority was to resist the *fiat* of the Omnipotent. It is by no means improbable that Jeremiah had now learned to appreciate the high qualities of Nebuchad-nezzar's statesmanship; and the letter to the exiles, written about this time, shows that he believed the vital interests of religion to be safe under his just and tolerant rule.

From this time onward, then, Jeremiah advocated the policy of voluntary submission to the Babylonian yoke as the only way to mitigate the horrors and agonies of the final dissolution. When the rebellion broke out, and the siege of Jerusalem was begun, he must have seen that resistance was hopeless. He stedfastly affirmed that the city must fall into the hands of the enemy, and that only a timely surrender would save it from being destroyed by fire. Behind the serried ranks of the Chaldean army he beheld the form of Yahwe fighting for them and through them against His own people (ch. xxi. 5, 6). His confidence was not for a moment shaken by the suspension of the siege caused by the approach of Hophra with his relieving army. 'If you should smite all the troops of the Chaldeans that fight against you, so that only mortally wounded men remained of them, each in his tent, they would arise and burn this city with fire' (ch. xxxvii. 10). But Jeremiah went much further than this. Not only did he urge the hopelessness of resistance, and advise the king to surrender, but when the king was unable or unwilling to take this course, he counselled private citizens to save their lives by deserting individually. 'See, I set before you *the way of life and the way of death*. He that remains in this city shall die by sword or famine or pestilence; and he who goes out and deserts to the Chaldeans who are besieging you shall live, and have his life for a prey' (xxi. 8, 9, xxxviii. 2). It is no wonder that the men at the head of affairs, who were responsible for the defence of the city, denounced as worthy of death the man who thus 'weakened the hands of the men of war that remain in the city, and of all the people' (xxxviii. 4).

Modern readers, too, have been scandalised by the conduct here imputed to Jeremiah, and many excellent scholars have refused to believe that he could have been guilty of it. To advocate a policy of capitulation on the regular government is one thing; but to incite soldiers or civilians to break their allegiance and go over to the enemy is a disloyal and treasonable act, which every right-minded man would condemn as inexcusable under any circumstances whatsoever. Yet the language of xxi. 9 and xxxviii. 2 admits of no other interpretation[1], and before pronouncing it impossible, or 'shameful,' or unworthy of a prophet, there are several things to be considered. Two ethical questions are involved. The first is whether it is the duty of the individual to subordinate his conscientious convictions to the demand of the State for unanimity in face of a common public danger; and the second is whether, if the State is committed to a course wrong in itself and sure to end in its own destruction, it is ever right for the individual to leave it to its fate and save himself. To the first question the answer of all prophecy, as of all personal religion, is an uncompromising negative. To the prophets of Israel, especially, the preservation of the two Hebrew States, so far from being a supreme object, was an aim inconsistent with their deepest convictions. They saw in these communities hindrances to Yahwe's reign of righteousness, and looked on their overthrow as a moral necessity. The preaching of this doctrine might be described as sedition from the point of view of secular statesmanship, or it might be called enlightened patriotism in so far as it was a call to the nation to repent and escape destruction. But when the call was refused no prophet fell back on the specious maxim of a hectic patriotism, 'My country, right or wrong!' As the last

---

[1] Cornill argues, very unconvincingly, that if in xxi. 9 we omit the phrases ונפל אל and הצרים עליכם (which are wanting in the parallel verse, xxxviii. 2) the verse contains nothing which Jeremiah might not have said. There is no justification for omitting these words; and even if we do omit them the fact remains that it is an incitement to *individual* surrender. It is true that יצא אל is the technical term for 'capitulate' or 'surrender,' and *might* be used of the city as a whole; but that it is not so used here is as plain as words could make it.

of these prophets Jeremiah maintained their attitude
through the agony of the final catastrophe; and it is not
surprising if in the tragic situation he had to face his
indifference to the integrity of the State carried him
further than any of his predecessors had had occasion
to go.

The other question is perhaps not so easily answered.
Whether ''tis nobler in the mind' to call for the sacrifice
of the individual in the common ruin, or to go to the
extreme in the endeavour to save innocent lives and
avoid needless suffering, is a problem of casuistry which
cannot be settled by general rules. We must remember
that Jeremiah himself did not follow the advice he gave
to others. The accusation of falling away to the Chaldeans he repudiated with honest indignation (ch. xxxvii.
14). He knew that his place was in the doomed city.
The inward voice which guided all his actions prompted
him to remain at the post of duty, and drain his country's
cup of misery to the bitter dregs. Those whom he
counselled to save themselves by individual surrender
were the private citizens who with their wives and
children were being sacrificed to political ambitions in
which they had no share, and for which they had no
responsibility. 'And why,' asks Dr Peake, 'should he
not have advised the people to surrender, when he was
certain that resistance was hopeless? He was not the
victim of modern military punctilio, common sense and
humanitarianism were wholly on his side. It is quite
true that those responsible for the defence were justified
in their complaints of his utterances from their point
of view; but Jeremiah was quite consistent in drawing
the practical inference from his prophetic certainty[1].'

Jeremiah's persistent advocacy of a 'defeatist' policy
has led some historians to represent him as an agent of
the Babylonian government, who under the cloak of

[1] *Century Bible* on Jeremiah, II, 24 f.

religion and prophetic inspiration carried on an insidious propaganda in the interest of his country's foes. Dr Hugo Winckler who was, if not the author, the leading exponent of the general view of prophecy on which this opinion rests, wrote of Jeremiah as follows:

If a Jeremiah was consulted by the king about the line of conduct to be followed towards Nebuchadnezzar, the reason is not that he was a 'prophet' or a wise man of any kind. As a man of property and influence and as one of the leaders of the Chaldean party Jeremiah had communications with Babylon which enabled him to form a clearer judgment of the political situation than the king, who surrounded by the anti-Babylonian and pro-Egyptian party was not in a position to arrive at a clear decision. Standing outside the court-camarilla, Jeremiah as a *politician* had a more comprehensive outlook on international affairs, because he had the necessary diplomatic connexions, and was able to maintain uninterrupted intercourse with the influential Babylonian circles, whether in Babylon itself or in the immediate vicinity, where Samaria was already the seat of a Chaldean viceroy[1].

It is unnecessary to discuss here a theory of prophecy which eliminates from it the moral and spiritual elements in which its real significance lies, and tends to degrade it to the level of a political agency in the service of oriental diplomacy. It may be admitted that Jeremiah is the prophet in whose public action the theory finds its most plausible support; but Jeremiah is at the same time the prophet whose experience and teaching taken as a whole render it utterly incredible. It is impossible to believe that the man who wrote the 'Confessions,' to whom the word of God was as a fire in his bones,

[1] *Die Keilinschr. u. d. Alte Testament* (3rd Ed.), p. 170. In justice to Winckler I call attention to an earlier utterance of his, too long to quote (*Geschichte Israels*, 1, 110 ff.), where he gives an estimate of Jeremiah which in my opinion is erroneous, but which does at least recognise that his activity was based on principles of a semi-religious or ecclesiastical kind.

who had braved every indignity and outrage at the
hands of his opponents because of his unflinching stedfastness in delivering his message, would prostitute his
gifts and influence to the service of a foreign power.
Traitors and intriguers are not the stuff of which martyrs
are made, and however advantageous to the Chaldean
interest Jeremiah's action may have been, we are sure
that it was inspired by purer motives and loftier aims
than to further the policy of the councillors of the king
of Babylon. He had stood in the council chamber of a
greater than any earthly potentate, and all the principles
which governed his conduct were based on the knowledge he had there acquired of the mind and purpose
of the Almighty. It remains for us to consider somewhat
more closely what were the fundamental prophetic ideas
which find expression in his public and political action.

Like all the prophets, Jeremiah had broken with the
popular delusion that the bond between Yahwe and
Israel was naturally indissoluble, so that Yahwe must
in the last resort intervene to prevent the annihilation
of His people by a heathen power. He had also, as we
have seen, risen above the more subtle delusion of the
Deuteronomists that an ethical bond with Yahwe could
be established by a superficial reform of religion under
the sanction of a national covenant. With his mind
thus freed from the illusions that blinded other men to
the signs of the times, he was able to face the stern
realities of the political world, and discern the trend of
events through which Yahwe was working out His
purpose on the stage of history. And there is no denying
that an enlightened political judgment, and a clear
perception of the forces that were shaping the immediate future, had a large share in determining the policy
which he urged upon the nation. He realised the
immense resources at the disposal of the Babylonian
empire, the weakness of any possible coalition against

it, and the folly of the attempt to assert the independence of Judah by armed force. It is probable also that he knew enough of the character of Nebuchadnezzar to be confident that the true interests of religion would not suffer through submission to his rule. Only it must be recognised that this clear-sighted political judgment was itself the outcome of a deeper prophetic insight. What Jeremiah was fundamentally sure of was that in the purpose of Yahwe the kingdom of Judah was doomed, and his observation of the march of events only gave precision to his conception of the manner in which that purpose was to be executed. Thus far there is no material difference between Jeremiah's political attitude and that of the great prophets who had preceded him. They had all foreseen the chastisement of Israel by the world-power of the time; and one of them, Isaiah, had striven to direct the policy of the country in accordance with that prevision. But in Jeremiah prophecy had made an advance which profoundly influenced the whole of his outlook on the future of God's kingdom. He had attained a knowledge of the nature of religion which saw that many things hitherto deemed essential and indispensable belonged to the realm of 'things that are shaken.' The bearing of this element in his experience on his political action must now be considered.

It is here that a comparison with Isaiah becomes specially instructive. It was long ago pointed out by Robertson Smith that Isaiah revived an ancient function of prophecy which had been in abeyance in the work of his two great predecessors. He had combined the announcement of what Yahwe was about to do to Israel with directions as to what Israel as a nation ought to do. This must be due to his grasp of some constructive principle which was absent from the thought of Amos and Hosea; and we find such a principle in the idea of the Remnant, expressed in the name of the son, Shĕăr Yāshûb, who accompanied him to the memorable interview with Ahaz, where the lines of all his subsequent political activity were laid down. To Isaiah the conception of the Remnant embodied the truth that in the national life of Israel there was enshrined an element of permanent value, a principle of continuity between the present and the future, which was indestructible because the preservation of the true religion in the world depended on it. The redeemed community of the future already existed *in nuce* in the Israel of the present, and although the nation as a political entity had to be cut down and its stump to pass through the fire, there was that within it which Yahwe would not suffer to be destroyed. Or, in another metaphor, the foundation of the new kingdom of God was already laid in Zion, and therefore Yahwe would break the power of Assyria when it threatened to sweep away that precious corner stone. This community of the true religion, already formed within Israel, and gathering up in itself all that was of spiritual value in the national life, supplied Isaiah with the motives which inspired his efforts to guide his country in affairs of state. It may not be always easy to see the precise connexion between his fundamental idea and its practical developments; but there is no doubt that the consolidation and conservation of the Remnant was a primary aim of Isaiah's exhortations to the rulers to exercise quiet and confident faith in Yahwe under the direction of the prophetic word.

Now there is nothing corresponding to this in the thinking of Jeremiah. For him there was no 'remnant' in Isaiah's sense—no seed, that is, of the future in any part of the nation, nothing capable of carrying forward the religious heritage of the past into the perfect religion of the latter days. It had been his mission to test and try every section of society by the word of the Lord, and he had found nought but 'refuse silver,' rejected of Yahwe (ch. vi. 30). To him there was no sacred, inviolable mount Zion, symbol and pledge of the spiritual building which Yahwe had founded and would protect. Every national institution of Israel, every form by which tradition had welded the people into political and religious unity—priesthood, prophecy, monarchy, temple and sacrifice, law—all had been found wanting; the whole fabric of the nation's life was worthless for the ends of God's kingdom. It cannot be, indeed, that Jeremiah held every individual lost to the divine purpose; but the individual had value only in virtue of his spiritual humanity, not in virtue of his inheritance in the privileges of the commonwealth of Israel.

We may expect, therefore, that in spite of superficial resemblances Jeremiah's political teaching will be of a different complexion from Isaiah's. Isaiah exerted himself to save the State, and in the end did save it, for the sake of the blessing that was in it. Jeremiah was indifferent to the preservation of the State, because he knew that it neither could be saved nor was worth saving; and he gave advice which undermined its stability. And again, while both prophets counselled political quietude and submission to a foreign yoke, they did so for opposite reasons. Isaiah denounced opposition to Assyria in the assurance that in the very hour of its triumph Yahwe would intervene for the deliverance of His people. Jeremiah discountenanced resistance to Nebuchadnezzar because he knew that Yahwe would *not* intervene: because Yahwe had delivered Jerusalem into his hand, and the path of life was surrender to his will. Each prophet was right for his own day: Isaiah in holding that the interests of religion demanded the continuance of the Hebrew State; Jeremiah in perceiving that the time had come for State and State-religion to be done away.

We can now see that the political activity of Jeremiah was rooted in the deepest region of personal experience. He had learned that religion is independent of national institutions and legal forms; he had learned by observation that these things were positive hindrances to that knowledge of God in which true religion consists. He had found the secret springs of religion in his own soul, in fellowship with the God who searched him and knew him, whose word was the joy and delight of his heart. What was true for him must be true universally. Religion lives in the sense of the divine which is implanted in the human spirit, and draws it upward to its home in God. And hence the new community of religion must be composed of men in whom this direct relation to God is a living reality, who have His revelation in their inward parts, and written in their hearts. To draw out the implications of this conviction in the sphere of eschatology, as they are unfolded in Jeremiah's teaching on the future of religion, is a task reserved for later chapters of this volume. We see enough to explain how he could not only contemplate calmly the disappearance of the Jewish State, with all its venerable institutions and traditions, but even help forward its dissolution, as the only way to liberate religion from its entanglement in the forms of a merely national worship of Yahwe[1]. In this we have the key to his attitude on the great political issue of his later years.

The defence of Jerusalem was maintained with the courage of despair for two and a half years. It was only when its powers of resistance had been weakened by famine that the besiegers succeeded in making a breach in the walls. Then the pusillanimous king, who could never bring himself to choose the 'way of life' through honourable surrender pointed out to him by Jeremiah,

[1] See W. Robertson Smith, *Prophets of Israel*, pp. 262 f.; Welch, *Religion of Israel, etc.*, pp. 237 ff.

deserted his post, and made a last effort to save his life
by breaking through the Chaldean lines, surrounded
by his men of war. He was overtaken and sent to
Nebuchadnezzar's headquarters at Riblah, where he
suffered a crueller fate than Jeremiah had warned him
of (2 Kings xxv. 7 = Jer. lii. 10 f.; cf. Jer. xxxiv. 4 f.).
A month later Nebuchadnezzar sent Nebuzaradan, the
captain of his bodyguard, to Jerusalem, with orders to
dismantle the fortifications and reduce the Temple and
the city to ashes. Jeremiah's predictions were thus
fulfilled to the letter. We have no prophecy of his which
can be securely dated from the time of the city's
destruction. There is a poem in ch. xxx. 5–7 which, if
it be a genuine work of Jeremiah, probably belongs to
this period; but its authorship is too doubtful, and its
religious significance too slight, to make it worth while
to quote it here. There is another in ch. xv. 5–9 which,
although its actual date be doubtful, will form an
appropriate conclusion to the present chapter. It depicts
the desolation of Jerusalem as already accomplished,
and in such moving terms that even if its language be
only the language of prophetic anticipation, it must
express the feelings with which he looked back on the
history which had culminated in this immeasurable
tragedy. It opens with an apostrophe to Jerusalem
sitting desolate and solitary, no man turning aside to
condole with her in her widowhood and misery. The
moral causes of her affliction are indicated: she has
exhausted Yahwe's patience by her persistent rebellion,
and now at last He has stretched forth His hand to
destroy her children. The lurid pictures of horror and
bloodshed which follow represent the judgment as past,
and it is obviously the final judgment on the nation
that is spoken of. The passage reads as follows:

5 Who takes pity upon thee, Jerusalem?
  Who bemoans thee?

And who turns aside from his way
　　To enquire of thy health?

6 Since thou hast rejected Me, saith Yahwe,
　　And wentest backward,
With uplifted hand I crushed thee:
　　I was tired of relenting.

7 So I winnowed them out with the shovel
　　In the gates of the land;
Have bereaved and destroyed My people,
　　Who turned not from their ways.

8 More are their widows in number
　　Than sand by the sea.
I brought upon them****
　　A spoiler at noonday;
Upon her I sent full suddenly
　　Anguish and terror.

9 She that bare seven doth languish,
　　She breathes out her soul;
Her sun has gone down while yet it was day:
　　She is shamed and dismayed!
And their remnant I give to the sword
　　Before their foes.

CHAPTER XIV

WITH THE REMNANT AT MIZPAH

THE circumstances of Jeremiah's release after the capture of Jerusalem are twice recorded in the book. In ch. xxxix. 14 we are told that one of the first acts of the Chaldean officers when they took formal possession of the city was to send for the prophet from the court of the guard, and hand him over to the care of Gedaliah, the son of Ahikam, who had already been appointed governor of the province of Judah[1]. But according to ch. xl. 1–5, Jeremiah had been marked for deportation to Babylon, and had reached Ramah in fetters, before Nebuzaradan had his attention called to his exceptional position among the captives. The captain of the guard immediately set him free, and gave him his choice either to proceed to Babylon under his own personal protection, or to join the newly appointed governor Gedaliah at Mizpah. Jeremiah chose the latter alternative, and threw in his lot with the impoverished remnant that remained in the land.

This second narrative is generally discredited by critics as a late legend, throwing an exaggerated emphasis on the deference shown to Jeremiah by the Chaldean authorities (cf. the spurious verses xxxix. 11, 12). It must be owned that it lays itself open to suspicion by the unskilful and indirect manner in which the facts are

---

[1] The statement of vv. 11 f., that Nebuchadnezzar had specially charged them to see to his safety, is undoubtedly apocryphal. The whole section vv. 4–13 is a late addition to the Hebrew text, not found in the LXX, in which v. 14 immediately follows v. 3, which in its turn is the continuation of the last clause of ch. xxxviii; xxxix. 1, 2, although found in the LXX, being clearly an interpolation from the book of Kings.

presented. It is introduced as a word of Yahwe to
Jeremiah (*v.* 1); but it really resolves itself into a
sermon by Nebuzaradan, in which the heathen general
instructs the prophet in the principles which the latter
had inculcated all his life. The situation in which the
speech was delivered is only indicated casually, as if it
were well known, in subordinate clauses of the superscription; and the main transaction is left to be inferred
from the speech itself. All this detracts seriously from
the historicity of the narrative, and compels us to
recognise an element of legendary embellishment in its
composition. Yet there are good grounds for thinking
that it rests on a sound tradition and preserves the
actual circumstances of Jeremiah's liberation more
faithfully that the abridged statement of xxxix. 14.
Can we suppose that Jeremiah was so well known to
the Babylonian commissioners that their first concern
on taking over control of the city was to set him at
liberty? Was Gedaliah in a position to act as Jeremiah's
protector at so early a stage in the settlement? It is
conceivable, no doubt, that he had been chosen as the
future governor of Judah before the termination of the
siege, and was ready at once to take up the duties of
his office. But from 2 Kings xxv. 22 we learn that his
appointment was one of the administrative acts performed by Nebuzaradan, who did not arrive on the
scene till a month after the fall of Jerusalem[1]. Taking
this view of the incident the second account of Jeremiah's
discharge is perfectly intelligible. At first he suffered
the common fate of an unknown citizen, and was
destined for transportation to Babylon. A considerable
time must have elapsed before Nebuzaradan could
complete his arrangements for the departure of the

[1] He is not mentioned in xxxix. 3, and the mention of his name in
xxxix. 13 is due to the author of the interpolation *vv.* 4–13, who was
aware from xl. 1–6 that Jeremiah owed his release to this official.

captives, whom he gradually assembled at Ramah.
Meanwhile Gedaliah would have made enquiries about
Jeremiah, and then applied for his release partly on the
ground of personal and family friendship, and partly
perhaps because he needed his support in the difficult
task that lay before him. Such a request, accompanied
by information about the prophet which could not fail
to commend him to the Babylonian government, could
not reasonably be refused, and Jeremiah was accordingly
set at liberty to go where he would[1].

The brief episode of Gedaliah's governorship is so
closely bound up with the personal fortunes of Jeremiah
that it is necessary to dwell for a little upon its tragic
story. It was an experiment in local autonomy which
exhibits in a very favourable light the pacific tendency
of the Babylonian imperialism. It vindicated, when too

[1] The attempts to harmonise the accounts, or to combine them in a
single narrative, seem to me unsuccessful. Mowinckel (*Zur Komposition
des Buches Jeremia* [1914], p. 24) tries to establish a connexion by
omitting xl. 1 as a mistaken duplicate of xxxix. 15, the heading of the
oracle on Ebed-melech in *vv.* 16–18, and reading xl. 2 as the continuation of xxxix. 14. But (1) Nebuzaradan was not in Jerusalem at
the time of xxxix. 3, 14; (2) in xxxix. 14 the other two officers had
already handed Jeremiah over to the care of Gedaliah, and it would
have been too late for a third official, even if he had been present, to
offer him a choice of two alternatives; and (3) the distinctive feature of
the narrative—that the captive train had reached Ramah before Jeremiah's fetters were struck off—remains unexplained. It is hardly less
unsatisfying to suppose that in the temporary absence of Gedaliah at
Mizpah Jeremiah had been left behind and was carried off by an
official oversight. Duhm and others, who accept the first statement as
historical, are therefore fully justified in regarding xl. 1–5 as legendary,
and taking xl. 6 as the continuation of xxxix. 14 in its original form.
But it is better to recognise them as two variant traditions of the incident,
the second of which, in spite of its legendary setting, gives correct
details which have been suppressed in the first. The case is closely
parallel to the duplication of xxxvii. 11 ff. and xxxviii, and confirms
the view that two strands of tradition have been interwoven in the
biography of Jeremiah (see p. 258 *n.* above).

late, the soundness of Jeremiah's repeated counsels to surrender the capital to the Chaldean armies. Even now, in spite of the severity with which he had crushed and punished the rebellion, Nebuchadnezzar had no thought of exterminating the Jewish people. There are not sufficient data on which to base a reliable estimate of the extent to which the country was depopulated; but it is clear from many indications that the great majority of the inhabitants were left in the land. They are described as 'the poorest of the land,' but the statements of the book of Kings are consistent with the assumption that they were the bulk of the Judean peasantry, apart from the citizens of Jerusalem and the well-to-do landowners throughout the kingdom. Over this not inconsiderable population Nebuchadnezzar set a governor of their own race, a member of one of their noblest families; and into his hands he committed the task of restoring order and confidence in the still unpacified province.

In Gedaliah the son of Ahikam the Babylonians appear to have found a man of outstanding character and ability, thoroughly sympathetic with their policy, and capable, if he had lived longer, of working it out successfully. He may have been one of those who had taken Jeremiah's advice, and gone over to the Chaldeans before or during the siege. At all events he was on the side of Jeremiah against the pseudo-patriotic faction which had forced the king into the struggle with Babylon. He was convinced like the prophet that the one hope of national regeneration lay in submission to the irresistible yet lenient sway of the king of Babylon, in whose clemency he had unbounded confidence. And he showed the courage of his convictions by his willingness to undertake the arduous and dangerous duty of building up a new commonwealth out of the wreck which war had made of the kingdom of Judah. He

fixed his residence at Mizpah, commonly identified
with the elevated site of *Neby Samwîl*, in the territory
of Benjamin, about five miles north-west of Jerusalem [1];
from whence as a centre he hoped gradually to con-
solidate his rule over the unsettled districts. There were
still scattered posts or commandos throughout the
province—*francs tireurs*, who had taken the field against
the Chaldean invaders, and had never been hunted
down. As the leaders of these bands came in one by one
and tendered their allegiance, Gedaliah treated them
with a frank magnanimity which completely won their
confidence. Instead of arresting or disarming them, he
sent them back to the villages they had occupied,
urging them to settle down to the peaceful occupation
of harvesting the produce of the vineyards and orchards
as the season of the year demanded. And, as if to assure
the new community of Yahwe's benediction on their
enterprise, the fruit-harvest of that autumn was unusually
abundant. In Mizpah itself 'they gathered wine and
summer-fruits very much'; and the fertile valleys and
terraced hillslopes rang with joyous vintage music which
celebrated the return of peace and prosperity to the
war-stricken land.

In another chapter [2] we shall examine a series of
poems which, if they be rightly dated from this period,
show that Jeremiah not only shared the new-born hope
of the little community, but saw in it a foretaste of the
perfect felicity of the Messianic age. The judgment
which for forty years he had predicted, the shadow of
which had hung over him like a cloud, darkening all
his horizon with the presage of its illimitable possibilities of woe, and quenching his sympathy with

[1] Another suggested identification is with *Tell-en-Naṣbe*, seven miles
due north from Jerusalem, commanding from a considerable altitude
the road to Nablus (see Schmidt, *op. cit.* p. 366, who refers to Alt,
Palästina-Jahrbuch, VI, 46 ff.).　　　　　　　[2] Chap. XVI.

common human joys, had taken place. The corrupt
social and political organism which had sheltered so
many evils and fostered so many false ideas, was a thing
of the past; the Temple and the holy city were in ruins;
the godless leaders of the people, his opponents and
persecutors, had gone to death or captivity; the last
remnant of Hebrew nationality had been swept away.
To what could he now look forward? Was he too little
of an optimist to expect that the millennium had
dawned with the settlement under Babylonian auspices
of a new Jewish community on native soil? He may
have been. Yet we know that as regards the ultimate
purpose of God he certainly was no pessimist. His faith
in the future of religion and a future kingdom of God
was deeply rooted in his experience, and had found
explicit utterance in his teaching. Moreover, as we
learn from ch. xxxii. 6–15, he had already formed the
conviction that an ordered commonwealth would arise
at no distant date around Jerusalem. The Chaldean
dominion would not last for ever, and after it had
passed away a new Israel would inherit the land of
promise, when each man would sit under his own vine
and fig-tree enjoying the reward of his labour. Even if
the precise eschatological value of the settlement under
Gedaliah be doubtful, Jeremiah unquestionably believed
that the blessing of Yahwe rested upon it[1], and that it
contained the promise of permanent good. Putting all
these things together, it is reasonable to suppose that
he recognised in this chastened and humble remnant,
emerging from the convulsions of the national dissolution, the nucleus of the new people of God in which
religion would find its perfect embodiment.

It is a mistake at all events to regard Jeremiah's
decision to share the fortunes of Gedaliah as the choice
of a worn-out old man whose work was over, and to

[1] Ch. xlii. 10–12.

whom it was a matter of indifference whether he spent the fag-end of his life in Babylon or in Canaan. A time had been when he held that the hope of the future lay with those who had gone into captivity; but the fall of Jerusalem had opened up a new prospect and given a new direction to his thought and activity. The advice which he had formerly sent to the exiles on the Euphrates—to 'build houses and dwell in them, to plant orchards and eat their fruit,' in loyal submission to the heathen power with which their interests were identified —could now be followed in Palestine itself. It was in fact the precise policy which Gedaliah had adopted and urged on his people. For once in the history of Israel the prophetic and the secular authority were in complete accord, and the counsel of peace was between them both[1]. The fact is interesting as an indication that there was no such radical opposition between Jeremiah and the better members of the Deuteronomic school as many writers have supposed[2]. Their one difference in principle had been on the question of the salvability of the Jewish State (pp. 176 f.); and when that issue was decided in Jeremiah's favour by the capture of Jerusalem all that was good in the movement would naturally rally to the prophet whose reading of the religious situation had been vindicated by the march of events. Of this *rapprochement* we seem to have an instance in the partnership of Gedaliah and Jeremiah. The new governor was by family tradition a Deuteronomist, but one who had never broken with Jeremiah. There were doubtless many reasons why he might have desired the presence of the venerable prophet with him at Mizpah when he undertook to organise the new settlement, though we can hardly believe that Jeremiah would have consented unless he had been in sympathy with his aims. The prophet's thoughts may have dwelt

[1] Zech. vi. 13.   [2] See Chap. vi above.

more on the ideal future while the statesman's were engrossed with the practical problems of the hour; but that was a difference which would only make their co-operation more stimulating and fruitful. Jeremiah had felt himself called from the first to pluck up and break down and destroy, but also to build and to plant: the negative side of his commission had been discharged, at what agonising cost to his sensibilities we have in some measure realised; he could now devote himself to the more congenial task of strengthening the hands of a true patriot and servant of God in building up a new Israel on the ruins of the old.

We may well imagine, therefore, that these short autumn weeks spent at Mizpah were the happiest period of Jeremiah's long life. Tradition has pictured him sitting disconsolate among the ruins of Jerusalem, pouring forth his grief in the plaintive and haunting strains of the Hebrew elegy. But although the second and fourth poems of the book of Lamentations present every mark of having been composed by an eye-witness of the Chaldean overthrow of Jerusalem, the ascription of them to Jeremiah rests on no better foundation than a heading in the Greek version. Internal evidence is almost decisive against the view that he was the author. The anonymous poet who wrote these verses has a feeling for the calamity of his people perhaps as sensitive as Jeremiah's, but his poetic genius is inferior and his religious temper of a different cast. He adopts the artificial form of the acrostic, and elaborates his lines with a nicety of which Jeremiah shows no trace. Above all, he writes from the viewpoint of those on whom the catastrophe had come as a bolt from the blue, to whom it was an unexpected and incredible thing that Yahwe should allow His holy place to be profaned by a foreign foe. Far different were the thoughts that at this time occupied the mind of our prophet. He was not at

Jerusalem but at Mizpah, amid rural scenes like those in which his boyhood had been spent, at the centre of a cheerful and industrious community, intent on repairing the ravages of war and laying the foundations of a new civil order. And the poems which may be most plausibly assigned to this part of his career are no dirges over the irretrievable past. They are attuned, as we shall find, to the festive songs of the husbandmen as they gathered in the precious fruits of the season which were to Jeremiah the earnest of higher blessings in store for the redeemed people of Yahwe.

All this fair promise of returning prosperity was blighted in an evil hour by the treacherous murder of Gedaliah, a deed so foul and senseless that many have thought it could only have been conceived in the brain of a lunatic. The narrative, however, suggests motives probable in themselves which bar the plea of insanity on behalf of the perpetrator. Among the field-commandants who came to make their peace with the governor the first named is a certain Ishmael, the son of Nethaniah[1], a prince of the blood, who was known or suspected by his companions of being in treasonable correspondence with the king of the Ammonites. When these men warned Gedaliah that Ishmael had been bribed to assassinate him, the brave young nobleman refused to believe them; and when Johanan ben-Kareah proposed to 'mak' siccar' by secretly doing away with the traitor, the governor peremptorily forbade him, telling him that his suspicions did injustice to Ishmael. There is no reason to doubt that Johanan's information was correct. Baalis of Ammon had an obvious interest in preventing the rise of a new Jewish state between him and the Mediterranean, and may also have hoped

[1] The narrative would read more intelligibly if we suppose that the name is inserted in ch. xl. 8 by mistake, and that the first appearance of Ishmael was that recorded in xli. 1.

to extend his dominion to the west of the Jordan. He dared not openly defy Nebuchadnezzar by making an attack on the small Chaldean garrison stationed at Mizpah; but if he could bring about the death of his deputy by the hand of a Judean he might hope that the vengeance of the supreme power would be turned against the Jewish remnant, and that out of the confusion something might accrue to his advantage. In Ishmael he found an instrument fit for his purpose. The hot-headed fanatic, with royal blood in his veins, resented the humiliation inflicted on his family by the elevation of a commoner as head of the administration, and was ready 'to do contrived murder' in his mad thirst for revenge. In due time he arrived at Mizpah with a band of ten desperadoes, and was hospitably entertained by the too confiding governor. In the night the assassins rose and carried out their bloody design. Gedaliah and his retinue perished in a general massacre of the resident Jews and Chaldeans, in which, however, the royal princesses and some others were spared and made prisoners. A still more ghastly and revolting tragedy was enacted on the following day, when eighty unsuspecting pilgrims going up to the ruined sanctuary at Jerusalem were lured out of their way and butchered in the streets of Mizpah, with the exception of ten men who saved their lives by disclosing secret stores of corn and fruit concealed in caves and cisterns in the neighbourhood.

The outrage was promptly, but only partially, avenged. The guerilla chiefs who had been won over by the generosity of Gedaliah, with Johanan ben-Kareah at their head, swiftly collected their forces, and intercepted the flight of Ishmael at Gibeon, where the cowardly ruffian abandoned his captives and his booty, and made his escape with eight of his ten accomplices across the Jordan to Ammon.

But the mischief done by the ruthless act was irreparable, or seemed to be so to Johanan and his fellow soldiers, on whom the leadership of the remnant now devolved. They felt very naturally that their standing with the suzerain power had been hopelessly compromised by a crime which they could not prevent, but from which they must find it difficult to clear themselves. If they had kept their heads and stayed on in the country, trusting to an impartial investigation by Nebuchadnezzar's government, all might yet have been well. But their strength had perhaps been exhausted by years of unsuccessful fighting, and this crowning disaster plunged them in despair. They turned longing eyes to the peace and security and plenty of Egypt, where they would 'see no war, nor hear the sound of the trumpet, nor have hunger of bread' (xlii. 14). Indeed, from the present form of the history, they would seem to have been on the way thither before they bethought themselves of consulting Jeremiah on their project. It is noteworthy, however, that in the narrative, so far as we have followed it, Jeremiah is never once mentioned. This suggests that we have here again an overlapping of two documents, of which the first (closing with ch. xli) gives a condensed account of the migration to Egypt, while the second (ch. xlii) relates in amplified detail Jeremiah's unavailing opposition to the resolve of the military leaders. But since that incident marks the beginning of a new phase of the prophet's attitude to his countrymen, we may pause at this point to discuss some important elements of his theology which seem to have come to maturity and expression during the later years of his ministry.

One possible objection to the view taken in this chapter may, however, be noticed before we leave the subject. The picture drawn above of the state of things in Palestine after the deportation is in strong contrast to another picture from the contemporary pen of Ezekiel, which apparently is based on information obtained from a survivor of the national overthrow (Ezek. xxxiii. 21, 24–26). Ezekiel describes the men left in possession of the desolate land of Israel as men who 'stand upon their sword,' who practise idolatry, ceremonial impurity, immorality and bloodshed, and who justify their claim to be the legitimate heirs of Canaan by a strange appeal to the remote history of their race. 'Abraham was one,' they defiantly argued, 'and yet he inherited the land; but we are many; to us the land is given for a possession.' That is to say, the smallness of their numbers as compared with the old population of the country was no argument against the validity of their title to the inheritance of Canaan: they were still many in comparison with the solitary patriarch whose seed had so wonderfully multiplied. Now, if this refers to the two months of Gedaliah's rule it certainly contradicts the impression which the record in the book of Jeremiah makes on the mind; and it represents a state of affairs in which we can hardly suppose that the prophet himself would have felt at home. And such a difference of judgment between two prophets would be no unprecedented phenomenon: it is of a piece with the opposite estimates of the Exodus period formed by Hosea and Jeremiah on the one hand, and by Ezekiel on the other. There were doubtless facts of the situation which would justify either estimate: all depends on the point of view. It is possible that Jeremiah might have seen in the varied life around him the promise of a bright future for Israel, while Ezekiel from a distance knew only of the dark blots on the picture, which must draw down further judgments on the sinful remnant. It is a question, however, whether the two descriptions correspond in point of time. Since the death of Gedaliah took place in the seventh month (Sept.–Oct.), and the arrival of the 'fugitive' in Babylonia is dated in the tenth month (Dec.–Jan.) of the same year, there was ample time for that somewhat shadowy personage to have gained a knowledge of later conditions in Palestine before he set out for Babylon. We know nothing of what actually happened there after the departure of Johanan and his company to Egypt; but we read in Jer. lii. 30 of a further deportation of Jewish captives five years after the conquest of Jerusalem; and it is permissible to suppose that in the interval the province had been a scene of anarchy and rebellion which had to be suppressed by a punitive expedition from Babylon. In so far as Ezekiel's invective rests on an objective acquaintance with the prevalent feeling in Judea, it is in this period of disorder that we must look for the men of blood and violence whose proud language had stirred the indignation of the prophet. In any case it is impossible to believe that such language expresses the tone of the settlement at Mizpah; and consequently there is nothing in Ezekiel's denunciation that forbids us to hold that Jeremiah cherished the most sanguine hopes of a national restoration as he contemplated the good work begun under the peaceable and enlightened rule of Gedaliah.

CHAPTER XV

THE FUTURE OF RELIGION:
I. THE LETTER TO THE EXILES

THE last three chapters have been mainly historical; and they have brought us to a point beyond which it is impossible to form a clear picture either of the outward circumstances of Jeremiah's life, or of the inner movement of his thought. With the descent into Egypt, it looks as if the cloud of despondency had settled permanently on the prophet's spirit, blotting out every gleam of hope that had ever brightened his sky. That impression may of course be quite misleading. The discourses contained in chs. xliii and xliv deal only with the fate of the Jewish colonies in Egypt; and their spiritual future was in Jeremiah's view as black as it could possibly be painted. It does not necessarily follow that he saw no light in any part of the horizon, or that his private reflexions were as gloomy as his public utterances. Nevertheless the fact remains that henceforward no word of hope from his lips is recorded, and it is difficult to think that the evening of his life was as a time of clear shining after rain. It is probable that he did not long survive his forcible removal to Egypt; and before we pass on to that closing chapter of his career we have to consider at some length an aspect of his message which comes to light in some of his later prophecies, viz. his eschatological conceptions, or the forms under which he was led to contemplate the final expression of religion as fellowship between God and man.

Now, in one sense Jeremiah may be said to be the

least eschatological of the prophets. Not that he is less concerned than others with the future of religion or of Israel. But his vision is free from the cataclysmic element which enters so largely into eschatological representations. There is abundant poetic imagination in his prophecies, but hardly a trace of apocalyptic imagery. He does not deal in lurid pictures of praeternatural gloom and terror—'As when some great painter dips His brush in hues of earthquake and eclipse.' It is a significant fact that the standing prophetic phrase 'Day of Yahwe' does not occur in any genuine utterance of Jeremiah. The Day of Yahwe as described by Isaiah (ch. ii) or Zephaniah (ch. i; cf. Isa. xiii, Micah i, ii) is a revelation of the presence of Yahwe in a great physical and political catastrophe, in which the order of nature is broken up, the nations are convulsed, and 'the whole aeon sinks in blood.' To say that such descriptions are purely figurative, and express nothing more than the onslaught of a formidable military power, does not seem to me to exhaust their meaning; but even on that view the absence of such images from the pages of Jeremiah would be a distinguishing feature of his eschatology. It is only in his youthful period, when he was shaken by the terrors of the Scythian invasion, that some writers have thought that an approach to apocalyptic can be detected, and that opinion is very doubtful. As life went on, and his historical vision became more clear and experienced, his view of the judicial intervention of Yahwe resolves itself into an anticipation of the overthrow of the Jewish State by the armies of Nebuchadnezzar. And the same note of sober realism characterises his conception of the era of salvation. Just as the eschatology of judgment moves on the plane of history and the providential ordering of events, so the eschatology of salvation unfolds itself in idyllic pictures of the future people of God under conditions which are

entirely natural, including no miraculous transformation of the physical environment such as we meet in
the prophecies of Hosea and Isaiah and (if the epilogue
to his book were genuine) even of Amos.

The teaching of Jeremiah on the consummation of
the divine purpose of redemption may be considered
under four heads: I. The emancipation of religion from
the national institutions of Israel. II. The restoration
of the Hebrew commonwealth on the soil of Palestine.
III. His negative attitude towards the expectation of a
personal Messiah. IV. The formation of a New
Covenant between Yahwe and His people. The first
of these is the subject of the present chapter.

I

That the essential religion of Yahwe is independent
of the privileges of Jewish citizenship, and is even
consistent with loyalty to a foreign power, is the theme
of Jeremiah's memorable letter to the recent exiles in
Babylonia which is preserved in ch. xxix. This document, whose text appears to have been considerably
altered and expanded in the course of transmission, may
have read originally somewhat as follows:

> 5 Build houses and dwell therein;
>   Plant orchards and eat their fruit;
> 6 Take you wives and beget children,
>   That you may wax and not diminish.
> 7 And seek the good of the land
>   To which I have led you captive;
>   And pray for it to Yahwe,
>   For with its welfare is yours bound up.
>
> 11 For well do I know the thoughts
>   That I think concerning you—
>   Thoughts of weal and not of ill—
>   To give you a future of hope.

¹² When you pray to Me I will hear;
When you seek Me you shall find:
¹³ When you seek with all your heart,
¹⁴ I shall be found of you, saith Yahwe[1].

In order to understand this pronouncement aright we must of course have regard to the circumstances which called it forth. Jeremiah's immediate purpose was to allay a dangerous revolutionary agitation which had sprung up among the Exiles in sympathy with a project of rebellion which was being fomented in Jerusalem[2]. Since the movement was largely inspired by religious fanaticism, the prophet seeks to counteract it by a finer and more spiritual conception of what true religion is. He counsels hope and patience, founded on faith in the purpose of grace which he knows to be in the heart of God towards His banished ones. He urges them to take long views, and not to murmur against the slow working of providence, saying that it is 'a long drawn-out affair' (xxix. 28), but to lead sober contented and godly lives under the protection of a foreign rule. Hence the letter, so far as it bears on our present subject, falls into two equal parts: The first (*vv.* 5–7) is an injunction to behave as peaceable subjects of the Babylonian Empire, identifying their material interests with its prosperity, and counting it a religious duty to seek its good. The second (*vv.* 11–14) is an assurance

---

[1] There is a prose appendix which reads (*vv.* 15 ff.):

'As for your saying, "Yahwe has raised us up prophets in Babylon": thus saith Yahwe concerning Ah'ab ben-Koliyah and Zedekiah ben-Ma'aseyah, "Behold I will deliver them into the hand of the king of Babylon and he will slay them before your eyes. And a curse will be derived from them by all the Jewish Exiles in Babylon, in these words: 'Yahwe make thee like Zedekiah and Ah'ab whom the king of Babylon roasted in the fire.'" Because they have wrought scandalous folly in Israel, and have committed adultery with their neighbours' wives.... And I have known it and bear witness': 'tis Yahwe's oracle.

[2] See pp. 253 f. above.

that God is as near to the devout Israelite in Babylon
as in Jerusalem, that they have still a share in His
gracious purpose, and that at all times they have access
to Him through prayer. The complete emancipation
of the spirit of religion from the forms of national
worship could not be more clearly enunciated than in
this twofold exhortation to expatriated Jews living in a
foreign land. It is the idea expressed in the second part
of the letter which is of importance for Jeremiah's
conception of the future of religion. There are two
questions which may be asked, and must be carefully
considered.

1. In the first place we have to inquire whether the
principle here enunciated is new to prophecy, and if so
how far it is the outcome of Jeremiah's personal experience. That prayer can be offered in any place seems at
first sight an obvious dictate of natural religion; and
there is clear evidence that even in the preprophetic
period men's minds had grasped this truth in Israel.
In the patriarchal narratives of Genesis there are
examples of prayer answered, and a relatively complete
religious life lived, at a distance from the Holy Land
and its sanctuaries. Elijah in a Phoenician town wrought
a miracle by the power of prayer to Yahwe (1 Kings
xvii. 20 ff.). It is not fair to set down such cases to the
naïve inconsequence of a popular theology which did
not reflect on the effect which a change of *venue* (so to
speak) must have in the worship of a national deity.
Nor is it quite convincing to say that what was conceived possible to heroes of religion like the patriarchs
and Elijah was beyond the reach of the ordinary
Israelite. We must admit that the idea of prayer to
Yahwe in a foreign land presented no difficulty to the
faith of pre-Exilic Israelites. The pagan maxim, *cujus
regio ejus religio* (in spite of an utterance like 1 Sam.
xxvi. 19), was no longer an accepted axiom of practical

religion. If Jeremiah's message involved no more than this it could scarcely be held to mark an advance in the apprehension of the spirituality and universality of true religion.

But we must observe that in Jeremiah's pronouncement the principle is applied to a wholly unprecedented situation. The men whom he addresses were congratulating themselves that Yahwe had raised them up prophets in Babylon. It was evidently a surprise to them that prophetic inspiration was not limited to the land of Israel, nor exclusively bound up with the political institutions on the preservation and recovery of which all their hopes were concentrated. In an entirely wrong way they imagined they were experiencing the presence of Yahwe in their exiled condition. Jeremiah seeks to convey to them a conception of the *true* way to cultivate the presence of Yahwe. His premiss is not that as individuals or as a community under an alien sky they may still retain some shreds of their religious heritage; but that in the privilege of prayer the whole reality of religion is theirs: that in the impending destruction of all the externals of their nationality—the Temple, the sacrifices, the Holy City—God still lives, and having intercourse with Him they have all. Prayer is not merely petition for special material blessings; it is the search for God—an earnest and whole-hearted search: 'When ye seek *Me*, ye shall find me'; 'when ye seek for Me with all your heart, I will reveal *Myself* to you.' Where God is thus revealed in experience, there all the powers of religion are, and nothing essential can be added thereto. That is the core of Jeremiah's teaching in this passage; and it is by no means clear that any previous prophet or thinker could have given it as well as he.

How far this doctrine rose above the prevailing beliefs of the age is best seen from a comparison with

the ideal of the Deuteronomic reformers. The contrast
has been so well brought out by Dr Welch, in the
closing paragraphs of his lectures on *The Religion of
Israel under the Kingdom*, that I might almost content
myself with a reference to his lucid and convincing
statement (pp. 231–241). He shows that the Deuteronomists had failed to grasp the fundamental prophetic
conception of a divine intervention to sweep away the
national life of Israel; it 'had no meaning for them,
save as a threat or warning to hasten their work' (p.
234). They could conceive of nothing higher than a
national religion; hence their supreme aim was to
preserve the State as the indispensable basis of religion.
They saw the need for a radical purification of religious
institutions from the abuses which had perverted them
from their true functions; but these institutions had
nevertheless a final value in the eyes of these men as
'forms of Israel's worship,' without which religion as
they conceived it would cease to be. From their point
of view, therefore, the State, which maintained these
institutions, was essential to the continuance of religion;
and a divorce between the religion of Israel and its
political organisation was unthinkable[1]. Now the
Deuteronomic party contained some of the best elements
in the life of the time. It had assimilated, as far as
average minds were able, the teaching of the prophets,
and sought to legislate in accordance with it. We found
reason to believe that Jeremiah sympathised largely

---

[1] All this, of course, is asserted only of the original promoters of the
reformation. Their successors of the same school of thought not only
contemplated but actually experienced the dissolution of the State, and
it is to their hands that we must attribute most of the anticipations of
exile and restoration which are found in the introductory and concluding
discourses of the book. But while these men learned that the State could
not be saved by a reform of its public religion, it is clear that none of
them entertained the idea that religion could exist except under the
forms of a revived Jewish nationality.

with their aim, and went some distance with them. But we saw also that he was fundamentally of a different spirit from theirs, and became more and more conscious of the difference as the results of the movement came to light. Nothing reveals the gulf that separated them more clearly than the principles laid down in the letter to the Exiles.

The question now is whether Jeremiah, in opposition to the Deuteronomists, represents the common standpoint of the prophets with regard to the connexion between religion and the State, or whether he goes beyond it. Dr Welch holds that all the prophets had contemplated a reconstitution of religion on a purely humanistic basis to the exclusion of the claims of Israelitish nationality. It appears to me that while this principle is latent in the prophetic theology no prophet had explicitly carried it to its logical conclusion before Jeremiah; and indeed we shall see later that even Jeremiah could not dispense with the idea of a restored Israel as the religious community of the future. The discussion would turn on the following points: (a) The prophets were conscious of an immediate personal relation to Yahwe, which must have been essentially independent of local or political conditions. It might seem impossible that they should have felt themselves cut off from this direct converse with God if they had been isolated from the life of Israel in a foreign land. Yet on the other hand the prophet had his *raison d'être* in a call to deliver Yahwe's message to Israel; and it is hazardous (especially in the light of Jeremiah's own experience) to assume that he would have realised his personal relation to God apart from his solidarity with the nation to which he was commissioned. And even if he attained this position for himself, we cannot infer that he would have extended the same principle to all Israelites, except in virtue of their membership in

Yahwe's people. It is doubtful if even Jeremiah went so far; and there is certainly no proof that any prophet before him did so.

(*b*) Again, the prophets undoubtedly announced the destruction of the State and therefore, it might be argued, they must have held that religion is independent of the State. It is unquestionable that they believed it to be independent of the *existing* State. It does not follow, however, that religion as conceived by them was capable of expression in any form that did not involve the continuance of the nation of Israel, purified by judgment from the sin of the past, and renewed in spirit in accordance with the righteous and holy character of Yahwe (cf. Isa. i. 26).

Nor (*c*) does the fact that in the teaching of the prophets the conditions of communion with God are exclusively ethical necessarily imply that these conditions could be realised in the corporate life of any other people than Israel, or in Israel without a political organisation. What Yahwe demands is morality; and morality is universal; but the practice of universal morality is not the whole of religion as the prophets conceived it. 'The sin of Israel,' says Robertson Smith, 'is not merely that it has broken the laws of right and wrong patent to all mankind, but that it has refused to listen to these laws as they were personally explained to it by the Judge Himself' (*op. cit.* p. 138). Religion is the gracious fellowship into which Yahwe has entered with the people of His choice; and while social immorality dissolves that relationship there is nothing to suggest that a new religious fellowship could be established on any other basis than God's revelation of Himself in the life and history of that nation[1].

---

[1] The prophet with regard to whom the above statement might most readily be questioned is Amos, whose thought of God as the sustainer of the moral order of the universe might seem to exclude the idea of a

(*d*) Another point at which the prophets loosened the bond between religion and the State is their repudiation of cultus as a means of intercourse with Yahwe (see pp. 178–183 above). A God who must be worshipped in spirit and in truth is one who can be worshipped equally in Samaria and in Jerusalem. But once more it is uncertain whether the prophets drew this inference from the principles of their teaching. Hosea seems to regard the suspension of cultus during the exile as equivalent to a *moratorium* in religion: 'Ephraim shall return to Egypt, and they shall eat unclean food in Assyria. They shall not pour out wine to Yahwe, neither shall they arrange their sacrifices to Him; their bread shall be to them as the bread of mourners; for their bread shall be for their appetite: it shall not come into the house of Yahwe. What will you do in the day of solemn assembly, and in the day of the feast of Yahwe?' (Hos. ix. 3–5). That is to say, the whole life of the people will be secularised for want of the religious observances by which it was sanctified, and which were dependent on possession of the land of Israel. And even if it be possible that the prophet is here expressing the consciousness of the popular religion, and not uttering his own conviction, still his silence as to the possibility of maintaining fellowship with Yahwe when national institutions are dissolved is significant, and marks a distinct difference between him and Jeremiah.

There seems therefore no reason to believe that any particular relation between the deity and any one people. The negative character of Amos's eschatology renders it impossible to speak with confidence as to his view of the religion of the future: if the epilogue to the book were genuine he looked for a restoration of Israel, and if it be spurious we know nothing at all of the matter. But Amos is not indifferent to the historic election of Israel by Yahwe, nor does he ignore the personal bond which gives morality a religious value: compare the quotation from Robertson Smith given above.

prophet occupied a purely universalistic standpoint, or permanently dissociated religion from its national embodiment in the Israelite commonwealth.

The conclusion to which these considerations point would seem to be that while the Deuteronomists fell far below the level of prophetic thought, inasmuch as they made religion dependent on the *existing* political system, Jeremiah rose above it in the explicit declaration that religion is essentially independent of *every* political bond, and exists in all its potency wherever devout Israelites turn with all their hearts to seek their covenant God. Though this is in itself an implicate of the prophetic teaching, it may well be that a peculiar experience of personal religion such as Jeremiah passed through was necessary to bring it out into clear consciousness. It was because he himself had known the power of prayer, and the answer to prayer, and so discovered in himself the foundations of individual piety, that he was able to assure his brethren that God was as near to them in their exile as in Jerusalem, and that even loyal submission to a heathen power was consistent with the only homage which He demanded —the devotion of the heart which seeks its true good in Him.

2. This brings us to the second question, which may be more briefly disposed of. It is, whether the programme of the letter to the Exiles is strictly eschatological at all, or whether it be of the nature of an *Interimsethik*, holding good only for the interval which must elapse before the establishment of the new Israel in its own land. It is possible, by eliminating *v.* 10 of ch. xxix (as I have done in the translation, and for which plausible reasons can be urged) to suppose that the 'future of hope' promised to the Exiles has nothing to do with the prospect of a restoration to Palestine, but refers to an indefinite future of blessedness in the land

of their adoption. Such a view might seem more in accordance with the implicit universalism of Jeremiah's teaching than the narrower one which makes a revival of nationalism the culmination of the prophet's hopes. But here we come upon a deep-seated ambiguity in Jeremiah's eschatological conceptions. His distinctive contribution to religion lies in his discernment of the permanent nature of religion as a spiritual relation between the human soul and God; and this points forward to a time when 'neither in this mountain nor yet in Jerusalem shall men worship the Father,' but the true worshippers 'shall worship Him in spirit and in truth.' But though the letter to the Exiles marks a clear advance along that line, it is more than doubtful if it expresses Jeremiah's view of the final form of religion. There are other elements in his outlook which make it incredible that he ever discarded the principle of nationalism, and extremely improbable that he abandoned the hope of a national restoration. That being so, there is little to be gained by ignoring it in the interpretation of this passage. The reasonable conclusion is that what he impresses on the Exiles is simply that while the Babylonian domination lasts, their religion must be of the purely spiritual and denationalised character here described, while he still cherishes the expectation that the ultimate embodiment of religion will be in a new Israel established before the eyes of the world on its ancient soil.

It may be interesting, before we pass from this subject, to consider the probable effect of Jeremiah's letter to the exiles on the permanent attitude of Judaism to the Holy Land. The 'Zionist' controversy of our day is no new phase of Jewish religion; it dates from the Babylonian captivity. When, in much less than seventy years, Babylon's power was broken, and the opportunity presented itself to return to Palestine, large numbers

of Jews, and these not the least devout, chose to remain
in their foreign home, while cherishing the most ardent
interest in the fortunes of those who had chosen to
return. Did they find in Jeremiah's missive the justification of their attitude, and the charter of their liberalism?
We cannot say. The necessities of the case would
probably in any event have produced a theory to justify
what was a plain counsel of expediency; and the theory
actually evolved was not precisely that of Jeremiah; for
it proved necessary for the preservation of national
identity to insist on the outward badges of circumcision
and the observance of the sabbath, as the two distinctively Jewish ordinances which could be retained in
exile. Nevertheless it is quite possible that historically
the influence of Jeremiah was a factor in initiating the
movement which played so large a part in leavening the
world with the principles of the religion of Israel.

CHAPTER XVI

THE FUTURE OF RELIGION (*continued*):
II. THE RESTORATION OF ISRAEL

THE Letter to the Exiles marks an advance towards the conception of a universal religion, free from local and politico-ecclesiastical conditions and based on the light that lighteth every man that cometh into the world. But it also reveals certain limitations which seem to restrict the scope of its underlying principle. For one thing, it does not discard the principle of nationality. The prophet's advice is given to Jews as such, and with all its catholicity of political outlook it is an exhortation to the practice of a religious attitude possible only to members of the chosen people. Again, we have seen that, explicitly or implicitly, it contains the promise of a fuller disclosure of Yahwe's purpose of grace in the form of a national restoration. To the further development of this idea in Jeremiah's prophecy we now turn our attention.

Perhaps the first assurance of a speedy return of material prosperity to the land of Canaan came to Jeremiah in the inspiration which prompted him to purchase a part of the family inheritance from a near relative during the siege of Jerusalem. The instructive incident is recorded in ch. xxxii. 6 ff. Jeremiah was then a prisoner in the court of the guard; his public work was suspended; he had leisure for reflexion while he waited for the inevitable capture and destruction of the city. We may imagine that he experienced something of that strange sense of relief and rest which was said to be felt by Russian revolutionists when they exchanged

a life of feverish and dangerous activity for the quiet of
'some deep dungeon's earless cell.' His mind was set
free to look beyond the storm of judgment to the hope
of a brighter day. At all events, no sooner did his cousin
Hanamel make his appearance in the guarded court
than Jeremiah recalled to mind a mysterious premonition of the visit and of what he had come to say; and
when he stated his business the prophet 'knew that it
was a word of Yahwe.' Unhesitatingly, therefore, he
made the purchase, sealing it with all the legal formali-
ties, and adding this oracle: 'Thus saith Yahwe of
hosts, "Yet again shall houses, fields and vineyards be
bought in this land!"' It is a remarkably sober anticipation of the Golden Age! Nothing more than settled
order and security of property, such as might well be
looked for under a Babylonian administration. But it
is at least a solid foundation for an aspect of Jeremiah's
teaching which must be admitted to hang otherwise
somewhat in the air.

For the higher flights of his prophetic imagination
in this direction we are dependent on a series of poems
in chs. xxx and xxxi, which chapters with the *addenda*
in xxxii and xxxiii are almost the only bright pages in
the book of Jeremiah. The analysis of these chapters is
beset by formidable critical difficulties. They are said
to form a 'book' containing all the words which Yahwe
spoke to the prophet, and which he was commanded to
write because Yahwe was about to 'restore the captivity
of His people Israel and Judah,' and bring them back
to the land which He gave to their fathers (xxx. 2, 3).
Now it is quite conceivable that Jeremiah might have
written such a Book of Consolation for the encouragement of true Israelites during the dreary years of their
banishment; just as in the reign of Jehoiakim he had
written a Book of Doom containing all the words he
had uttered *against* Israel and Judah (xxxvi. 2). But it

is not credible that he wrote *this* book in the form in which we now have it. There is no room for doubt that its final compilation is the work of an exilic or post-exilic author. The only question is whether we can distinguish a nucleus of prophecies actually uttered by Jeremiah. On that point scholars have been much divided in opinion, although there is a growing disposition to recognise a genuine element at least in ch. xxxi. It will be sufficient for our main purpose to examine a few selected passages, the authenticity of which is acknowledged by the majority of recent commentators [1].

(1) xxxi. 2–6

The Renewal of Yahwe's Loving-kindness

2 The people found grace in the desert—
    A people escaped from the sword.
 While Israel marched to his rest,
    3 From afar did Yahwe appear.
 'With a love from of old I love thee;
    Therefore in kindness I draw thee.'

4 Once more I will build thee securely,
    O virgin of Israel!
 Once more thou'lt come forth with thy tabrets
    And dance with glee!
 5 Once more thou shalt cover with vineyards
    Samaria's hills!

*   *   *   *   *   *

6 Yea, there comes a day
    When watchers call
    On Ephraim's hills:
 'Let us rise and go up to Zion—
    To Yahwe our God!'

---

[1] Giesebrecht, Duhm, Cornill, Erbt, Peake, Schmidt.

(2) xxxi. 15, 16
The Weeping of Rachel

15 Hark! In Ramah is heard lamentation—
  Bitterest weeping!
'Tis Rachel o'er her children weeping,
  Refusing comfort!

16 (Thus saith Yahwe):
'Refrain thy voice from weeping—
  Thine eyes from tears!
For a guerdon awaits thy labour;—
  Their return from the enemy's land!'

(3) xxxi. 18–20
Ephraim's Repentance and Forgiveness

18 I have heard, I have heard
  Ephraim bemoaning:
'Thou hast punished me, and I took correction,
  Like an untamed colt.
Restore me, and I will return:
  Thou art Yahwe, my God!

19 For after I turned I was sorry—
  I smote on my thigh;
In shame and confusion I bear
  The reproach of my youth.'

20 Is Ephraim my favourite son,
  A darling child?
That as oft as I mention his name
  His memory haunts Me!
Thus does My heart yearn for him
  My pity is stirred.

(4) xxxi. 21, 22
A Summons to return

21 Set thee up way-marks,
  Raise thee posts!
Heedfully mark the highway,
  The road thou hast gone!

> Come back, O Virgin of Israel!
> To these thy cities return!
> 22 How long will thy hesitance last,
> Thou erring daughter?

The fact that these poems have been preserved in a section of the book which has obviously been edited for a special purpose in a later age does not weigh very heavily against the assumption that they were written by Jeremiah. We might expect that a compilation of this nature under the name of Jeremiah would contain a kernel of genuine words of that prophet; and if we can find a series of passages whose literary qualities are on a level with his best work, we must regard it as probable that these at least are genuine. That this is the case with the four passages quoted will hardly be denied by any competent judge of poetry. For originality of conception, vividness of imagination, and depth of feeling, they are unsurpassed by anything in the book, or even in the whole Old Testament. And when we discover further a coincidence of ideas, and striking stylistic affinities, with other writings of Jeremiah[1], the presumption that he is the author far outweighs any considerations that can be advanced to the contrary.

The problem before us is first of all a biographical one, or at least one that can be most easily stated in terms of biography. It is to find a period in Jeremiah's history which would account for the sudden outburst of joy and hope which is characteristic of these poems, as well as the specific direction taken by the prophet's

[1] Note the close parallel between the third poem above and ch. iii. 20 ff.; and between xxxi. 2 f. and ii. 2–4. Of stylistic resemblances the most marked is the pleonastic sequence of the passive on the active verb (or the simple form on the causative) (xxxi. 4, 18 *bis*; cf. xi. 18, xv. 19, xvii. 14, xx. 7). We may note also in xxxi. 20 the characteristic Jeremianic idiom of the alternative question followed by the circumstance which suggests it, as in ii. 14, 31, viii. 4 f., 22, xiv. 19, xxii. 28; and a slight reminiscence of ii. 25 in xxxi. 16.

anticipation: in particular the predominant, if not exclusive, interest in the restoration of the northern tribes.
Now it was suggested in Chap. xiv (pp. 276 f.) that the
narrative of Baruch supplies a situation which corresponds to the conditions under which such hopes as
are here expressed might naturally originate. If there
was any time of unalloyed happiness in the life of
Jeremiah, it was the few months spent with Gedaliah
at Mizpah after the destruction of Jerusalem. The
long-threatened judgment on the nation was at length
accomplished, and under the protection of the Babylonian power the survivors of the catastrophe were
permitted to form a new community, stripped of earthly
might and all pretension to secular magnificence, but
capable of being moulded into harmony with the prophetic ideal of a true people of God. There is every
probability that in this fresh start in the national life
Jeremiah recognised the germ of the future kingdom
of Yahwe, and the dawn of the golden age to which the
prophets had looked forward. It was indeed the day of
small things, but it was sufficient in a mind like Jeremiah's to inspire the hope of the greatest things, even
the inbringing of the final salvation, the acceptable year
of the Lord. In such a time of simple contented industry
and dawning agricultural prosperity we can best understand the breaking into song of the prophet's long
repressed but inextinguishable affection for his nation,
and the glowing pictures of Samaria's fertile hills
clothed with vines, and happy maidens dancing to the
music of their tambourines.

It is much more difficult to find a satisfactory explanation of the prophet's steady gaze to the north as the
theatre of the coming blessedness—a feature which is
plain on the surface of the first three poems, and is
probably to be assumed in the fourth. We remember,
of course, that he was a Benjamite, with a warm feeling

for the religious traditions that clustered round the ancient sanctuary of the Rachel tribes at Shiloh. We realise also that he was living (as we assume) at Mizpah, itself in the territory of Benjamin, with a wide outlook toward the richer uplands of Ephraim still further north, and within four miles at most of Ramah where the tomb of their common ancestress Rachel was shown. But how far is he dealing with ideal abstractions—with Rachel and Ephraim and the Virgin of Israel as personifications of the present and future inhabitants of these regions? Or how far is the return of which he speaks a literal return of the hopelessly scattered Israelites who had been carried captive by the Assyrians so long before? In order to find some light on these questions a few notes on the exegesis of the four poems may be necessary.

In the first poem, the meaning of the opening stanza is very obscure. It may be understood either as a reference to the first meeting of Israel with Yahwe in the desert of Sinai (cf. Hos. ix. 10), or as a figurative description of the present condition of the people in exile, and its impending restoration through the inexhaustible grace and kindness of Yahwe. Neither view yields a perfectly clear sense; but it seems probable that both situations are combined in the prophet's mind: the 'ancient love' of Yahwe for Israel, first manifested in the wilderness sojourn (cf. ch. ii. 2–4) is the ground and pledge of its ultimate redemption. The next strophe gives a picture of the future prosperity and felicity of the restored nation, in which the point to be noted is the concentration of the prophet's interest on the central district of Palestine (v. 5). Yet the following verse implies that the religious centre of the new Israel will be Jerusalem (v. 6). Now we learn from ch. xli. 5 that at the very time when Jeremiah was at Mizpah men went on pilgrimage from northern cities—Shechem,

Shiloh, Samaria—to the ruined shrine of Yahwe on
Mount Zion. The prediction of *v*. 6 might thus be
explained as a projection of the actual condition of
things into the ideal future: pilgrims would then go
up to the house of God, no longer with signs of mourning on their persons, but with the joy of the multitude
keeping holy day. On this interpretation the poem
might deal with the restoration of Israel as a unity,
without reference to a return of the lost Ten Tribes,
the only return from exile contemplated being that of
the Judeans recently deported by Nebuchadnezzar.
But whether this view does justice to the series as a
whole is a matter which will call for further consideration.

The verses on the *Weeping of Rachel* present a similar
ambiguity. The meaning may be that Rachel, the
ancestress of the central tribes, is still mourning over
the long-lost children of the Assyrian captivity, and
that it is their return which is predicted. But the passage
might be read differently in the light of an attractive
conjecture which has been put forward by some writers[1].
It is pointed out that it was just at Ramah that Jeremiah
was released from the gang of prisoners who were being
transported to Babylon, among whom there must have
been many Benjamite inhabitants of Jerusalem. It certainly gives an additional interest and significance to
this touching poem if we suppose that the idea came to
Jeremiah on the spot; so that the weeping of Rachel is
not a purely imaginary lament over a distant past, but
is a reflexion of the actual lamentation heard over those
who were even then being torn from her bosom. It is
difficult to say which of these conceptions gives the key
to the meaning of the poem. The first definitely implies
the expectation of a literal return of the northern exiles

[1] Hitzig, *Kurzgefasstes exeg. Handbuch, ad loc.*; Schmidt, p. 354;
so Delitzsch, Orelli and others.

from 'Halah and Habor, the river of Gozan, and the cities of the Medes' (2 Kings xvii. 6), while the second is consistent with the view that the hope of a return is limited to the Judeans recently banished by Nebuchadnezzar.

In the third poem the subject is Ephraim, the masculine personification of North Israel. It is again doubtful whether the name stands for the exiled descendants of Sargon's captivity or for the population of the territory once occupied by the tribe of Ephraim; and the doubt is not resolved by a comparison with the parallel passage in ch. iii, where the same uncertainty has to be reckoned with. There is here, however, no mention of a restoration from captivity; the return spoken of is a spiritual process of penitence and regeneration in the heart of the people.

The last passage is a *Summons to return*, which can hardly be understood except in a physical sense. Indeed, the twenty-first verse taken by itself reads like an exhortation to the departing captives to mark carefully the road by which they travel, so that they may find their way back; and in that case the reference must be to the recent deportation after the fall of Jerusalem. But that impression is not borne out by the language of *v.* 22, which seems addressed to a people that has long hesitated to choose the narrow path of return to God by genuine repentance and confession.

We observe, then, throughout the series a fixed expectation of a return of exiled Israelites, along with a marked and intelligible bias of interest in the future of the central tribes, or at least of the central region of the land. Now undoubtedly the simplest view to take of the prophet's outlook is to identify the subjects of these two aspirations, and hold that the exiles whose return is prophesied are the descendants of the northern Israelites, who are to reoccupy their ancient abode. The

alternative explanation is to separate the subjects,
applying the promise of return to the Jewish captivity
as representative of the historic nation of Israel, and
taking the conversion of Ephraim to mean a revival of
the true religion among the actual inhabitants of the
northern province, and their incorporation in the new
Israel whose centre was in Jerusalem. It is difficult on
either view to harmonise the conflicting indications
which we have pointed out in the poems; and the issue
is only complicated by a reference to the very similar
dilemma in which we were placed by the criticism of
ch. iii. We saw in the exposition of that chapter[1] that
according to one analysis its theme is the restoration of
Israel as distinct from, and indeed in contrast to, Judah;
while another analysis leads to the conclusion that the
conversion of Judah, alone or as representing the ideal
unity of Israel, is contemplated. Now ch. iii is commonly
regarded as an early prophecy of Jeremiah, and if we
are right in assigning the poems of ch. xxxi to his
latest years, we must recognise that the situation had
been entirely changed by the overthrow and captivity
of the kingdom of Judah. In regard to ch. iii it was
arguable that the idea of a return of the Ten Tribes
came into Jeremiah's mind through reflexion on the
deeper guilt of Judah, which suggested that the less
guilty sister-nation, who had already suffered the
penalty of her apostasy, would be first recalled to her
divine husband's love, and would prove responsive to
the call. But that motive would cease to operate when
Judah also had been banished for her sins; and in any
case it is too casual in its suggested origin to account
for the expectation of a return of the northern tribes as a
permanent feature of the prophet's eschatology. If on
the other hand we disconnect the latter part of ch. iii
from the appeal to North Israel, and take it to be a

[1] pp. 79–83 above.

description of the repentance of Judah, we lose touch entirely with the idea of a restoration of the northern tribes which is prominent in ch. xxxi; for the striking correspondence between iii. 21–25 and xxxi. 18–20 will prove nothing except that Jeremiah's conception of repentance is the same whether the subject be Judah or Ephraim. The question in regard to ch. xxxi is not whether a restoration of North Israel be predicted, but only what kind of restoration is meant—a literal return from exile, or a spiritual return of the remaining children of Rachel and Ephraim to the true religion of Israel. On the whole it seems safest to adhere to the literal interpretation: that Jeremiah living within sight of the ancient and hallowed centres of the worship of Yahwe was filled with a passionate longing and hope for the return of the disinherited and scattered sons of the north who were the rightful heirs of the promises made to the fathers.

The main point, however, is that in some sense a restoration of the Israelite nationality was the form in which Jeremiah conceived the future kingdom of God. The idea of a world-religion in which there should be neither Jew nor Gentile, 'barbarian, Scythian, bond nor free,' was not reached by him. A conversion of the heathen world to the religion of Yahwe was indeed within his vision, as the following isolated oracle shows (xvi. 19 f.).

> 19 Yahwe, my fort and my fortress,
>   My refuge in time of need!
> To Thee shall nations come
>   From the ends of the earth, and say:
>
> 'Mere lies have our fathers possessed,
>   Vanities that profit nothing.
> 20 Can a man make gods for himself,
>   Though they really be no gods?'

What the relation of these converted idolaters to the future people of God will be is nowhere indicated[1]; but it would certainly be a mistake to suppose that the reinstatement of Israel as a nation is a mere local incident of a new age in which the knowledge of the true God shall cover the earth as the waters cover the sea.

This concentration of interest on the new Israel is due to a limitation inherent in the Old Testament point of view which even Jeremiah was unable to transcend. The limitation springs from a fundamental truth of religion, that religion has a social aspect, and cannot unfold its full powers except in a community; and nationality was the only form of religious community known to the men of the Old Testament. The idea of a new community created by the spirit of religion itself and founded on a relation to God common to all its members, was beyond their grasp, because the conditions for the formation of such a community did not yet exist. They therefore clung to the traditional idea of Israel as the people in whose history the true God had revealed Himself, and within whose fellowship their personal communion with God was realised. This we must hold to be true of Jeremiah. The individualism which comes to light in him more clearly than in any other Old Testament writer proved incapable of breaking finally with the principle of national religion, for the reason just indicated, that it was powerless to create a new spiritual fellowship in place of the old. Thus while to Jeremiah the nation is no longer the *unit* of religion, it is still the *sphere* of religion, within which its aspiration after fellowship in work and worship is satisfied. This will appear more clearly when we come to consider his prophecy of the New Covenant.

[1] In ch. xii. 14–17—a passage of more doubtful genuineness—the neighbouring heathen nations are spoken of as being incorporated (under conditions) in the people of Yahwe.

CHAPTER XVII

THE FUTURE OF RELIGION (*continued*):
III. THE MESSIANIC KING

THE figure of the Messiah holds a very subordinate, and indeed precarious, position, in the eschatology of Jeremiah. In speaking of his attitude to that ideal as 'negative' I did not mean to assert absolutely that it has no place in his scheme of the future; but only, first, that the few passages in which it occurs are all doubtful, and, secondly, that even if some of them be genuine the portrait appears in faded colours, and shorn of the ideal grandeur and religious significance which it has in the Messianic prophecies commonly attributed to Isaiah. We may pass over the obviously secondary prophecy of ch. xxxiii. 15, which occurs in a long section wanting in the LXX and representing a sacerdotal interest in religion utterly inconsistent with the spirit of Jeremiah, and rests on a misinterpretation of ch. xxiii. 5 f. (see below). Equally destitute of originality is the Messianic allusion to the future David in xxx. 9. The combination of Yahwe as God and David as king is characteristic of Ezekiel (xxxiv. 23, 24, xxxvii. 23–25), and the exact phrase here used is found in Hosea iii. 5. The latter reference might suggest that Jeremiah himself has borrowed it from Hosea; but apart from the doubtful authenticity of the Hosea passage, the whole context in which xxx. 9 stands shows it to be the result of somewhat illiterate editorial manipulation. In the obscure twenty-first verse of the same chapter we have a striking description of the future *'Addîr* or *Môshēl* as one who, being of genuine Israelite descent, is endowed with the priestly prerogative of access to the immediate presence of Yahwe. Whether the passage is in any sense Messianic, whether it refers to a unique individual or to a line of theocratic princes, it is difficult to tell; but it implies an experience of foreign rule, and an estimate of the privileges of priest-hood, which are irreconcilable with the times and the teaching of Jeremiah. The only passage, in short, of strictly Messianic import which can plausibly be assigned to Jeremiah is ch. xxiii. 5 f.; and this demands a careful examination. The oracle runs as follows:

Lo, days are coming, saith Yahwe, when I will raise up to David a genuine Scion (צמח צדיק), and he shall reign as king and prosper, and execute right and justice in the land (or world). In his days shall Judah be saved, and Israel dwell in security; and this is the name by which he shall be called, 'Yahwe is our righteousness.'

Apart from the question of its authorship, this passage has a general interest as expressing the per-sistent central features of Israel's Messianic ideal: some utterances may rise above it, and others fall below it; but the main elements of the conception are those here registered. The Messiah is the ideal king of the future, ruling in virtue of a unique personal relation to Yahwe, which is here symbolised in his name. He is 'of the house and lineage of David,' and wields the sceptre of righteousness, and prospers in all his undertakings. His reign is the pledge of his people's welfare and victory through Yahwe's gracious presence with them through him. Whether universal dominion be an essential of the notion is open to question, and the uncertainty is reflected in the ambiguity of the word ארץ in *v.* 5, which may mean either 'land' or 'world.' At all events his reign confers on Israel a primacy among the nations; and it is probably in accord with

the deeper thought of the Old Testament that there is
here no hint of military or despotic domination over
the Gentiles. We may therefore accept the passage as
an adequate expression of the prophetic doctrine of the
Messiah, and proceed to inquire whether such a conception harmonises with the general principles of
Jeremiah's thinking[1].

[1] The literary evidence for and against the genuineness of the verses
is pretty evenly balanced, and has led different writers to opposite conclusions. The main points are these: (1) The oracle is introduced by an
eschatological formula (הנה ימים באים) which occurs 16 times in
Jeremiah, 3 times in Amos, and also in 1 Sam. ii. 31, 2 Kings xx. 17
(= Isa. xxxix. 6), and which in the great majority of cases is a mark of
late origin. (2) This impression is strengthened by the fact that *vv*. 5 f.
do not form a natural sequel to *vv*. 1–4: in these latter we read of
'shepherds' in the plural, who shall be raised up to replace the evil
shepherds who have wasted the flock of Yahwe (cf. Ezek. xxxiv. 1 ff.,
xxxvii. 15 ff.); in *vv*.5 f. of an individual 'Sprout' who shall be raised to
protect and govern the people. That there is an irreconcilable contradiction between these representations it would be too much to affirm,
but nevertheless they seem to belong to different circles of ideas. Cornill
endeavours to save the genuineness of *vv*. 5 f. by denying that of *vv*.
3, 4; but *vv*. 1–4 form a much more homogeneous oracle than *vv*. 1,
2, 5, 6, and to my sense of poetic form *vv*. 1, 2, are not one whit more
metrical than 3, 4. That *v*. 3 could not have been written by Jeremiah
would therefore only prove that the whole section is spurious, not that
what remains is genuine. No motive can be assigned for the insertion
of *vv*. 3 f. between *v*. 2 and *v*. 5, if these had been originally connected,
and their excision would only be justified if there were positive grounds
for believing that what precedes and what follows were from Jeremiah's
hand. (3) In favour of Jeremiah's authorship the strongest argument is
the occurrence of the name צמח as a Messianic title applied to Zerubbabel
in the prophecies of Zechariah. It is contended that Jer. xxiii. 5 f. is
an intermediate link between the use of the word (in its literal sense of
'vegetation') in Isa. iv. 2 and its use as a technical designation of the
Messiah in Zech. iii. 8 and vi. 12. But to prove that our prophecy is
earlier than Zechariah is not to prove that it is Jeremiah's. It is quite
conceivable that all the passages are post-exilic and of a date more nearly
contemporary with Zechariah (*c*. 520 B.C.). (4) Another argument, on
which Cornill lays great stress is based on a supposed cryptic allusion to
the last king of Judah (צדקיהו) in the name here given to the Messiah

That question can be most usefully discussed in connexion with a thesis still more general, which has been most elaborately maintained by Volz[1]: viz. that the idea of a personal Messiah is inconsistent with the presuppositions of pre-Exilic prophecy as a whole. According to Volz Jeremiah is the first prophet in whom we detect the influence of current Messianic ideas which had taken possession of the popular mind. He supposes that the expectation of the Messiah was a recent outgrowth of the revived spirit of nationalism which marked the later part of Josiah's reign. It originated in court circles, with the leaders of the patriotic party, whose chief concern was the outward aggrandisement of the nation; it was then adopted by the more strictly religious party which carried through the Deuteronomic reformation; and finally the true prophets of Yahwe yielded to the force of opinion, and found a place for the Messiah in their pictures of the future. The first to adopt the conception expressly was Ezekiel;

(יהוה צדקנו). It is pointed out that the prophecy stands at the end of a series of oracles on the later Judean kings, just where we should expect one on Zedekiah, that Jeremiah had good reasons for refraining from a personal attack on that weak but well-meaning king, and that therefore he directs his polemic against the courtiers and aristocrats (רעים) who enforced their will on the monarch, and contents himself with showing by a covert allusion to his name that he had not left him altogether out of account! I do not think that this rather fantastic hypothesis will bear comparison with the much more rational view of Duhm: that xxiii. 1–4 is the work of an editor, summing up the section on the kings of Judah with the promise of better days to come, and that this was afterwards supplemented by prophecies of a more explicitly Messianic character in 5 f., 7 f. (It should be noted that *vv*. 7 f. have a closer connexion with 1–4 than with 5 f.). The critical arguments tend on the whole to undermine confidence in the authenticity of the passage, but the negative conclusion is not so certain as to render superfluous a consideration of Jeremiah's attitude towards the Messianic hope. There is always the possibility that *vv*. 5, 6 are an independent prophecy of his.

[1] *Die vorexilische Jahweprophetie und der Messias* (1897).

but the manner in which it appears in his writings (xvii. 22 ff., xxi. 27) shows that it is not original but must have been borrowed from some quarter; and since it is not found in previous prophets it must have been derived from the popular eschatology of the time. The position assigned to Jeremiah in this development is a peculiar one. The deeper elements in his thinking—his knowledge of God, for example, and his perception of the spirituality and inwardness of true religion—reacted against Messianism in all its forms, and prevented him from actually accepting the idea of the Messianic king; nevertheless in certain aspects of his eschatology he approximates to the range of ideas in which the hope of a Messiah was born. This appears chiefly in his view of the future people of Yahwe as a politically organised community, with a ruling class purified from the vices of the old regime (iii. 15, xxiii. 4), as a necessary condition of the enjoyment of the blessings of salvation. Although that anticipation is not Messianic in the full and strict sense, it is an accommodation to those tendencies of the age which gave rise to the prevalent belief in the Messiah. Thus, while Jeremiah was conscious of the radical opposition between the genius of prophecy and the spirit which nourished the Messianic hope, we can see at the same time how that idea exercised a disturbing influence on his mind, and began to deflect the fundamental principles of pre-Exilic prophecy from their proper orbit.

Whatever may be thought of these clever speculations, it cannot be said that they spring from a very exalted or penetrating estimate of the character and teaching of Jeremiah. That the prophet whose whole life was spent in solitary opposition to public opinion, who was never known to falter in fidelity to his own convictions, who had seen and fearlessly exposed the subtle dangers of the Deuteronomic movement, should have compromised with the far less specious pretensions of national chauvinism, is a supposition which would require very strong evidence to induce any intelligent admirer of the prophet to entertain it. But in truth Volz's theory is but an ingenious solution of difficulties which are not in Jeremiah's real attitude at all, but only in the false situation into which he is forced by the theory itself. There is not the slightest affinity between Jeremiah's descriptions of the future religious community and the dream of a powerful military State which is alleged to be the basis of the Messianic expectation, nor on the other hand is there any disharmony between the former and the ruling ideas of the prophetic theology. Volz admits (p. 73) the sobriety of the pictures of the last days presented by Jeremiah: of a people assured of no outward splendour but only of a quiet and peaceful life in the land of Canaan, of a government devoid of might and glory and charged only with the maintenance of internal order and the unimpeded exercise of religion. But he makes the mistake of identifying the prophetic denunciations of the existing political system with opposition to State organisation of any sort; and thus is led to regard the very few and uncertain allusions in Jeremiah to a new government (iii. 15, xxiii. 4) as a toning down of worldly aspirations alien to the principles of the prophets, instead of a natural projection of these principles into the ideal future. The whole construction is governed by the assumption that Jeremiah is a stepping stone from the blank negation of the earlier prophets to the express recognition of the Messianic ideal by Ezekiel; and hence it was necessary first to account for the origin of the ideal outside prophetic circles, and then to show how it gradually succeeded in naturalising itself in the environment of prophetic thought. But it is pure conjecture that the figure of the Messiah was a creation of the time of Jeremiah; or that it was first inspired by the character or prowess of Josiah; or that it was fostered by the impulses which led to the Deuteronomic reform: each of these positions is beset by difficulties which Volz has hardly faced. And here, indeed, his arguments may be turned against his own theory. For if—as is very possible—the idea was taken over by the canonical prophets from the current religion of their day, this was just as likely to have happened in the time of Isaiah as in the time of Jeremiah and Ezekiel; there being absolutely nothing to forbid the supposition that the hope of a personal Messiah formed a part of the prevalent eschatology in the eighth century as well as in the sixth: the silence of the documents is the same in both cases. In any event it seems to me highly improbable that the Messianic expectation foisted itself on the consciousness of the prophets by a process which involves a weakening hold of the moral essence of religion on the part of a man like Jeremiah.

The root fallacy of Volz's position seems to be that he draws a distinction between the political and the religious which is foreign to the Old Testament point of view. To him the Messiah is essentially a political figure, not a directly religious factor of the final salvation. He belongs not to the category of properly spiritual blessings, but to that of external benefits conferred by Yahwe on the nation. He is nowhere represented as a prophet or a teacher; he stands in no immediate relation to the individual, but only to the community as a whole. He is the Deliverer from oppression, the Ruler of the golden age. He is, in short, a symbol of the particularistic aspect of the eschatological hope—of Israel's aspiration after material greatness and world-power. There is of course much in this that is perfectly true. That the Messiah is a political personage is one of those things which no one has thought of denying.

He is a King, and the office of a king is necessarily
political. The mistake, as I have said, is to separate two
things which are never separated in the minds of Old
Testament writers. It is no doubt an imperfection of
the Hebrew religion that it was unable to conceive a
nation's communion with God otherwise than as medi-
ated through temporal blessings, among which are
included the political blessings of good government and
a measure of earthly might and dominion. But the
limitation lies in the facts of the case. Volz admits that
there is a vein of particularism in the teaching of the
prophets; so that even if the Messiah were in the first
instance a projection of nationalist feeling there is no
necessary incongruity between the ideal and the prophetic view of the future. He even acknowledges that
a certain religious significance does attach to the idea
of the Messiah, although he considers this to be a
secondary and subordinate aspect. A personage who
governs by the power of Yahwe, who is endowed with
the spirit of God, who causes the divine will to prevail
by his rule, and is himself a model of true piety and
morality, is as distinctly a religious figure as any known
to the Old Testament. Whether these aspects of the
ideal be primary or secondary makes little difference.
We may say that the Messiah of the prophets is primarily
a political figure to which a religious significance was
necessarily attached, or that he is primarily a religious
ideal to which political features were added: on neither
view is the assertion justified that the conception is
irreconcilable with the presuppositions of pre-Exilic
prophecy.

On the other hand Volz is right in insisting that the
distinctive features of Jeremiah's prophecy are not congenial to the Messianic idea in its Old Testament
forms. In his profoundly personal experience of religion
he seems to break through the limits of nationalism,

and to reach forward to a conception which is at once universal—embracing the heathen in the divine purpose of salvation (xvi. 19)—and individual, having its source in the fellowship of the human soul with God. We have seen that this side of his thinking is developed in an eschatological direction in his assurance to the Exiles in Babylon that the essential exercise of religion was possible for them under conditions which excluded the appearing of a Messiah. In so far as the Messianic idea represents the combined elements of nationalism and particularism it is out of harmony with the deepest tendencies of Jeremiah's teaching. Yet we have also seen that the principles of individualism and universalism are not carried out to their logical issues by Jeremiah. He shares with all the prophets the belief that the religious community of the future is to be a new people of Israel. Hence we cannot assume *a priori* that his outlook leaves no room for a restored Davidic monarchy, or for an ideal King of the last days: that is for a personal Messiah.

Whether he actually cherished that expectation remains doubtful, for the reasons we have stated. It depends on the authenticity of the single oracle in which it finds expression (xxiii. 5, 6). Two observations may be made. In the first place, the form in which the idea is presented is not inconsistent with the subdued colours in which Jeremiah elsewhere depicts the future blessedness of Israel. The Messiah as here described is no warrior king, or conquering hero, who vanquishes foreign nations and establishes a mighty empire on the earth, but a just and pious ruler who maintains righteousness in the land, and in virtue of his relation to Yahwe is the medium of divine succour and security to his people. There is nothing here unworthy of Jeremiah, or out of keeping with his conception of a peaceful and well-ordered commonwealth enjoying the blessing of

Yahwe in its own land and under its own government.
But, in the second place, the fact that the idea appears
only in one doubtful passage, and is absent from the
late prophecies of ch. xxxi, shows that it can never have
laid a very strong hold on the imagination of the prophet.
It is at best extraneous to the vital truths of his message,
not organically related to them, and still less arising out
of them, but adopted from tradition with an antithetic
reference to the unworthy occupants of the kingly office
in Jeremiah's time. When we compare the passage with
the lofty idealism of the Messianic prophecies in Isaiah
(ix. 1–6, xi. 1–8), we feel that the idea has lost something
of the glamour of its first inception. To Isaiah the
Messiah is a semi-divine personage, the radiant source
of supernatural powers which regenerate nature and
human society; in Jeremiah he is an ordinary good
king, and in a religious sense is merely the symbol of
the truth expressed in his name, that 'Yahwe is our
righteousness.' The contrast suggests that the passage
in Jeremiah belongs not to a waxing but to a waning
phase of the Messianic hope in Israel, but a phase in
which it still remains true to the ethical and spiritual
character impressed upon it by the inspiration of Isaiah.
Great ideals like this do not as a rule make their way
into religion by a gradual assimilation and transformation of the material by the spiritual, as Volz supposes
to have been the case with the Messianic idea. They
commonly burst in all their splendour on the mind of
a great religious genius, and fade into the light of
common day as new aspirations and ideals are evoked
by the living spirit of revelation, fulfilling himself in
many ways.

CHAPTER XVIII

THE FUTURE OF RELIGION (*continued*):
IV. THE NEW COVENANT

WE come in the last place to the *locus classicus* of Jeremiah's eschatology, the passage which has generally been held to express his deepest insight into the final manifestation of religion—the prophecy of the New Covenant in ch. xxxi. 31–34. The genuineness of this oracle is energetically disputed; and standing as it does in a series of disconnected and critically doubtful utterances, one cannot but feel with Cornill that it is no light matter now-a-days to maintain that it was written by Jeremiah. To establish that position proof would be required that the ideas are so intimately related to the structure of Jeremiah's thinking as to make it highly improbable that they should have been expressed by any other than he. Unfortunately the questions of authorship and of meaning are so bound up that the exegesis is apt to be biassed by assumptions as to the authorship, and *vice versâ*. Thus we may read into the words a view of religion so profoundly spiritual and personal that it is hardly conceivable that any one else than Jeremiah could have written them. On the other hand they may be interpreted in a trivial and formal sense which would stamp them unmistakably as the composition of a late Jewish legalist. The problem has therefore to be approached from two sides, and a satisfactory solution will only be reached if we find them to converge on one result.

We begin by inquiring whether the conception of religion as *based on a covenant* is in any degree charac-

teristic of Jeremiah; and if so in what way the idea
may have entered his mind. Unless the first question
can be answered affirmatively, it is clear that nothing
will be gained by ascribing the prophecy to Jeremiah.
Now, neither of these questions is so easily answered as
they were supposed to be at the time when Guthe wrote
his standard Latin dissertation on the Jeremianic notion
of the covenant (1877). At that time the book of
Jeremiah was generally accepted as in the main an
authentic record of the prophet's ministry; and it was
possible to cite 24 occurrences of the word *Běrîth*
which had not been seriously challenged by critics.
But now there is hardly one of those passages in which
the word is found which has not been declared spurious
by one eminent scholar or another. It does not follow
that they must all be summarily rejected: there are
many to which exception is taken on grounds that are
far from convincing; and the point to be determined is
whether there are enough to warrant the conclusion
that the idea formed an integral element in Jeremiah's
view of religion.

The idea of the covenant appears first in Jeremiah
in connexion with Josiah's reformation. In the pre-
Deuteronomic discourses, represented broadly by chs.
ii–vi, we find no trace of it. There the relation between
Yahwe and Israel is conceived in personal terms, as
resting on mutual affection—*héṣed*, which means kindness or grace on the part of Yahwe and loyal piety on
the part of Israel. For this view of religion the appropriate image is the marriage-bond, with its implications
of love and fidelity and trust. It should not be overlooked, however, that we also find the conception of
religion as a discipline—a yoke which had been cast off
(ii. 20, v. 5); and in this we may perhaps recognise a
point of affinity with the Covenant-idea. Indeed, the
figure of marriage itself, with its formal abrogation by

a 'bill of divorcement,' has a legal aspect which under certain circumstances might develop into the more abstract conception of the Covenant.

Be that as it may, the earliest express mention of the Covenant occurs in ch. xi. 1–8, a passage which we have already examined in discussing Jeremiah's attitude to the Deuteronomic movement[1]. The result there reached is not of vital moment for the point now to be insisted on, so long as it is admitted that the narrative contains at least a kernel of genuine words of Jeremiah. Whether the real fact be that Jeremiah accepted the national Covenant with its documentary basis as having divine authority, or whether he merely adopted and gave a wider range to the 'general idea of Deuteronomy, that of the covenant between Yahwe and Israel'; on either view—and on the second even more obviously than on the first—he recognised the validity of the Covenant-idea as a formal expression of the religious bond between God and His people. Now, the sudden emergence of the idea at this particular juncture can hardly be accidental. It suggests that the notion did not originate with Jeremiah, and was not a product of his spontaneous reflexion. It was due to the impression made on his mind by the great transaction of the year 621, in which for a time he saw a return to the purity of the national faith, which was full of promise for the future. With the previous history of the conception we are not here directly concerned. It is not a direct inheritance from the older prophets, although Hosea (viii. 1) may have been acquainted with it. Most probably it belonged to the oral and literary tradition of the Mosaic period, and through priestly influence it may have become the property of the combined prophetic and priestly party which carried through the Deuteronomic reform. In the seventh century it must have

[1] pp. 97–102.

met some deeply felt want of the age, so that when a great religious reformation was contemplated it took by common consent the form of a renewal of the Covenant with Yahwe.

It is a further question whether the conception became a permanent element of the thinking of Jeremiah; and on that point the evidence is less decisive than might be desired. In the sequel of ch. xi (*vv.* 9, 10), written probably in the reign of Jehoiakim, the people are said to have returned to the sins of their fathers, and thereby broken Yahwe's Covenant, as if they had entered into a 'conspiracy' to do so. There seem to be no good reasons for denying the originality of this utterance; and it clearly implies that the thought of the Covenant retained a certain place in the prophet's mind. Similarly in xxii. 8, 9 (but in a more doubtful context: = Deut. xxix. 23 f.), the fate of Jerusalem is ascribed by the nations to the fact that the people have 'forsaken the covenant of Yahwe their God, and worshipped other gods.' In xiv. 21, the people under the shadow of some great calamity implore Yahwe to remember and not break His Covenant with them, a testimony perhaps rather to the popular belief than to that of Jeremiah. Lastly, ch. xxxiv. 13 is a clear and important reference to the Mosaic Covenant; and the only pertinent objection that can be urged against it is that being taken (probably) from the narrative of Baruch it does not necessarily reproduce the *ipsissima verba* of Jeremiah. In all these cases the prophet is dealing with breaches of the covenant; and it is conceivable that with the failure of Deuteronomy staring him in the face he might have thrown his indictment into this form without attaching much intrinsic value to the idea. The remaining passages all refer to the New Covenant; but with the exception of the classical *locus* in ch. xxxi they are all of very doubtful originality (xxxii. 40, xxxiii. 20, 21, 25, l. 5).

It is thus a very slender line of proof-texts which leads from the covenant of Josiah to the anticipation of a New Covenant as the permanent form of religion in the future. Is it sufficient to show that the idea was a living principle of Jeremiah's teaching, so that out of it could have sprung his general conception of the relation between God and His people? To put the question in that form is almost to invite a negative answer. It is not, however, altogether a matter of proof-texts, but much more of affinities of thought between the teaching of Jeremiah and the circle of ideas to which the Covenant belongs. And such affinities appear to exist in his later prophecy. The most distinct is contained in the phrase 'I will be a God to them, and they shall be to me a people,' which is the specific formula of the Covenant, and (with variations) occurs not only in ch. xi. 4, but also in vii. 23, xxiv. 7, xxxi. 33, [xxx. 22, xxxi. 1, xxxii. 38]. Although the last three instances may be secondary, the genuineness of vii. 23, xxiv. 7, if not xi. 4, cannot reasonably be questioned, and there is no justification for regarding the formula as in itself a mark of Deuteronomic editorship. Again, the representation of the land of Canaan as a gift to the nation or to the fathers is a constant element in the Covenant conception, and is found in passages which we need not hesitate to attribute to Jeremiah (vii. 7, xvii. 4, xxiv. 10, xxv. 5— [doubtful: iii. 18, xii. 14, xvi. 15, xxx. 3, xxxii. 22, xxxv. 15]). Once more, the obligation of obedience— listening to the words or the *Tôrā* of Yahwe—as a condition of well-being, is frequently emphasised in the book, and has at least an affinity with the idea of the Covenant. To assign these features wholly to the Deuteronomic redaction as is done by some writers, is really to prejudge the issue with which we are occupied, besides overlooking the probability that the editors must have found some point of contact for their phraseology in the actual words of the prophet.

The reluctance of many recent writers to admit that Jeremiah was influenced by the notion of the Covenant proceeds largely from a true perception of its inadequacy to express the deeper elements in his thought and experience. If anything is vital in Jeremiah, it is his experience of religion as immediate fellowship with God, and his conviction that the reality of it consists in a right inward disposition, in the instinctive response of the heart to the revelation of God. The Covenant, on the contrary, only establishes an external relation: the two parties standing over against each other, with nothing to unite them except a legal obligation. It represents a view of religion which was natural and beneficial in the early history of Israel, but could only produce a false sense of security in the age of Deuteronomy. How can we suppose that such a representation was accepted by the man whose constant effort was (in the words of Dr Davidson) 'to draw men's minds away from all that was external—sacrifices, Temple, ark and law-book—to that which was inward and real'? The objection is weighty, and would be decisive against the contention that the whole of Jeremiah's theology moves within the circle of the Covenant-idea. It is certain that his personal piety could never have expressed itself in terms of a covenant between him and God, and equally true that the religious instinct which he conceived to be native to the human soul, and which he desired to see liberated from the fetters of evil custom in the hearts of his countrymen, was incapable of embodiment in the forms of a statutory and dissoluble relationship.

But the difficulty disappears when we observe that the idea is used by Jeremiah only when speaking of religion as a national institution. It is a framework into which is fitted, not his whole view of religion, but only his view of the relation between Yahwe and Israel as a people. Now this national aspect of religion presented a problem from the point of view which the prophets, and Jeremiah in particular, had reached. In his early poems Jeremiah had dealt with it on the lines of poetic analogy, in the personification of Israel as formerly the devoted bride, but now the unfaithful and adulterous wife, of Yahwe. But it must have become plain to him that this representation of Israel as an ideal unity was inadequate to the practical situation with which he was faced. The conception of Israel as a moral personality, though true to the larger issues of national destiny, and therefore never abandoned by Jeremiah, failed to bring home to the individual his own responsibility for the apostasy of the people. It was as if there were a 'conspiracy' to thwart the purpose of Yahwe (xi. 9, 10); but the root of that conspiracy was in the perversity of the individual will. The idea of the Covenant afforded a certain relief from this embarrassment. It was given by the facts of history[1] and, as the initiative of the Deuteronomists showed, it was capable of practical application to the needs of the present. And while it conserved the national principle in religion, it nevertheless individualised men, laying on each man's conscience the duty which God required of him as a member of the covenant people. Whether Jeremiah approved of the Deuteronomic covenant or not there is nothing in his teaching antagonistic to the idea as a form in which Israel's relation to Yahwe might be expressed. It is perhaps not too much to say that it was the necessary transition from the purely national view of religion with which he started to the implicit

---

[1] 'Neither to the Deuteronomist nor to Jeremiah is the Covenant the direct content of immediate faith; to both it reflects a historic knowledge of the origin of the relation between Yahwe and the people of Israel' (Duhm, *Theol. d. Pr.* p. 237).

individualism which is characteristic of his mature reflexion.

These considerations make it credible that the conception of Israel's relation to God as founded on a historic covenant occupies a real, though not all-inclusive, place in the theology of Jeremiah. From this it is but a step to the anticipation of a New Covenant. It is clear from many passages that he was profoundly exercised by the failure of the national religion. He sets this failure 'in all possible lights' (Davidson): it is to him something inexplicable and frightful. He contrasts it with the stedfastness of the heathen religions (ii. 11), nay even with the fidelity of the Rechabites to their tribal code (xxxv. 14). He marvels that his people should forsake the Fountain of living water for the broken cisterns of an unreal faith; that they should be capable of for ever falling without rising again; that they are so destitute of the instinct that draws man to God. It is a monstrous thing that the virgin Israel has done in forgetting God and worshipping vanity (xviii. 13 ff.). It is true that he explains the portent by the inveterate sinful propensity of the people, but he must surely have been conscious that that was not the last word. The heart might be 'desperately sick,' but it was not naturally depraved; the spell of evil habit might be too strong for the human will to break (xiii. 23), but it could not destroy the essential affinity of man's nature with the divine. The very fact that evil habit had gained such an ascendancy in the life of the nation that it had to be consumed in the fire of judgment, pointed to some inherent defect in the old dispensation, which made it an ineffective means of communion between the nation and its God. The only hope for the future lay in a readjustment of relations between Yahwe and Israel—in a New Covenant, established, as the writer to the Hebrews puts it, 'on better promises.'

By a New Covenant, then, Jeremiah means a new religious relationship; and we have now to examine wherein the novelty of that relationship consists. We do not know for certain in what precise terms Jeremiah would have described the Mosaic covenant. The only explicit statement is in ch. xi. 1–8; and we have seen reason to surmise that these verses have been freely expanded by Deuteronomic editors. A comparison with other passages[1], however, yields the following features as constituents of the conception: (i) The covenant formula is 'I will be to them a God, and they shall be to me a people.' (ii) There are conditions to be fulfilled by Israel, viz. (*a*) exclusive allegiance to Yahwe, (*b*) obedience to His will as expressed in His Law (*Tôrā*), and in the continuous revelation of prophecy. (iii) The promises on the part of Yahwe are (*a*) to treat Israel as His peculiar people, and (*b*) to secure it in the possession of the land of Canaan. It will be seen that if this is a correct account of Jeremiah's conception of the Mosaic covenant, it is identical with that of the writers of Deuteronomy: that is, it agrees with the ideas of the circle from which he appears to have borrowed the notion.

The contrast between the Old Covenant and the New is set forth in the great prophecy of ch. xxxi, which I will now quote in full:

31 Lo, the time is coming, saith Yahwe, when I will make with the House of Israel [and the House of Judah] a New Covenant. 32 Not like the covenant which I made with their fathers when I took them by the hand to lead them out of the land of Egypt; seeing that they have broken My covenant, and I have rejected them, saith Yahwe. 33 But this is the Covenant which I will make with the House of Israel after these days, saith Yahwe: I put My *Tôrā* in their inward part, and write it in their heart; and I will be to them a God, and they shall be

[1] Ch. vii. 2, 7, 23, xi. 15, (xiii. 10), (xii. 14), (xvi. 15), xvii. 4.

to Me a people. 34 And they shall no longer need to teach one another, and every man his neighbour, to know Yahwe; but all shall know Me, from the least to the greatest, saith Yahwe; for I will pardon their guilt, and remember their sins no more.

It will be seen first of all that in two respects the New Covenant is simply a renewal of the Old. First, the principle of nationalism is carried over from the old dispensation to the New: the covenant is made with the House of Israel [and the House of Judah]. Again, the form of the New Covenant is identical with that of the Old: 'I will be to them a God, and they shall be to me a people,'—a formula, indeed, which is capable of no enlargement, but only of a fuller realisation. The distinction of the New Covenant, therefore, is that it provides the conditions which make fellowship with God real. As Vatke has expressed it, the difference lies 'not in the content of the covenant, but on the side of *reality*, of *subjectivity*' (*Biblische Theologie*, p. 526; quoted by Kraetschmar, *Die Bundesvorstellung im A.T.* p. 159). The ideal which the Old Covenant failed to make good will be realised under the New.

What, then, are the positive features of the religious relationship established by the New Covenant? There are three: (1) *Inwardness*: 'I will put My law in their inward part'; (2) *Individualism*: 'all shall know Me'; (3) *Forgiveness of sins*: 'their sins I will remember no more.' Now, all these are indispensable conditions of true fellowship with God; but in the present connexion the last two, which *follow* the covenant formula, appear to have a secondary emphasis. The second is an expansion or corollary of the first; and the third, introduced by 'For,' seems to characterise the whole relationship as founded on reconciliation with God. The central truth, therefore, on which the emphasis of the prophecy lies, is the inwardness of true religion—the spiritual illumination of the individual mind and conscience, and the doing of the will of God from a spontaneous impulse of the renewed heart. To Christian theology the promise has meant nothing less than this, and the prophecy of the New Covenant has therefore been regarded as one of the profoundest anticipations of the perfect religion that the Old Testament contains.

The objections to this view of the passage are stated with his usual perspicacity and incisiveness by Professor Duhm. After remarking that if the words were written by Jeremiah they would be of the highest importance as setting forth the contrast between the prophetic and the Deuteronomic conceptions of religion, Duhm proceeds to argue that they have no such significance. They betray no consciousness of the need for a higher kind of religion. If that had been in the mind of the unknown author, he would have spoken of a new *Tôrā* rather than of a new *Běrîth* or Covenant—a *Tôrā* which in virtue of its essentially different content and character would be better fitted than the old to be written on the heart. Since he says nothing of this we must assume that he is thinking only of the old law, with all its ritual prescriptions about clean and unclean foods, external holiness, and so forth; and when he speaks of it as written in the inward part he simply means that every Jew will know it by heart, and not at second hand through the instruction of professional teachers. Of a higher revelation of God, of personal communion with God, or of a regenerate heart in the sense of Christianity, Duhm finds in the passage no suggestion whatever.

Now quite possibly this is the interpretation which we should be obliged to put on the prophecy if we regard it as a product of post-Exilic Judaism. But is it a fair and natural explanation of its language and the sequence of its thought? On the contrary it appears to me that it empties its terms of their proper force and significance. Duhm's most fundamental argument lies in the assertion that if the passage had any meaning worthy of Jeremiah it must have promised a new *Tôrā*. But if it was *not* written by Jeremiah, it is very difficult to see why the legalist who wrote it should speak even of a new *Bĕrîth*. The old covenant surely afforded scope for the memorising of the old law to any conceivable extent (see Deut. vi. 6 ff.). Committing to memory is after all a purely human exercise, whereas what is promised in the text is a divine operation on the hearts of men. Moreover, learning by heart does not supersede the necessity for human instructors, so that the antithesis between *vv*. 33 *a* and 34 *a* becomes meaningless. The antithesis really implied in the language is between an external law, written in a book or on tables of stone, and the dictates of the inward moral sense informed by true knowledge of God. To 'know Yahwe' (*v*. 34) and to have His revelation written on the heart (*v*. 33) are the same thing; and the weakness of the old dispensation was that the mere inculcation of external precepts by priests or teachers or parents failed to reach the springs of action, and to produce that knowledge of God as the lover of mercy, righteousness and justice (ch. ix. 23 [24]) which makes His will the guiding principle of the life. If this is not to create a new heart in the Christian sense, it is only because the figure employed is inadequate to express the fulness of the idea which the writer has in his mind. And to ask, as Duhm does, why God did not provide for this in the first covenant is surely an astonishing lapse from the historical view of religion, which has had no more brilliant exponent than Duhm himself.

A word or two may be added on the contention that this implies a new revelation—a new *Tôrā*—and that no such expectation is expressed in the prophecy. I venture to think that this objection is met by an understanding of the sense in which Jeremiah (and perhaps the prophets generally) use the word *Tôrā*. I hazard the suggestion that this is closely analogous to the manner in which Jesus speaks of the law as in essence eternal and immutable, but in form imperfect and needing to be 'fulfilled' and in part abrogated. To Jeremiah the true *Tôrā* of Yahwe is not Deuteronomy nor any written code, nor priestly oracle, nor prophetic message, but something which has been partly expressed in all these ways and yet transcends them all—the revelation of the essential ethical will of God. *Bĕrîth* and *Tôrā* are related to each other as form and content. The old covenant was based on an imperfect manifestation of the law of God in the form of external commands; the New Covenant will be established by a better revelation of that will in the spirit of man. If this be a true representation of Jeremiah's attitude to the *Tôrā*, and if Jeremiah be the author of the verses before us, there was no occasion to announce a new law capable of being engraved on the heart in a better way than committing it to memory. The *Tôrā* of Yahwe is the living principle of religion which is ever new, which exists perfectly in the mind of God, and is therefore capable of being reproduced in the minds of men who 'know Yahwe' in spirit and in truth.

On the view which I have tried to expound the high importance assigned to the passage in the New Testament (Heb. viii. 8–12, x. 16 f.; Rom. xi. 27; Mat. xxvi. 28; Luke xxii. 20, etc.)—an estimate endorsed in the main by the *consensus* of Christian scholarship—is amply vindicated. It is the announcement of a new and final stage in the manifestation of God's purpose of redemption, at which His gracious relation to His people will be realised in a perfect fellowship of heart and will, based on the forgiveness of sins. It must have been written by Jeremiah, and is rightly regarded as his most noteworthy contribution to the ideal religion

of the future. In it we find a synthesis of the two
tendencies which we have seen to run through his
eschatological conceptions: on the one hand his clinging
to the national idea as the only form in which the
religious community was conceivable to him; and on
the other hand the conception of religion as direct
contact between the individual soul and God. Both are
represented in the New Covenant; it is a national
covenant, made with the house of Israel; and at the
same time it is individual, resting on the possession by
each member of the community of personal knowledge
of God. This no doubt involves a formal incongruity,
but it is one which runs through the whole of the Old
Testament, and belongs to the inherent limitations of
the old dispensation. The prophet has to put new wine
into old bottles. In terms of the covenant he has to
express truth which transcends the covenant idea, and
cannot be adequately embodied in its forms. The whole
notion of a compact between God and man, which was
the prevalent view of religion in the age of Jeremiah,
is broken through by the promise of an intimate union
of mind and will brought about by God Himself, and
represented here as the writing of His law on the heart.
The real nature of this divine operation on the human
soul Jeremiah probably could not have explained. He
had learned by experience the need of it, if religion was
to be; and his faith was stedfast that the creative power
of God would effect the renewal, and as he says in
another place, give the people a heart to know Him
(xxiv. 7).

It may be but one aspect of the perfect religion that
is here set forth, its inwardness, but that aspect is
fundamental. The individualism of Christianity is not
a secondary and incidental feature: it is of the essence
of the Gospel. It affirms the infinite value of the individual soul, its potential freedom from the realm of

nature and the environment of evil into which it is born, and its capacity for realising that freedom in communion with the Father of spirits. Something of this Jeremiah had learned in his own life; and if he saw but dimly, he perceived that what religion was to him it must be to all men—the response of the heart to the voice of God within. The vision of an ideal community with a right mind towards God he held in common with all the prophets, and like them he conceived it as a restored and purified Israel. His peculiar contribution to the prophetic hope is the thought of a direct action of God on the heart of each Israelite, bringing it into harmony with His own character and will. He may not have seen that this thought must burst the bond of nationality, and be fulfilled in an invisible fellowship of spirits based on that knowledge of God which he knew to be the ultimate reality of religion. But in projecting his own personal experience into the future as the form which true religion must assume universally, he threw a bright beam of light across the ages; and it falls at last on One who is the Yea and the Amen to all the promises of God—on Jesus the Mediator of the New Covenant, and the Author of eternal salvation.

CHAPTER XIX

LAST DAYS OF JEREMIAH

WHAT remains to be told of the history of Jeremiah seems to set the seal of failure on the work of his life. We see the prophet engaged in a last hopeless protest against the unbelief and superstition which permeated every fibre of the popular sentiment, and found even in national disaster a fresh stimulus to its vitality. The record is doubly melancholy when we contrast it with the bright anticipations which he had cherished of a new people of God arising on the foundation of the good work done by Gedaliah at Mizpah. Like Dante at the outset of his pilgrimage, he had seen near at hand the sunlit summit of the 'delectable mount' of an earthly kingdom of righteousness and peace, but when he essayed to climb its slope he found his way impeded by the 'peaceless beast' of his countrymen's unregenerate mind, which thrust him back into the darkness from which he had emerged[1]. In very truth

[1] *Inferno*, Canto I, ll. 13–18, 55–60:

> Ma poi ch' io fui al piè d' un colle giunto,
> Là dove terminava quella valle
> Che m' avea di paura il cor compunto,
> Guardai in alto, e vidi le sue spalle
> Vestite già de' raggi del pianeta
> Che mena dritto altrui per ogni calle.

> * * * * * *

> E quale è quei che voluntieri acquista,
> E giugne il tempo che perder lo face,
> Che in tutt' i suoi pensier piange e s' attrista:
> Tal me fece la bestia senza pace,
> Che venendomi incontro, a poco a poco
> Mi ripingeva là, dove il Sol tace.

it was only by way of the eternal world that Jeremiah could enter on the fruition of his hopes.

The turning-point in his relations with the community whose fortunes he had so willingly shared was the resolve of its leaders to migrate to Egypt. This, we have seen, was their almost instinctive impulse as soon as they realised the probable consequences of the assassination of the Babylonian governor in their midst. If they had succeeded in capturing the murderer they might have hoped to establish their innocence by handing him over to the strong arm of Chaldean justice; but with the real criminal undetected how could they feel themselves safe from Nebuchadnezzar's indiscriminate vengeance? Besides, they were weary of the incessant turmoil, the harassing uncertainty of their precarious existence in Palestine, and longed for a security and comfort to which they had long been strangers. We cannot say that such fears were groundless, or such desires in themselves reprehensible. We have to consider what sinful element lurked in their purpose to make it the occasion of an irreparable breach between them and the prophet whom they had learned to revere as the inspired interpreter of the will of God to their generation.

It appears quite plainly that Jeremiah himself was at first in some doubt regarding the propriety or rightness of the step that was meditated. When the people approached him with a humble request for divine guidance on the 'way that they should walk and the thing that they should do' at this critical juncture of their destiny, he had no answer ready. Ten days he spent in prayer and meditation before the mind of God was perfectly clear to him (ch. xlii. 1–7). It is an instructive, though unique example of the process by which a prophet might attain to certainty of the message he was to deliver as the word of God; and it is one that lies very near to the region of common religious experience. It suggests an analogy between prophetic inspiration and that assurance that God has spoken to the soul which comes in answer to prayer for light in some perplexing situation—an analogy which, even if it be not complete, is perhaps the nearest that can be found to the operation of the divine spirit on the mind of a prophet. It may be difficult to say how far we are entitled to extend this idea; but we see at least that on the highest level of prophecy illumination might be the result of prolonged mental conflict, and that final certitude was reached in a way not essentially different from that in which light dawns on the mind, or duty becomes plain, in rapt spiritual communion with God.

We can partly understand the issues which so profoundly exercised the mind of Jeremiah at this time, and the considerations that might incline his judgment in one direction or the other. This project of seeking refuge in Egypt—was it from God or of men? Was it in the line of Yahwe's purpose for His people, or was it contrary thereto? Would it strengthen faith and true religion in the hearts of the men who were yielding to it, or would it mean their exclusion from the commonwealth of Israel? To every Israelite the very thought of a return to the land whence Yahwe had brought His people at the first must have been repellent: it was a reversal of the providential order of the nation's history. Yet Jeremiah had taught the exiles in Babylonia that their religion was independent of climate, that Yahwe could be worshipped in a foreign land as truly as at Jerusalem. Might not that which was true of compulsory exile in Babylon be equally true of a voluntary exile in Egypt? Was not Yahwe as near to those who sought Him with all their heart in Egypt as in Palestine? But no! Egypt was not Babylon, nor were the men who consulted him of a kind to hold fast their faith when

deprived of its outward symbols and traditional associ-
ations. It was a settled conviction of Jeremiah's later
ministry that the Babylonian empire was the power
ordained by Yahwe for the maintenance of civil order
in the world, and his belief in the character of Nebuchadnezzar assured him that he would act worthily of his
high mission, and would show mercy to them and
reinstate them in their possessions, if they remained
under his rule. To seek safety beyond the pale of the
great world-empire was to flee from the presence of
Yahwe, and renounce the hope of a place in His
kingdom. The men who did not perceive this were
blind to the signs of the times, and deaf to the voice of
prophecy. The purpose they had formed was rooted in
unbelief, in distrust of Yahwe's power to protect them,
and indifference to His claim on their allegiance. As
the issues gradually cleared themselves in the prophet's
mind he came to see that more than material interests
were at stake in the matter submitted to him. The men
who proposed to forsake the land were on the point of
forfeiting their religious heritage. If they persisted in
their intention not only would the good work begun
under Gedaliah be undone, but they themselves would
be lost to the cause of Yahwe and the future of Israel.

When the answer came it was clear and peremptory.
To abide in the land, trusting to the promise of Yahwe
and the clemency of the king of Babylon, was the
course of safety and of duty; to go down to Egypt was an
act of apostasy and rebellion, which would be punished
by all the evils they sought to escape. But meanwhile
an opposite process of conviction had been going on
in the minds of the fugitives. There is no reason to
question the sincerity of their solemn promise to yield
implicit obedience to the word of the Lord, whether it
were in accordance with their wishes or not (ch. xlii.
5 f.). But as the days passed, and no answer was received,

they became so sure of the rightness of the step they contemplated that nothing would persuade them that an adverse decision was an authentic oracle of Yahwe. Moreover they suspected that Baruch was bringing pressure to bear on the prophet, and swaying him in a direction opposed to the opinion of the majority. So when Jeremiah announced to the assembled community the message he had received, he encountered a hard-faced resistance against which he could make no headway. The spokesmen of the assembly boldly charged him with falsehood, in trying to palm off as a divine communication the policy of Baruch the son of Neriah. This interesting and unexpected tribute to the influence of Jeremiah's self-effacing biographer led Canon Cheyne to conjecture that Baruch had latterly gained an undue ascendancy over his master, obscuring with worldly wisdom his communion with his God, and deflecting his mind from its better intuitions by the false expectation that under Gedaliah Israel as a nation could yet be built up in its own land[1]. There is no evidence to support so sweeping a conclusion, although there is enough to show that Baruch was a person of more consideration and force of character than we should have gathered from his own modest pages. It may well have been that by his zeal and activity in the service of the now aged prophet he had of late taken a prominent part in public affairs, and had created the erroneous impression that he was the more energetic personality of the two. At all events it now suited the purpose of the self-willed captains to put on him the responsibility for an oracle which they were determined to disobey. Their minds were already made up; and without further parley they gathered their company together, and set out for Egypt, taking Jeremiah and Baruch with them.

[1] *Jeremiah: his Life and Times*, pp. 191 f.

We are told nothing, and can imagine little, of the reception which this miserable band of Jewish refugees met in the land of the Pharaohs, or of their manner of life there, or even how long they were able to maintain a separate existence. The interest of the narrative is concentrated entirely on Jeremiah's attitude to his expatriated countrymen, and is restricted to two incidents, both of which must have taken place soon after the migration. Two illusions appear to have sustained the spirit of the leaders in their headstrong and hazardous adventure. One was that in Egypt they would be beyond the reach of Nebuchadnezzar's vengeance, under the protection of a friendly and powerful monarch. The other was that they could still remain true to the religion of their fathers—why else did they compel Yahwe's greatest prophet to accompany them? In the two scenes recorded by Baruch we seem to see Jeremiah setting himself to shatter these illusions, one after the other.

On the first (ch. xliii. 8–13) we need not dwell at great length. It was apparently a night-scene[1], enacted in front of the royal palace at Tahpanhes or Daphnai, the frontier fortress where the wanderers first found a resting-place on Egyptian soil. In presence of a few Jewish men, Jeremiah is directed to perform a singular action. He is to take great stones and bury them secretly at the entrance of the palace. He is then to announce that a day will come when the dreaded Nebuchadnezzar will set up his throne over these very stones as the conqueror of Egypt. It is a symbolical prophecy of the invasion of Egypt by the king of Babylon from whom his hearers had thought themselves secure. He will

---

[1] So at least if with the Greek versions of Aquila, Symmachus and Theodotion, and the Vulgate we read בַּלָּט, 'in secrecy,' instead of the unintelligible במלט במלבן of the Massoretic text. See the commentaries.

ransack the land of Egypt as easily as a shepherd clears
his sheepskin cloak of vermin, and having finished his
work he will retire in safety. It did not require great
political knowledge to foresee that a conflict between
the two great powers was inevitable in the near future,
or to tell on which side the victory would lie. The same
expectation was entertained and more definitely expressed by Ezekiel in an oracle dated about the year
570 B.C. (Ezek. xxix. 17–20). The predictions seem to
have been partially fulfilled within the lifetime of some
of Jeremiah's hearers, though not till after the prophet
himself had passed from the scene. Obscure references
in both Babylonian and Egyptian inscriptions combine
to make it probable that a Babylonian invasion of Egypt
took place in the year 568, in which the land was
ravaged as far as the southern frontier at Syene (Ezek.
xxix. 10)[1].

The second incident requires closer study, both for
its intrinsic religious importance, and because of the
difficulty of unravelling the situation presented to us
in ch. xliv. As it stands it reads at first like an encyclical
written by the prophet to all the Jewish residents in
Egypt, from Migdol and Tahpanhes in the north, to
Memphis in the centre, and Pathros or Upper Egypt
in the south. The purpose of the letter seems to be to
drive home the lesson of the destruction of Jerusalem,
and announce the extinction of the remnant which
perpetuated in Egypt the iniquities of their forefathers.
There is nothing incredible in the supposition that
numerous Jewish settlements were already scattered
over this wide area. But when we reach *v.* 15 we find
that the words are *spoken* to a vast concourse of Jews
assembled in one place, and this narrows itself down
further to an altercation between Jeremiah and the

---

[1] Meyer, *Geschichte des Alterthums* (1884), p. 497; Winckler,
Geschichte Babyloniens und Assyriens (1892), pp. 312 f.

women of the assembly, who hotly asserted their determination to return to the worship of the Queen of
Heaven in fulfilment of a vow which they had made.
It might not be altogether impossible to effect a rough
harmony of these discordant indications, by imagining
a great representative gathering of Jews from all parts
of Egypt, met to celebrate the resuscitation of the cult
of the Queen of Heaven, on which the female element
among them had set its mind. But even with that
assumption it would be difficult to read the chapter as
the composition of a single author. The diffuse homiletic
style which pervades the chapter bears the marks of
literary origin, and is ill-suited to the requirements of
oral address under such circumstances as are suggested;
and the abrupt introduction of the women with their
favourite form of idolatry in *v.* 15 throws the whole
scene into confusion. Recent expositors are agreed that
the passage has suffered expansion and consequent
modification at the hands of Jeremiah's editors, although
the extent of these editorial operations is variously
estimated by different writers. The most drastic, but
at the same time the most satisfying, solution seems to
be that given by Erbt, who finds the genuine historical
kernel of the narrative in the passage dealing with the
worship of the Queen of Heaven, which was afterwards
converted by amplification into an oracle against
Egyptian Judaism as a whole. Of the two speeches put
into the mouth of Jeremiah he rejects the first (*vv.*
20–23), and finds the real answer of the prophet to the
argument of the women in *vv.* 24–28, which, with some
alterations of text he reduces to metrical form (see
below, p. 345)[1].

---

[1] In detail Erbt's analysis (which is adopted in the main by Schmidt)
is nearly as follows: He assigns to the redaction the whole of *vv.* 1–14,
except the heading, and the second half of *v.* 4 ('Do not this abominable
thing which I hate'), which he retains as the expostulation of Jeremiah

There is no more vivid illustration in the Old Testament of the deep-seated antagonism between the prophetic and the popular interpretations of providence than this remarkable dialogue. It proves the utter failure of the Deuteronomic reformation to reach the heart of the people. The worship of the Queen of Heaven—the goddess Ishtar, represented by the planet Venus—was a specifically Babylonian form of idolatry which had come into vogue in the reign of Manasseh, and had laid a firm hold on the imagination especially of the women of Judah. Its interesting rites had often been witnessed by Jeremiah in the cities of Judah and the streets of Jerusalem (ch. vii. 17 f.). It must have been suppressed during the later years of Josiah; whether it had been restored in the reaction under Jehoiakim we do not know. At all events it must have been to the earlier period that the women referred when they alleged that all the disasters which had overtaken the State dated from the time when this cult was abandoned (*vv.* 17 f.). Perhaps it is taking a too serious

---

to which the women retort in *vv.* 15 f. In *vv.* 15–19 the only material alteration is the clearing from *v.* 15 of the misleading clauses 'all the men who knew that their wives sacrificed to other gods, and all,' and 'and all the people that dwelt in the land of Egypt in Pathros'; thus making the women the only speakers in *vv.* 16–19. Similarly, in *v.* 24 he deletes (with LXX) 'all Judah which is in the land of Egypt'; and in *v.* 25 reads (again with LXX) 'Ye women' instead of 'Ye and your wives,' and (besides some minor changes) turns the masculine suffixes into feminine in what follows. *V.* 26 is reduced to its last clause, 'My name shall no more be in the mouth of any man of Judah, saying "As Yahwe liveth," in all the land of Egypt.' *Vv.* 27 and 28 *a* are omitted entirely, and in 28 *b* the words 'that are come into the land of Egypt to sojourn there,' and at the end 'Mine or theirs' (LXX). *Vv.* 29, 30 can have formed no part of the original address. See Erbt, *Jeremia u. s. Zeit*, pp. 77 ff., 107, and compare Schmidt, *Die grossen Propheten*, pp. 372 f. Many of these emendations and excisions are supported by other scholars (Stade, Duhm, Cornill, etc.), and the gain in clearness is unmistakable.

view of this feminine theology to suppose that it involves a belief in the Queen of Heaven as a more potent deity than Yahwe, or a deliberate repudiation of the national God. What the women objected to was not the acknowledgment of Yahwe as the supreme God, but only that *exclusive* worship of Him which the prophets and Deuteronomy demanded and which had made illegal an innocent and picturesque piece of ritual which experience had now shown to be necessary for the welfare of the State. That they could look back to the reign of Manasseh as a time of ease and happiness in the nation's history evinces a depth of religious callousness, an aloofness from the struggles and sufferings of the prophetic party at that time, which we might expect to find in the secluded upper *coteries* of society and nowhere else. Since we read of royal princesses who had been left in charge of Gedaliah and been escorted to Egypt by Johanan and his men of war (ch. xli. 10, xliii. 6), we may imagine that these court ladies were chiefly influential in starting this paganising movement among the women of the caravan. Probably on the way to Egypt, they had registered the vow to which they here allude, to return to the worship of their favourite goddess at the first opportunity and it would seem from Jeremiah's words to them that he had interrupted them in the act of carrying out their resolution. He would see once more 'the children gathering wood, and the fathers kindling the fire, and the women kneading the dough, to make cakes to the Queen of Heaven' (ch. vii. 18).

Read in the light of this dramatic situation, the words of Jeremiah are charged with terrible import. He has tried to dissuade the women before him from carrying out their purpose, and has been met with clamorous and insolent defiance. He makes no further attempt to expostulate with them, but with scathing irony he hands them over to their reprobate and superstitious mind (*vv.* 25–28):

25 Thus speaks Yahwe, Israel's God:

> Ye women! Ye have spoken with your mouth,
>> And performed it with your hands!
> 'We will assuredly fulfil our vows which we have vowed,
>> To burn sacrifice to the Queen of Heaven
>> And pour out to her libations.'
> Hold, then, to your words,
>> And do according to your vows!

26b By My great name I swear,
>> Saith Yahwe!
> That My name shall no more be heard
>> In the mouth of any man of Judah
>> In all the land of Egypt.
28b Then shall all the remnant of Judah know
>> Whose word it is that stands!

The point of the oracle is the announcement of the extinction of the Yahwe-religion among the Jews of Egypt. Thus the second illusion cherished by the leaders of the migration is dispelled by the inexorable logic of the prophet. They had flattered themselves that they could still hold fast to the religious inheritance of their race, although they went to sojourn in a strange land. They knew not what spirit they were of. Their wives and daughters, with their frankly pagan proclivities, more truly expressed the real religious attitude of the community; and the men, by countenancing the revival of heathen rites in their midst, had shown where their sympathies lay. They drew a lesson from the late disasters which was diametrically opposed to the teaching of the prophets and the mind of God; and soon the empty profession of the national faith would give place to open and complete apostasy. The name of Yahwe would no more be in the mouth of any Jew in the land

of Egypt. The long controversy between Yahwe and
Israel closes with the abandonment of His worship by
the last survivors of the national catastrophe. Then it
will be seen which of the two readings of history—the
prophetic or the popular—holds the field. They shall
know 'whose word stands, Mine or theirs.'

This was probably the last, as it is the last recorded,
public utterance of Jeremiah. In hurling the sentence
of final rejection against his fellow-exiles he lays down
his work as a prophet. Of his private feelings in these
closing days of his life we have perhaps a revelation in
what is probably the last message that has been preserved from his lips: the oracle on the faithful friend
of his declining years and companion of his exile,
Baruch the son of Neriah (ch. xlv). The passage is
undoubtedly very obscure in its allusions, and the date
is uncertain. The heading assigns it to the fourth year
of Jehoiakim, when Baruch is first introduced as Jeremiah's amanuensis; but that notice is one that might
easily have been inserted by an editor who mistook the
writing of the prophet's biography for the writing of
the roll of his prophecies in 604; and the supposed
situation hardly does justice to the language of the
oracle. We do not know what fresh sorrow Baruch
complains of in v. 3, and still less can we conjecture
what personal ambition of his is rebuked in v. 5. But it
seems to me that we can best appreciate its tone and
significance if we hold that it stands in its proper
chronological place at the close of Baruch's biography,
and contains the last words of Jeremiah to his devoted
disciple. It reads, in short, like a farewell oracle, perhaps
even a death-bed charge. The last verse strongly suggests that the friends are about to separate, and that
Baruch will tread a lonely and perilous path through
life, deprived of the guidance on which he had so long
leaned. The fresh grief which has desolated his heart

is the prospect of separation from his beloved master; and the 'great things' which he is tempted to seek for himself might be a position of influence which he had hoped to occupy by the side of Jeremiah in the reconstruction of the new Israel. We may at all events read the chapter by the help of this hypothesis, and try to catch something of its sombre and chastened spirit.

¹ The word which Jeremiah the prophet spoke to Baruch the son of Neriah, as he wrote these words in a book: ² This is Yahwe's oracle concerning thee, O Baruch:

3 'Thou hast said, "Ah, Woe is me!
　　　That Yahwe adds anguish to my pain!
　　Weary am I with sighing,
　　　And find no rest!"'
4 Thus shalt thou say to him:
　　　Thus saith Yahwe:
　　'Behold, what I have built
　　　That I pull down,
　　And what I have planted
　　　That I pluck up¹!
5 And wilt thou seek great things for thyself?
　　　Seek them not!
　　Behold, I am bringing evil on all flesh,
　　　Saith Yahwe;
　　But to thee I give thy life as a prey,
　　　In all places whither thou shalt go.'

If these be indeed the last words of Jeremiah, they are a fitting *finale* to the life of incessant strife and contention, of defeat and disappointment, the successive phases of which it has been the object of these studies to portray. They yield us a last glimpse into that 'lake of sorrow' which lay within the breast of the prophet. But they are more than that. They sum up the verdict of prophecy on God's dealings in mercy and judgment

¹ The closing words of *v*. 4 in the Heb., 'and that is the whole earth,' are not in the LXX; and ought clearly to be omitted.

with the impenitent people of Israel. Its creation and
its destruction were alike the work of Yahwe of hosts,
the God of Israel and the God of the universe. In that
truth Jeremiah's faith finds anchorage, and to the end
he is a man 'very sure of God.' If He who formed
Israel from the womb had found it necessary to destroy
the work of His own hands, if divine patience and love
had failed in the effort to mould the intractable clay of
a nation's character into a vessel fit for the Master's
use, what is left for the protesting human heart but to
be still and know that He is God? The resources of
infinite wisdom and goodness cannot be exhausted; and
God who fulfils Himself in many ways will yet make
Himself known as the God of salvation to all the ends
of the earth. Hence, although the descent from the
rapturous poetry of ch. xxxi to the gloomy resignation
of ch. xlv be almost too painful to contemplate, we are
not to conclude that Jeremiah had lost hope in God or
in the future of His kingdom. No more could he hope
to see with his eyes the good of Israel, since Yahwe had
torn down what He had begun to build; and for himself and Baruch nothing remained but a resolute facing
and endurance of calamity to the uttermost. But Yahwe
still lived, and was 'wakeful over His word' to build and
to plant, as He had been to pull down and to pluck up
(xxiv. 6, xxxi. 28). Jeremiah had been disappointed in
his recent expectation of seeing the material foundations
of the new kingdom of God laid in Palestine; but he
could still believe that its spiritual foundations would
be laid in a change of heart among the exiles in Babylonia[1], and that in God's good time all that he had

[1] On the assumption that ch. xlv is a parting oracle to Baruch, Erbt
builds a conjecture which would bring the oracle into direct connexion
with Jeremiah's hopes for the Babylonian exiles. He thinks that Jeremiah
sent Baruch to Babylon to convey to the Jewish colony there his literary
testament, and that this chapter marks the termination of their long

dreamed of the blessedness of Israel would be fulfilled, when the people turned to Him with their whole heart.

Thus we leave the last great prophet of Judah, worn out by the labours and sufferings of forty years, in darkness though not in despair, awaiting death. It were vain to attempt in closing an estimate of his character and many-sided-genius, or of the value of his contribution to the religious experience of the people of Israel. From the point of view from which we have mainly sought to present his life, as the culmination of the prophetic movement in Israel, no fitter words could be found to sum up the significance of his work than Ewald's eloquent and sympathetic tribute in his *History of Israel*, which is here quoted *verbatim* from Dr Estlin Carpenter's translation (vol. iv, pp. 249 f.):

This renders Jeremiah, the greatest prophet of this age, the truest type throughout his whole career of the inevitable dissolution of the kingdom. Possessed of the most perfect prophetic spirit of all, unstained by any perverse tendency, his noblest utterances, nevertheless, fell fruitless from his lips; his worst forebodings, his severest threats, were vain. Unwearied by any disappointment or catastrophe, he ever collected his energies afresh for simple labour at Yahwe's work; and yet at times

intercourse. 'Sein Wirken ist beendet, er ist ein alter Mann, dem Scheiden nahe. Da schickt er seinen Jünger aus, den er eben, was ihm noch denkwürdig erschienen, hat aufzeichnen lassen, nach Babel an die Gola. Dort soll er sein Zeuge sein, den Exulanten soll er die Hinterlassenschaft des Mannes überbringen, der den Ausgang Judas mit seinen Mahnungen, Warnungen, Drohungen und Hoffnungen begleitet hat. Die *allgemeine* aufregung ohne Ende hat ihre *besondere* Form für Baruch: für ihn bringt sie Unruhe, gefahrvolle Wanderung und den Abschied von dem greisen Meister....Er wird glücklich nach Babel gelangt sein, er hat dort die Zeugnisse von der Wirksamkeit des Propheten verbreitet so dass sie uns erhalten geblieben sind. Die Trennung von ihm ist Schuld daran, dass wir nichts über den Ausgang Jeremias wissen. Baruch hat wohl selbst nichts mehr von ihm gehört' (*op. cit.*, p. 86). I agree, however, with Cornill that this original and ingenious interpretation finds little support in the words of the oracle itself.

bowed down by the overwhelming burden of the age, and the bitter anticipation of the inevitable end of Israel's long course, he almost lost the iron power and confident composure of an ancient prophet, and bowed down in despair, as though under a curse. Through a career of half a century he preserved and increased in his own person the honour of prophetism; yet its results turned out exactly opposite to Isaiah's, for his labours proved less and less successful, and his own lot was one of increasing sadness. Precisely similar was the decline of the whole State; although it concealed within itself some mysterious higher possibility, yet it ever sank more and more irretrievably into the yawning abyss, beyond the power of human vicissitudes and exertions to raise it again as they had done some hundred years before in Isaiah's time. In Jeremiah the kingdom lost the most human prophet it ever possessed. His heavy sorrows and despair, his noble yet fruitless struggles, and his fall, were those of the whole of prophetism, and, so far as prophetism constituted the inmost life of the ancient State, those of the State itself. If any pure soul could still save the State, that soul was Jeremiah's whose period of greatest vigour fell in those three and twenty years of its dying agony; but even for the noblest of the prophets the time was now gone by, and the last great prophet and all the remains of the ancient kingdom of Israel, which had been preserved amid the storms of centuries, were engulfed in a common ruin.

Jeremiah, as has often been said, is the prophet of a dying nation; his poetry with its dominant elegiac note is the swan-song both of Hebrew nationality and of Hebrew prophecy. Prophecy, it is true, was destined to rise phoenix-like from the ashes of the national conflagration; and in the soaring idealism of the second Isaiah, and the rigorous, doctrinaire, but constructive genius of Ezekiel, it evinced a power and originality not unworthy of its glorious past. But the new prophecy was not a revival of the old, from which nevertheless it borrowed most of its light: it had a different function to perform, and a less penetrating message to deliver. The essential task of the prophecy which reached its complete development amid the death-throes of the kingdom of Judah was to separate the vital truths of religion from their embodiment in the institutions of a decadent social organism; and its characteristic message had been that Yahwe was about to break down that which He had built and pluck up that which He had planted. That task was finished in the work and life of Jeremiah—in his life even more than in his work; for it was only in a tragic personal experience such as he passed through that the reality of religion could be apprehended and verified. Greater than all the teaching of subsequent prophets in its influence on the piety of following generations was the spirit of Jeremiah, which breathed out on his people after his death, and bore fruit in an experience of fellowship with God which satisfied the deepest aspirations of the human soul. In his life of unrewarded labour, of unparalleled endurance, and absolute fidelity to God men even read lessons of which his own writings betray no consciousness. They learned from contemplation of its long tragedy a truer insight into the great law of vicarious suffering, which led them on to the conception of the mission of Israel as the oppressed and afflicted servant of Yahwe, and still further to the idea of the one perfect and sinless Servant of the Lord—the Man of sorrows and acquainted with grief, the Lamb of God which taketh away the sin of the world.

SCRIPTURE PASSAGES DISCUSSED
OR REFERRED TO

N.B. The order of books is that of the English Bible

INDEX